The New York Times.

JAPAN WARS ON U.S. AND BRITAIN; MAKES SUDDEN ATTACK ON HAWAII; HEAVY FIGHTING AT SEA REPORTED

THE STARS AND STRIPES 3D.

President's Son in London

Pay Boost Is Passed In Congress

THE STARS AND STRIPES 3D.

Celebrities to Entertain Troops

Japs Lose Heavily In Sea Battle

The New York Times.

U.S. DEFEATS JAPANESE NAVY; ALL FOE'S SHIPS IN ONE FLEET HIT; MANY SUNK; BATTLE CONTINUES

Lorita B. Wenzlaff
7532 Pleasant Ave.
Richfield, MN 55423-4122

FACES OF VICTORY

PACIFIC: 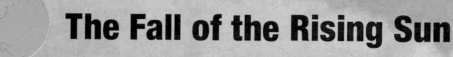 **The Fall of the Rising Sun**

From the Editors of *VFW Magazine*

Bob Snodgrass
Publisher

Richard K. Kolb
Executive Editor

Gary L. Bloomfield
Senior Editor

Michael McKenzie
Consulting Editor

Robert Widener
Design Consultant

Dan Hill
Research Consultant

Anita Stumbo
Design and Typography

Production Assistance: Sharon Snodgrass, Diana Rose, Steve Van Buskirk, Vern Pall, Pat Brown, Betty Bachand, Peggy Allee, Jamie Montgomery, David Sumner, Jack Smith, Jerry Steely, Kristina Brisendine, Clark Nungester, Laura Bostrom, Lydia Steinberg, Kris-Ann McKenzie, Timothy Dyhouse, Jeannie Thompson

Contributing Photographers: Chris Vleisides, Chris Dennis

Original artwork courtesy Norman Rockwell Foundation and Jim Dietz

Gatefold map courtesy of U.S. Military Academy, West Point

Select photos courtesy of National Archives

Remaining photos courtesy the Veterans of Foreign Wars Archives

Published by Addax Publishing Group, Kansas City, Missouri

Library of Congress Catalog Card Number: 95-77869

ISBN: 1-886110-01-8 (General)
ISBN: 1-886110-03-4 (Limited)
ISBN: 1-886110-05-0 (Collectors)

ADDAX
PUBLISHING
GROUP

To the millions of Americans who served in the
Pacific Theater of Operations between 1941 and 1945,
and especially those who sacrificed their lives there
in defense of the nation.

Table of Contents

LEGEND

Listed below are some key terms commonly used in military writing. They apply to both unit designations and casualty categories.

UNITS

Term		Abbreviation
Platoon	(25–30 men)	Plt.
Company	(100–130)	Co.
Battalion	(600–900)	Bn.
Regiment	(1,800–2,700)	Regt.
Division	(10,000–15,000)	Div.
Infantry		Inf.
Airborne		Abn.
Armored		Armd.
Regimented Combat Team		RCT
Parachute Infantry Regiment		PIR
Combat Command A or B		CCA or CCB

CASUALTIES

Killed in Action	KIA
Wounded in Action	WIA
Died of Wounds	DOW
Missing in Action	MIA
Prisoner of War	POW

Photo credits: "Fighting Back at Ewa," page 1; "Best on Deck," pages 2–3, "Beach Head," pages 6–7 © Jim Dietz

Preface

Asiatic-Pacific Campaign Medal

FACES OF VICTORY: *Pacific — Fall of the Rising Sun* was underwritten by the Veterans of Foreign Wars with great pride. Honoring America's warriors, after all, has been one of the VFW's primary tasks over the past 100 years.

This volume, like the European Theater book, is dedicated not just to the more than 1 million VFW members who are WWII vets, but to all 16 million Americans — living and dead — who wore a military uniform during that critical time in U.S. history.

Creating this permanent literary tribute came naturally with the launching of VFW magazine's "50 Years Ago This Month" series, starting in December 1991. The series' intent, like this volume, is twofold: to remember those who served and sacrificed, and to provide a valuable reference for posterity.

WWII histories generally focus on the political/diplomatic, strategic/tactical and generalship of the war. But this is a chronicle of the average American fighting man. It centers on his experiences, views, hardships and sacrifices. Firsthand accounts form the book's heart and soul. Coverage is comprehensive — soldiers, sailors, airmen, Marines and Coast Guardsmen, and specialized unit members, all receive recognition.

Furthermore, rather than rehashing the best-known "big battles" exclusively, *Fall of the Rising Sun* highlights the seldom-chronicled combats and units. It's full of firsts, lasts and onetime events. It also is handsomely illustrated with photographs, art, sidebars and statistical compilations.

For easy reading and understanding, the story line is based on geographical theaters of operation, not strict chronological order. Recounting simultaneous campaigns is complex and confusing.

Publication of the book coincided with the end of the war in the Pacific because WWII was in the headlines and on the minds of the American

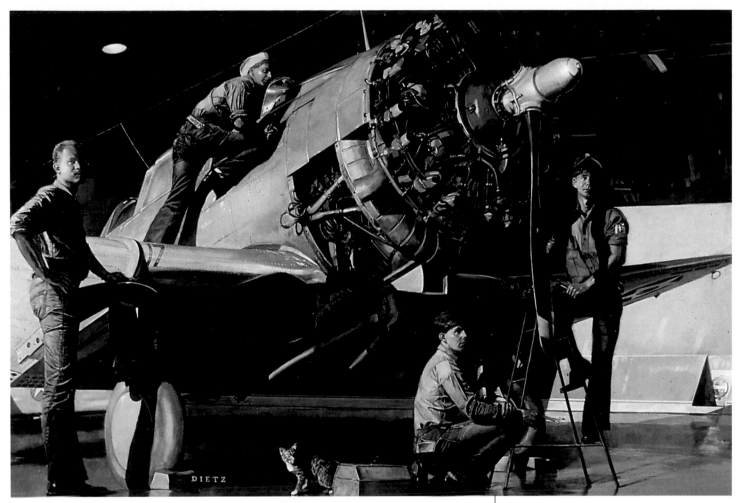

people. This volume appropriately placed the VFW in the forefront of commemorating this turning point in world history.

Fall of the Rising Sun is the dedicated work of *VFW* magazine's editorial staff, Addax Publishing Group and a half dozen free-lance authors. All pooled their proven research and writing skills to produce a book that the VFW is proud to promote. Years of in-depth research went into its development; painstaking attention was paid to detail to guarantee an accurate portrait of the Pacific fighting man.

Still, a single volume can cover only so much ground. The editors used their best judgment, based on letters received from WWII veterans during the past five years, along with the desire to offer a fresh perspective, to guide the book's contents. Any errors or omissions lie squarely at my doorstep.

Combat Infantryman Badge

— RICHARD K. KOLB
Editor-in-Chief
VFW Magazine
Kansas City, Missouri
September 1995

Foreword

Rear Adm. (Ret.) Chester W. Nimitz, Jr.

THE PACIFIC OCEAN during World War II provided the setting for the most enduring experience of my life. Like many of you who wore our country's uniform amidst those trying times, that experience was a high point in my life.

I am proud to be among the millions of Americans who served at sea or ashore in the Pacific Theater. My service took me to Australia, the Dutch East Indies (Indonesia), Solomon Islands, Philippines and South China Sea.

As a submariner aboard the *USS Sturgeon, Bluefish* and *Haddo*, I made 11 war patrols based out of Fremantle, Australia. Our war was undersea and often secretive. Surviving depth charges and sinking enemy ships were part of the job.

The men with whom I served made WWII specifically memorable. While the Navy Cross, Silver Star (three) and Bronze Star (two) will always have special meaning to me, the Navy Unit Commendation holds a place in my memory like none other. Because it was earned as part of a team — a team that helped America emerge victorious.

Exploits of the Submarine Service are almost legendary. Sub crews comprised less than 2 percent of all U.S. sailors, yet accounted for 45 percent of enemy merchant shipping and 29 percent of all warship tonnage sunk. But a severe price was paid: the "Silent Service" sustained the highest loss rate of any Navy branch in WWII. Of 17,750 submariners, 3,500 (19.7 percent) lost their lives.

The camaraderie among submariners, in truth, was characteristic of all American fighting units. And that includes Army infantrymen, Marines,

Army Air Forces' pilots and crews, naval aviators, Coast Guardsmen, Navy Armed Guards, sailors who manned the warships and logistical craft, famed frogmen of the UDTs, the Nurse Corps and Seabees.

It's that *esprit de corps* that *Faces of Victory: Fall of the Rising Sun* has so aptly captured. No other organization is better qualified to tell the story of the Pacific war than the Veterans of Foreign Wars. For among its ranks are the men and women to whom we are so greatly indebted.

Battle flags flying, the submarine *USS Tinosa SS-283* steams up to the Pearl Harbor submarine base after weeks of patrol in the Inland Sea of Japan. U.S. Naval Institute

— CHESTER W. NIMITZ, JR.
Rear Admiral (Ret.)
Boca Grande, Florida
September 1995

Acknowledgments

"PT Boat" © Jim Dietz

TAKING ON A PROJECT as massive as covering America's fighting man during World War II in the Pacific in one volume is challenging, to say the least. But because a wealth of information has been compiled and distilled by historians — both amateur and professional — over the past 50 years, it was made much easier.

As a result, the *VFW* magazine staff is indebted to previous researchers who diligently put the pieces of the Pacific Theater puzzle together. Without the excellent works they have produced, no chronicle of service personnel in Asia and the Pacific would have been feasible.

Of course, the primary contributing authors — Dominic Caraccilo and Michael Graham — must be singled out for authoring most chapters. Both of them invested a great deal of time and talent to make *Fall of the Rising Sun* a reality.

Moreover, Rear Adm. (Ret.) Chester Nimitz, Jr., was considerate enough to write the foreword. He, Gen. William Westmoreland and President Gerald Ford lent their names to the special collector's edition.

The Veterans of Foreign Wars had a unique reservoir on which to draw, too. Beyond doubt, the most valuable contributors to this volume were the former fighting men themselves — VFW members from across the nation. Their personal exploits and reminiscences made the pages come alive with action and authenticity.

During the last four years, the magazine's WWII series rekindled fading memories and revived countless members' interest in reliving their experiences in print. Many took the time to write — offering constructive criticism, setting the record straight and closing the historical gaps.

To the hundreds of VFW members who have donated incalculably to the magazine's archives, we extend our thanks. The insight of those who were actually there in those foreign fields, on the oceans and in the skies inspired this book.

Finding pictures and artwork is always an ordeal, and this effort was no exception. Once again, members sent their prized snapshots for use in the book. Most photos, however, were culled from VFW archives or obtained from the services and military museums.

The National Archives, U.S. Army Military History Institute, Naval Historical Center, U.S. Naval Institute, U.S. Marine Corps Historical Center, West Point Museum, U.S. Air Force Art Collection and the Smithsonian Air and Space Museum provided invaluable assistance. WWII combat artists and photographers also should be acknowledged for preserving on film the life and death struggles suffered by Americans overseas between 1941 and 1945.

James Dietz, who has produced exemplary WWII paintings, supplied many of the action-packed color prints that open many of the book's sections. The Norman Rockwell Museum and National Guard Heritage series also provided memorable scenes on canvas.

Everyone in the VFW's Publications and Public Affairs Department played a part in producing this book. Gary Bloomfield, Robert Widener, Timothy Dyhouse, Betty Bachand, Pat Brown, Peggy Allee, Vern Pall and Steve Van Buskirk all contributed to its success. Deadlines were made only because they were there to pitch in.

Ron Browning of VFW's Marketing Services and Walt Bates of the Information Technology Department helped reach out to members to make them aware of this special tribute.

A special thanks to Bob Snodgrass of Addax Publishing for understanding the value in producing *Fall of the Rising Sun*. His foresight and patience are worthy of praise.

VFW's leaders wholeheartedly endorsed this venture from the outset. Commander-in-Chief Allen "Gunner" Kent, Adjutant General Larry Rivers and Quartermaster General Joe Ridgley all instinctively sensed the need for paying tribute to World War II veterans on the 50th anniversary of the war's end. Recognizing military service and sacrifice has been a hallmark of the VFW throughout the 20th century.

★ ★ ★

"Kamikaze" © Jim Dietz

PREPARING
FOR THE
PACIFIC WAR

Mobilizing for the War Against Japan

Causes

Causes

"

We have learned a great deal about our American boy and the stuff he is made of. The wounded do not cry. Their buddies come first. The patience and determination they show, the courage and fortitude they have is sometimes awesome to behold.

"

— Unidentified Nurse
Army Nurse Corps

EVEN TODAY, more than 50 years after the fact, historians do not agree on the date when World War II began in the Pacific. Some consider the beginning of the war to have been in 1931–32 when Japan seized Manchuria.

Other historians date the start from Japan's invasion of China in 1937. Indeed, the *USS Panay* was attacked by the Japanese on the Yangtze River on Dec. 12 of that year, with the loss of two American lives and 12 seriously wounded.

For the U.S., the conflict began in 1941. Until then Americans tried hard to stay out of the fighting. But in July 1941, Japan threatened to conquer French Indochina and Siam (Thailand). As a warning, President Franklin Roosevelt halted oil sales to Japan and froze all Japanese assets in the U.S. Tokyo retaliated by freezing U.S. economic holdings in Japan.

Tension increased in October. Gen. Hideki Tojo, the leader of the most extreme faction of expansionists in the Japanese military, became prime minister and at once began preparing for war. Japan commenced large-scale troop movements in Southeast Asia and Tojo called on the Japanese Diet to legislate a huge military build-up.

Meanwhile, in Washington, D.C., negotiations between Japanese diplomats and U.S. Secretary of State Cordell Hull, intended to resolve the escalating crisis, made no progress. In late November, Hull warned President Roosevelt that the situation had gone beyond diplomacy and was now chiefly a military problem.

By then, however, a peaceful settlement appeared too late anyway. A large fleet of aircraft carriers and supporting warships and submarines had already secretly departed Japanese ports and were bound for Pearl Harbor in the Hawaiian Islands — the principal Pacific base of the U.S. armed forces.

Strategy

After the attack on Pearl Harbor, the Japanese pushed forward against little opposition. U.S. and Allied forces fought bravely, but they were outnumbered and outsupplied. Japan seized many important islands, which served as "unsinkable aircraft carriers" from which her ships and planes exercised control over much of the Pacific.

Allied strategy in the Pacific (including China, India and Burma), where the U.S. played by far the greatest role, began to take shape in summer 1942 when the naval victories in the Coral Sea and at Midway placed the Japanese on the defensive. From that time until the end of the war, U.S. forces were guided by the following three major aims:

- Drive through the Japanese positions in the Central and Southwest Pacific, and retake the Philippines.
- Cut Japan's lines of communication with its overseas bases, and its sources of war material such as oil, tin and rubber in the Netherlands East Indies and Malaya.
- Establish bases in the western Pacific for the final attack on the Japanese home islands.

This strategy required an entirely new set of coordinated land, sea and air tactics for amphibious warfare operations. These were necessary to fit the U.S. emphasis placed on island-fighting and winning command of the sea. Planners did not intend to capture each Japanese-held island separately, since this would have taken too long and cost too many lives.

Instead, plans were based upon the principle of "island-hopping," which required the capture of only a few key islands en route to Japan. Each island taken provided a base from which other islands could be taken. Planes and ships based on the newly captured islands made it impossible for the Japanese to operate from their nearby bases in the area.

A Japanese officer aptly described U.S. tactics: "The Americans attacked and seized, with minimum losses, a relatively weak area, constructed airfields and then proceeded to cut the supply lines to our troops. . . . The Americans flowed into our weaker points . . . as water seeks the weakest entry to sink a ship."

Leadership

The planning and implementation of U.S. operations against the Japanese was divided into three main commands:

- Gen. Douglas MacArthur commanded the Southwest Pacific Theater and carried out operations in New Guinea, the Solomons, the

Bismarck Archipelago, and other island groups south of the equator, as well as later in the Philippines.

- The direction of the South, Central and North Pacific campaigns lay in the hands of Adm. Chester W. Nimitz, Jr., commander of the U.S. Pacific Fleet.

MacArthur and Nimitz generally planned their operations so that they supported the same overall strategic pattern of attack set by the Joint Chiefs of Staff in Washington. In the later stages of the war, MacArthur's and Nimitz's forces often took part in the same campaigns and shared the same bases.

- Gen. Joseph W. "Vinegar Joe" Stilwell (and later Lt. Gen. A.C. Wedemeyer) was the principal U.S. field commander on the Asiatic mainland, commanding operations in the China, Burma and India (CBI) Theater.

Battleground

The environment in which the war against Japan was waged was probably the most inhospitable and varied ever encountered by such large opposing military forces.

The Pacific was characterized by innumerable groups of reef-encircled islands — some only a few hundred yards in diameter, others several hundred square miles in size; some jungle-covered, others sandy. On New Guinea and in the Philippines, troops contended with rain forests, spongy bottomless swamps, towering jungle-covered mountains, precipitous ravines, cliffs and deep gorges.

In the Aleutians, arctic winter conditions prevailed. GIs in China, Burma and India worked among some of the earth's worst terrain: mountains with peaks thrusting above the clouds, constantly flooding rivers, impenetrable swamps, bamboo-blocked valleys interspersed with thick jungle underbrush and labyrinths of knife-edged elephant grass.

Let's give him Enough and On Time

Poor sanitation and unhygienic conditions made all of the Pacific war zones breeding grounds of death-spreading insects and microorganisms. Disease was especially rampant in the Southwest Pacific and CBI where U.S. troops were stricken at average annual rates of up to 865 cases per 1,000 men.

Not surprisingly, most of the war's battlegrounds were sparsely inhabited. William Manchester, in his biography of MacArthur, *American Caesar*, recalled some of the harsh conditions. Guadalcanal and the Philippines were rocked by earthquakes. On Iwo Jima, volcanic steam hissed through the rocks.

On Bougainville, bulldozers vanished in muddy swamps, and at the height of the battle for Peleliu

Mead Schaeffer painted *Point of File*, his tribute to the American fighting man, in 1942.

For the men sent overseas in WWII, separation from family was perhaps the greatest hardship. National Archives

the temperature was 115 degrees in the shade. At Cape Cloucester, over two dozen Americans were killed — of all things — by huge falling trees. On New Britain, 16 inches of rain fell in a single day.

Army engineer aviation units sent to survey the Santa Cruz Islands for airstrips were practically wiped out by malaria. A typhoon that swept through the Philippines wreaked havoc on the U.S. Third Fleet. When ships went down, sailors risked death from marauding sharks.

As grim and unspeakably difficult as the far-flung theaters of operations against Japan were, U.S. troops in particular turned out to be much more adaptable than the enemy to the obstacles of terrain and climate.

Order of Battle

The comparative power and staggering array of U.S. land, sea and air forces that were deployed and enabled Allied victory against Japan were unprecedented and included:

Naval Forces

The Pacific Fleet, with its main base at Pearl Harbor, was divided into several fleets: the Third in the South Pacific under Adm. William F. "Bull" Halsey; Fifth, Central Pacific, Adm. Raymond A. Spruance; and Seventh, Southwest Pacific, Vice Adms. Arthur S. Carpender and later Thomas C. Kinkaid. During 1944–45, Third and Fifth fleets were actually the same force with command elements alternating between operations. These three fleets together comprised the bulk of the greatest navy that ever sailed the seas — a "Two-Ocean Navy" that during the war grew into an immense flotilla.

It included a main battle force of 27 heavy and eight light aircraft carriers and eight new fast battleships to win command of the sea, conduct air strikes, and isolate islands for amphibious assault. And 16 older battleships and 77 escort carriers gave landing forces direct naval gunfire support and close air cover.

Tremendous numbers of cruisers (92), destroyers (501), destroyer escorts (406), mining and patrol craft (2,703) and landing and district craft (105,398) also waged the war. The Submarine Service's 202 submarines sank 1,951 Japanese men-of-war alone. The fleet train of 1,541 fleet auxiliary vessels made it possible for the Navy to undertake the decisive Pacific offensive.

Naval aviation's 437,524 personnel and 75,000 planes also were arrayed against Japan, bombing naval and air bases and island defenses before they were invaded, transporting supplies and conducting air reconnaissance.

The Coast Guard put 1,677 vessels to sea (including 600 cutters and numerous small craft for escort work and harbor security) and 171,192 personnel. Many of them served in the Pacific in the naval troop transport service and aboard landing craft, emergency and rescue craft, tenders and tugs.

Naval Construction Battalions (the "Seabees," 326,000 strong) excelled at building docks, erecting barracks, building storage facilities and constructing and repairing airfields. The Naval Armed Guard, totalling 144,970 men, provided protective firepower aboard merchant marine vessels, which kept the lifeline to the fighting front filled with critical war material.

The Navy Medical Corps' surgeons and corpsmen worked both afloat and ashore, landing with assault waves and operating aid stations and hospitals. Underwater Demolition Teams (the famous "frogmen") reconnoitered beaches and removed landing obstacles and mines during amphibious operations.

Ground Forces

The Army provided the majority of U.S. troops in the war against Japan. But for practically the entire war, available U.S. ground forces at no time amounted to more than one-third of the overall Japanese ground forces opposing them. When Japan surrendered, there were only 21 Army and six Marine divisions in the Pacific.

The Marines were the spearhead in the Central Pacific. From one division at the time of Pearl Harbor, the Fleet Marine Force, Pacific, expanded to six divisions (1st, 2nd, 3rd, 4th, 5th and 6th) and the III and V Amphibious Corps, commanded by Lt. Gen. Holland M. Smith, the top Marine Corps commander in the Pacific.

Marines provided security forces afloat and ashore for the Navy, as well as ships' detachments in major combatant vessels and at virtually all shore-based naval installations.

Marine aviation elements employed 125,162 personnel in 132 squadrons distributed among carrier-based Marine air support groups and the shore-based 1st, 2nd, 3rd and 4th Marine Air Wings, together with the necessary supporting and logistic units. (A training wing, the 9th, remained in the U.S.)

Specialized units — raiders, parachute, pioneer, amphibious reconnaissance, base and anti-aircraft defense, joint assault signal, amphibian tractor and armored amphibian — rounded out the Marine contribution.

U.S. Army ground forces were incorporated eventually into three field armies:

- Sixth Army in the Southwest Pacific and later the Philippines under Lt. Gen. Walter Krueger, comprising: I Corps — 25th, 33rd, 41st Infantry divisions; IX Corps — 77th, 81st Infantry divisions; XI

You're in the Army now! Early on, public send-off ceremonies were staged for the freshly sworn-in soldiers, wringing many tears from wives and girlfriends. National Archives

During the battle of Midway, the Japanese carriers *Kaga* and *Akagi* come under attack by U.S. planes. The Japanese Imperial Navy stood superior to the Allies until this battle when these two flattops plus the *Soryu* and *Hiryu* were destroyed, turning the tide in the Pacific war on the water and shifting the strategic emphasis to island-hopping. *Naval Historical Center*

Corps — 43rd, Americal, 1st Cavalry divisions; Reserve — 40th Infantry and 11th Airborne divisions.

- Eighth Army, the Philippines, Lt. Gen. Robert L. Eichelberger: X Corps — 24th, 31st Infantry divisions; XIV Corps — 6th, 32nd, 37th, 38th Infantry divisions; Reserve — 93rd and 96th Infantry divisions.
- Tenth Army, centered in the Ryukyu Islands, Lt. Gen. Simon B. Buckner and after his death in action, Gen. Joseph W. Stilwell: XXIV Corps — 7th, 27th Infantry divisions; Reserve — 98th Infantry Division of U.S. Army Forces, Middle Pacific, based in Hawaii.

The Army also deployed other separate combat, logistical support and special units, including elite forces such as Rangers, Scouts and the *Galahad* and *MARS* task forces; detachments of the top-secret Office of Strategic Services; the famed engineer special amphibious brigades; Air Commando groups; military police; coast and anti-aircraft artillery; amphibious tractor and tank units; as well as medical, civil affairs, ordnance, quartermaster, signal, and transportation elements.

Army Air Forces
The job of suppressing enemy airfields, making harbors untenable for shipping, pounding down islands before invasion, providing support for assaulting forces and attacking economic and industrial objectives fell largely to the land-based U.S. Army Air Forces (USAAF).

The result was a war of attrition in the air marked by fierce battles, often embroiling hundreds of planes. The magnitude of the Pacific conflict in the air frequently resembled the struggle which the more numerous Army Air Forces waged in Europe.

In the air war against Japan, the USAAF included the Seventh Air Force in the Central Pacific under Maj. Gen. Willis H. Hale; Tenth, India and Southeast Asia, Maj. Gen. Howard C. Davidson; Eleventh, North Pacific (Alaska), Maj. Gen. William O. Butler; Fifth and Thirteenth, South and Southwest Pacific, Lt. Gen. George C. Kenney and Maj. Gen. St. Clair Street, respectively; and Fourteenth, China, Maj. Gen. Claire L. Chennault.

In addition, the Twentieth Air Force, based in the Marianas under Maj. Gen. Curtis E. LeMay, directed operations of the very long-range B-29 Superfortress bombers. The Far East Air Forces (FEAF), stationed in the Philippines, later operated out of Australia. Each of the Army Air Forces in the Pacific and Asia included large numbers of signal warning, engineer aviation and air service support units.

The scope and intensity of the USAAF effort is shown in its achievements: 670,000 combat sorties flown in all theaters against Japan, including the home islands themselves; a half-million tons of bombs dropped; 10,300 Japanese planes destroyed; and over a hundred square miles of the five largest industrial areas of Japan destroyed.

THE SATURDAY EVENING
POST

JULY 25, 1942   10¢

READ... ...ISSUE

AN...

BLACK M...KET

Norman Rockwell

Sword drawn, a Japanese officer leads his men into battle. Enemy commanders were quick to use their swords, like the *samurai*, and were given to leading maniacal, *Banzai* charges under the time-honored battle code of *Bushido* — which called for fighting to the death.
Courtesy of Mainichi Shimbun, Toyko

The Enemy

On the eve of war, Japan had 51 divisions, despite a prewar population of only 70 million, equal to about half that of the U.S. At sea, Japan had what amounted to one of the world's most formidable fleets, including 10 carriers, 10 battleships, 35 cruisers, 111 destroyers and 64 submarines.

By the time of their defeat, the Japanese had mobilized a total of 7.4 million men and put 120 divisions into the field. The Imperial Japanese Navy, which for centuries had never been defeated, simply no longer existed — having lost in action with the U.S. thousands of sailors and nearly all its ships.

As Meirion and Susie Harries put it in their book *Soldiers of the Sun: The Rise and Fall of the Imperial Japanese Army*, the first challenge to Allied forces in battle was understanding the unusual methods of fighting that the Japanese used. Japan's ancient *Bushido* code of warfare forbade troops to be taken prisoner and required them to fight to the death.

Consequently, Japanese soldiers were much less cautious than Western troops. They took fantastic risks because they believed that it was a glorious achievement to die in battle. Their senseless *Banzai* suicide charges in the face of unconquerable firepower after an action had been lost never failed to amaze American troops.

"Two features of the Pacific fighting differentiated it from that in Europe," concluded a WWII historical study. "The Japanese fought on in suicidal fashion if bypassed, even very small groups or individuals; and they killed wounded men without mercy. U.S. soldiers were aware of this and felt strongly about leaving wounded comrades in the wake of an advance, to fall victims to any bypassed sniper."

Speed in the form of sudden and violent offensive action, notes S.I. Mayer in *The Japanese War Machine*, was a cardinal tactical principle with Japanese troops, who were generally well-armed. Their tactics were often reflected in their weapons, which tended to be compact and light.

In the air, Japanese aircraft at first outclassed every Allied plane in the Pacific. The Zero fighter, in particular, was light and maneuverable, had a high rate of firepower and could fly in a fighter-bomber role. At sea, Japanese ships were well-designed and characterized by speed and heavy firepower.

Marine Capt. J.L. Zimmerman best summed up the Japanese fighting man who "fought, as an individual, as well and as bravely as any warrior the world has ever seen. He bore privation and hardship that would have put out of action most [men] . . . and attacked with determined ferocity whenever he came into contact with the American troops. In attack he was single-minded and reckless of his life; in defense he was bitterly tenacious. He was in all ways . . . to be respected" for the danger he represented.

The American Fighting Man

Despite popular Hollywood images, the burden of battle was shared equally by all the services — not just the Marines and Navy — in the Pacific Theater. Both Army ground and Army air units played vital roles in achieving the victory over Japan.

As a matter of fact, the Army's 20 combat divisions and eight air forces in the theater sustained exactly 50 percent of the Americans killed in action in the Pacific. Clearly, no matter what branch of the armed forces, all did their part. Soldiers, sailors, Coast Guardsmen, Marines and airmen alike were molded into a composite American fighting man who had all the essential qualities in common.

Just what made the typical serviceman who fought in the Pacific tick? Like his counterpart in Europe, he displayed the best of American traits. But what motivated him to fight and sustained him in combat, found researchers, was a rather subdued patriotism.

While most GIs "had little taste for discussions of the justness of the American cause," concluded one surveyor, a minority did express idealistic reasons for serving. A private on New Guinea, for instance, wrote, "We are fighting for what appears to be the strongest hope for advancing the status of the individual man the world over."

Regardless of personal motivation, all fighting men experienced fear and courage. One of Merrill's famed Marauders in Burma wrote: "Fear has an identifiable taste. At least it has for me. It is a taste of brass. Every time a shell exploded it was as if my tongue had been touched by two poles of a dry cell."

But through it all, men who had seen combat said they were fortified by prayer, companionship, duty, anger, a sense of do-or-die, faith in firepower and just plain luck. Observed one British officer: "The bravery and self-devotion of the American airmen and sailors and the nerve and skill of their leaders shocked the souls of the *samurai*."

Shortly before being killed, an Army nurse recorded: "We have learned a great deal about our American boy and the stuff he is made of. The wounded do not cry. Their buddies come first. The patience and determination they show, the courage and fortitude they have is sometimes awesome to behold."

These traits and more would be demonstrated time and again by the average GI as he fought to set the sun on the Japanese empire.

A Marine stares at the smoke barrage covering Peleliu in September 1944.
Painting by Tom Lea

Japanese aircraft conduct the surprise air raid on American ships in port at Pearl Harbor, Dec. 7, 1941.
Robert G. Smith, U.S. Naval Institute

From Pearl Harbor to the 'Pearl of the Orient'

U.S. NAVY Gunners Mate Leland Howard Burke, a crew member on the battleship *USS Arizona* for five months before Dec. 7, 1941, recalls that day vividly: "General Quarters had been sounded. I was trying to get to my battle station. But all I could see when I reached the top deck was smoke. There were small fires springing up all over the ship. I stumbled and almost tripped over the bodies of the dead and wounded.

"Orders were being screamed from all directions. We didn't know who was in charge. As I looked past the ship's main mast I saw a Japanese fighter plane coming toward us. There was a big red ball on its side. It dropped a bomb right on top of the magazine. Everybody was in near panic."

Joseph Taylangela, ensign on the *Arizona*, said, "I was one of those in charge of removing bodies from the sinking ship. It was a tough job. We were surprised, but I kept thinking that some of those in charge in Washington must have known it was coming. We did have some hints for weeks that the Japanese might attack. Our training did not prepare us for such an attack."

The major architect of the Pearl Harbor attack was Adm. Isoroku Yamamoto, commander-in-chief of the Japanese Combined Fleet. He urged a massive air attack from Japanese carriers as the first day of a decisive war with the United States.

He told his Imperial General Staff colleagues, "It is time to devote ourselves to the inevitability of a war with the United States. I must be wholly successful so that Japan would be dominant until a victorious conclusion."

When the Pearl Harbor attack planners met with Emperor Hirohito, they had to answer some hard questions. "What will be the cost in loss of life, and can you assure us of success? You told us a few years ago that our invasion of North China would end quickly. We are still there. We need to be assured and convinced," the monarch said.

Adm. Yamamoto said, "This attack will demoralize the Americans and destroy their will to fight. Surprise is the most important element in this plan. That surprise should destroy most of the American fleet and cause confusion.

"We must therefore decide the outcome of the war on the first day. The Pearl Harbor attack should be one of several successive acts, including an invasion of California and a drive to Washington, D.C. to dictate terms of peace in the White House." After the meeting with the emperor, Adm. Yamamoto told his aides that "the United States could be a formidable opponent. We must be successful and avoid any possible reversal of our initiative or arouse the anger of the Americans."

In Washington, President Franklin D. Roosevelt discussed possible Japanese first-strike against the United States. "We know that the possibility of an attack exists but we don't know where it would take place. We can't attack first, of course. The Japanese have to make the first move."

In the months before the attack, two Japanese envoys — Saburo Karuso and Adm. Kichisaburo Nomura — went to Washington to reach a peaceful settlement to disputes between the two countries. They were not aware of the planned attack on Pearl Harbor.

When the two envoys were told to get full agreement on Japan's demand for free reign in Asia and the Pacific by the end of November 1941, Nomura replied, "We cannot get the Americans to agree to all of these points on such short notice. The terms are too sweeping and absurd." But Nomura's superiors in Tokyo insisted and ignored the pleas for more time.

Ira Huntley, a seaman first class at the time of the attack, recalls life aboard ship in Pearl Harbor. "We had daily classes in ship and plane recognition, but none of those classes had anything to do with the mention of a Japanese air attack. We just didn't believe that Japan would take such drastic action and attack the American fleet. We were drilled at our

When Japanese planes attacked Pearl Harbor, the *USS Shaw* erupted into a fireball after its forward magazine exploded.

"

The only thing to do now is to lick the hell out of them.

"

— SEN. BURTON K. WHEELER
comment made shortly after the bombing of Pearl Harbor, December 1941

The battleship *Arizona*, burning out of control, sustained the most deaths of any U.S. ship hit during WWII: 1,014 — almost half of the total killed in the attack on Pearl Harbor.

battle stations on how to defend our ship, but we never believed it would happen."

Almost on a daily basis, the U.S. ambassador to Japan, Joseph Grew, cabled his view of the prospects of war. In late October 1941, Grew told President Roosevelt in a coded cable: "The present Japanese government may not be able to resist the demands of the military. If we are to find a solution to this crisis, it will have to be very soon. Everyone is tense here."

The Japanese government headed by Prince Konoye was trying to forestall a war with a major breakthrough in the U.S.-Japan negotiations. He proposed to Secretary of State Cordell Hull that Konoye meet with Roosevelt somewhere in the Pacific.

FDR liked the idea, but told Hull that such a meeting would have no advance guarantees. "I don't want to emerge from a meeting looking like [Britain's Neville] Chamberlain." Suitable terms for a meeting never materialized, and within weeks the Konoye government collapsed and was succeeded by a military-dominated one.

One person in Hawaii knew an attack would take place — Takeo Yoshikawa, a naval officer handpicked as a super spy to monitor U.S. naval and military maneuvers. Yoshikawa cabled detailed information every day

Wreckage piles up at the Naval Air Station in Pearl Harbor as explosions billow in the background.
National Archives

and sent scores of pictures back to Japan. He was virtually unnoticed as he mingled with thousands of other Japanese who lived in Hawaii.

One message from Tokyo to Yoshikawa said it all: "We need more detail on how many ships are in port every day, what planes land or take off from U.S. bases, and the location of carriers. No detail is too minute." But not even Yoshikawa knew the date of the attack.

The Navy flier chosen to command the air attack on Pearl Harbor was 39-year-old Mitsuo Fuchida. When given the command, he said, "I am honored by this decision. I will proudly carry our flag to the enemy."

Later in life Fuchida immigrated to the United States. He recalled his feelings when the first wave flew over Pearl Harbor: "I couldn't believe my eyes. I had seen and carefully studied all of the maps and photographs, but never fully comprehended how so much of the American fleet would be anchored in one small bay. I thought they deserved to be attacked to have been so foolish."

Paul E. Gan, also survived the Pearl Harbor attack. His remembrance of that fateful Sunday is still one of disbelief.

"I have often wondered, looking back 50 years, how anyone could have escaped from our ship, the *Arizona*, that day. Someone ran into us and

66

*What I thought was my neighbors'
loud radio was in fact the full fury of
the Jap Air Force. Our ordinary
Sunday morning turned immediately
extraordinary.*

99

— EJLIF SCHMIDT
Pearl Harbor Survivor

Above: Mess Attendant 1/C Dorie Miller, a cook aboard the *USS West Virginia,* sports the Navy Cross, which he earned at Pearl Harbor on Dec. 7, 1941. National Archives

Top: During the Pearl Harbor attack, a Japanese pilot shot this photo, which shows smoke from Hickam Field on the horizon as the devastation unfolds. National Archives

yelled we should get up on deck right way. My battle station was the ship's range finder.

"But the first thing I saw was a torpedo hitting the battleship *West Virginia* anchored near us. Fighter planes were strafing our deck and everyone jumped for cover. No words can describe the wreckage I saw. Many of our crew members jumped into the water as the abandon ship order was given."

One American caught in the confusion of the time was Coy Miller, who had written a letter to his family on Nov. 6. "I am on overtime in the Navy now. I have already been discharged, but the papers are not complete. I didn't re-enlist so I am just a civilian sailor.

"Things are about the same here. From what I read, if the Nazis win many more battles, we'll have to knock those Japanese for a loop. I wish we could go someplace and knock the hell out of someone." Miller was killed on Dec. 7.

Adm. Yamamoto received a message from the Japanese carrier fleet an hour after the attack: "Mission has been accomplished. Huge American losses and the attack was a complete surprise." Yamamoto turned to his aide and remarked, "That is good but not a word about the American carriers. We still don't know where they are. The future is still in doubt."

The Japanese attack force included 40 torpedo bombers, 30 horizontal

Survivors of the attack on the U.S. Naval Station in Kaneohe Bay at Pearl Harbor place wreaths on the graves of those who died. U.S. Navy

bombers, 54 dive bombers and 45 Zero fighters. U.S. material losses at Pearl Harbor were 162 planes, 85 U.S. Navy aircraft, eight battleships, three cruisers and three destroyers.

When news of the attack reached Washington, Secretary Hull was scheduled to meet with the two Japanese envoys, who were there to deliver Japan's declaration of war. Because of delays, Hull didn't read their ultimatum until after the attack on Pearl Harbor had started.

He told them, as they stood in front of his desk, "I must say that in all of my conversations with you during the last nine months, I never uttered one word of untruth. This is borne out absolutely by the record. But in all my 50 years of public service I have never seen a document that was more crowded with infamous falsehoods and distortions. These distortions are on a scale so huge that I never imagined until today that any government on this planet was capable of uttering them."

The next day, the President had his own response, calling the attack a "day that will live in infamy."

Counting Casualties at Pearl Harbor

Casualties	U.S.	Japan
Killed (total)	**2,403**	129 approx.
Navy	2,008	129 approx.
Marine Corps	109	—
Army	218	—
Civilian	68	—
Wounded (total)	**1,178**	unknown
Navy	710	
Marine Corps	69	
Army	364	
Civilian	35	
Ships		
Sunk or Beached*	8	6
(5 Battleships, 1 target ship, 1 repair ship, 1 minelayer)		(5 midget subs, 1 I-Class sub)
Damaged	13	
Aircraft		
Destroyed	188	29
Damaged	159	74

*All U.S. ships, with the exception of the *Arizona, Utah* and *Oklahoma*, were salvaged and later saw action.

Source: National Park Service

Framed in explosive clouds, Battleship Row
at Pearl Harbor on Dec. 7, 1941.

Battleship Row at Pearl Harbor took the brunt of the Japanese attack, sending seamen scurrying in a spectacle of smoke and flames. The *USS West Virginia* (left) and *Tennessee* are seen here. U.S. Navy

'More Important Than Life'

The big battleships of Battle Division 1, the *Nevada*, the *Oklahoma* and the *Arizona*, had returned to Pearl Harbor after war games in the open sea.

A young machinist mate on the *Nevada*, Don Ross, had just come on midnight engineering watch. His chief ordered, "Put the engine room on alert. Be ready to answer bells by morning." Ross suspected trouble. It was Sunday morning, Dec. 7, 1941.

"I was shaving when I heard airplanes racing outside my window," Ross remembered. Then he looked out and saw three Japanese Zeroes screaming over the east side of Ford Island, firing hot flames from their guns.

Ross ran down to the forward generator room. Within three minutes, the *Nevada* was on full combat condition ZED, or general quarters.

At 0805, the *Nevada* was blasted by a torpedo. A hole 60 feet long and 18 feet below the water line opened on the port bow near turret two, just 40 feet from the forward generator room.

"That shook things up a bit!" Ross recalled. The room heated up and smoke filled the compartment. Ross knew the generators had to be switched to the rear dynamo room as soon as possible. Deep in the bowels of the *Nevada*, he and his 27 men struggled for just a little more time to allow the rear units to get ready.

Suddenly, Ross heard a tremendous explosion. The impact far exceeded anything he had ever heard or felt. He didn't know until later that the battleship *Arizona*, moored right at the *Nevada*'s bow, had just blown up, killing more than 1,000 sailors.

Then a second group of Japanese bombers attacked the *Nevada*, rocking it with three bombs. More forward water gushed in and the pumps struggled to keep up. Then a fourth bomb flew down onto the armor deck at the "bull ring" where the ship's air centralized from the top side. Ross received a full torch of fire to the left side of his face, blinding his left eye.

He momentarily lost consciousness. Recovering, he realized the danger to his men and shouted his lifesaving order, "Get out men! Get the hell out of

Donald Ross, machinist mate aboard the battleship *USS Nevada*, received severe facial burns and was blinded in the left eye during the torpedo and bomb blasts of Dec. 7, 1941. His actions that saved the ship from exploding earned him the Medal of Honor. U.S. Navy

The *USS Nevada*, damaged but still able to sail, limped away from other burning ships along Battleship Row, nosed into a reef yet didn't sink. National Archives

here! Get out!" The men rushed up the ladder to escape. Ross was left behind alone.

The rear generators were not ready to come on line. Ross struggled to do the work of his entire crew as he fought to keep the forward dynamos working. If the *Nevada* lost power now, the whole ship would go dead in the water. The guns would stop, the pumps would stop and all communication would be lost. The battleship's survival depended on the efforts of this brave, young sailor.

Ross knew he couldn't last much longer. The rear generators were finally ready and he switched off to them as he started to fall. An electrician on the distribution board heard gagging followed by a faint, "God help me," and then silence. The electrician ran to the dynamo room, opened the hatch, jumped into the 140 degree heat and smoke, put the unconscious Ross over his shoulder and worked his way up the 18-foot ladder to safety. Ross wasn't breathing.

Artificial respiration was started. After three minutes, slowly, Ross started breathing again. When he regained consciousness, a terrible realization occurred to him — the exhaust in the forward condensers had not been secured. This could cause an incredible explo-

sion. Struggling to find his way back down into the darkness of the deadly smoke and heat where he had almost died, Ross found the pipe cut-off valve and turned it. The ship was spared.

The *Nevada* had nosed into a shallow coral reef so she wouldn't sink. The Japanese attack was ending and the big ship was severely damaged, but still afloat. Fifty-seven of the *Nevada*'s brave sailors died that morning, fewer than would have died if not for the clear and brave thinking of its young machinist.

Looking back, Ross remembered, "I didn't think about fear. I was frightened, but the fear didn't control me. The most important thing was my men and the ship. These were more important to me than my own life."

Through the actions of Donald Ross on Dec. 7, 1941, the *USS Nevada* and her crew lived to see more days of service to their country — in the Aleutian Islands, the North Atlantic and the beaches of Normandy.

Adm. William Halsey on April 14, 1942, presented to Donald T. Ross this country's highest award, the Medal of Honor. World War II had begun and for history and heroes, this day would never be forgotten. Donald Ross died May 27, 1992.

Wake Island: 'This Great Fight'

News about Japan's attack focused on Pearl Harbor. But another U.S. Pacific outpost — Wake Island, located 2,300 miles west of Hawaii — was also hit, on Dec. 8, 1941.

Intended as a forward base for submarines of the Pacific Fleet, Wake's fortifications were still being constructed when the first Japanese air raid occurred at noon, just hours after the attack on Pearl Harbor. "The pilots [Japanese] in every one of the planes were grinning wildly. Everyone wiggled his wings to signify *banzai*," remembered a Marine on Wake Island.

Marines of the 1st Defense Battalion and Marine Fighter Squadron VMF-211, plus Army and Navy personnel and civilian construction workers, braced for the assault.

Air raids would continue for four more days, until an invasion fleet arrived. Though vastly outnumbered and outgunned, the Wake defenders managed to repel the initial assault. Shore batteries sank the destroyer *Hayate*, and Marine pilots knocked out the destroyer *Kisaragi*. Three other enemy destroyers sustained damage. A Japanese commander called the action "one of the most humiliating defeats our navy ever suffered."

Despite continued shelling and bombing, the Americans held on until Dec. 23, when 1,500 soldiers of the Japanese Special Naval Landing Force stormed ashore. This first U.S. land battle of the Pacific campaign was savage: 122 Americans were killed, 49 wounded and more than 400 Marines captured. Also, 1,200 U.S. civilians there were imprisoned in China. (On Oct. 7, 1943, Japan executed 96 of the Wake defenders.)

Wake's defense blunted Japanese momentum and raised home front American morale. No wonder President Franklin Roosevelt called it "this great fight."

Far East Air Force Faces Destruction at Clark

Japanese air and naval forces reached out in all directions of the Pacific on Dec. 7 and 8, 1941. Pearl Harbor was the biggest prize, but Guam and U.S. airfields in the Philippines also were attacked.

Guam withstood two days of air attacks from enemy bombers based on Saipan before the island's defenders — 153 Marines, 271 Navy personnel, an 80-man Insular Guard Force and a volunteer militia, with little more than .30-caliber machine guns for firepower — surrendered to 6,000 men of Japan's South Seas Detachment, on Dec. 10. Guam was the first U.S. possession to fall into enemy hands during WWII.

Loss of Guam and Wake (13 days later) severed the lines of communication between the Pacific Command at Pearl Harbor and the Philippines, which would also come under attack.

Through military channels and public radio broadcasts, the news about

Four hours after attacking Pearl Harbor, on Dec. 7, 1941, Japanese planes bombed Wake Island. The defenders — primarily Marines of the 1st Defense Battalion and Fighter Squadron 211, plus civilian construction workers — fought off enemy air attacks for four days.

The Japanese then tried to land assault troops on Wake, but were repulsed, until Dec. 23, when 1,500 soldiers of the Japanese Special Naval Landing Force overran the island. U.S. Navy

An American soldier stands in a bomb crater at Cavite Navy Yard near Manila, the Philippines, after it was attacked on Dec. 10, 1941, by Japanese planes. The attack on Cavite — the primary U.S. naval base in the region — forced the U.S. Asiatic Fleet to head for the Dutch East Indies.

Three days earlier, and approximately nine hours after the attack on Pearl Harbor, Japanese planes destroyed bombers and fighter planes of the Far East Air Force, headquartered at Clark Airfield on Luzon.

National Archives

Pearl Harbor was flashed around the world. At Clark Field in the Philippines all units, and specifically the Far East Air Force, were put on alert.

With Japanese army and navy planes based on Formosa just 500 miles away, an attack could occur with little warning. Air Force Chief of Staff Gen. Hap Arnold even flashed a message to Clark Field, urging commanders there to take all precautions to ensure the Far East Air Force didn't suffer the same fate as the Pacific Fleet at Pearl.

At about the same time, reports of incoming enemy bombers were transmitted to Clark. Fighter planes from the 17th and 20th Pursuit squadrons were scrambled to intercept the invaders. Bombers also took off, without any bombs aboard, just to avoid being destroyed on the ground.

Instead of attacking Clark Field, the initial wave of enemy bombers struck at Davao Gulf on Mindanao.

All of the American planes aloft were called back to Clark to be refueled and armed for an air strike on Formosa.

While these planes were on the ground, though, an enemy force of 108 bombers and 84 Zeroes approached. Monitoring posts detected them, but warning messages were never received at Clark. It was approximately 12 hours and 40 minutes after the attack on Pearl Harbor.

Other air units received the warning and ordered their fighters to repel the invaders. But at Clark, B-17 bombers and all of the fighters of the 20th Pursuit Squadron were caught lined up on the runway as Japanese planes suddenly appeared overhead. Three P-40s of the 20th Pursuit managed to take off and shoot down several of the enemy fighters.

Casualties in the attack on Clark Field and other bases in the Philippines were 80 killed and more than 150 wounded. Half of the Far East Air Force was destroyed: 18 B-17 bombers, 53 P-40s and three P-35s plus numerous other aircraft (B-10s, B-18s and reconnaissance planes).

"The catastrophe of Pearl Harbor overshadowed at the time and still obscures the extent of the ignominious defeat inflicted on American Air Forces in the Philippines on the same day," wrote Louis Morton in *The Fall of the Philippines*.

"As at Pearl Harbor, the Japanese had removed in one stroke the greatest single obstacle to their advance southward. The Philippine garrison could expect little help in the near future. It was now almost surrounded. The only path open lay to the south, and that, too, soon would be closed."

Taste of Victory: Macassar Strait

Allied reconnaissance patrols had detected an enemy naval force of 20 troop and supply transports, accompanied by a dozen destroyers and several cruisers, bound for the Macassar Strait and the crucial oil fields of the Dutch East Indies (today Indonesia) in mid-January 1942.

With the bulk of America's warships either sunk or crippled at Pearl Harbor, the only ships available to challenge the approaching armada were six antiquated WWI four-stack destroyers and two light cruisers of the U.S. Asiatic Fleet.

Despite the impossible odds, this fleet — *Task Force Five, Striking Force* — steamed toward the east coast of Borneo. But soon the two cruisers dropped by the wayside — each had to be accompanied by one destroyer back to Java for repairs. This left only the four destroyers — *John D. Ford, Pope, Parrott* and *Paul Jones* — to pursue the attack in the Battle of Macassar Strait off Balikpapan. It would be the Navy's first surface action since the Spanish-American War.

Without radar or any air cover, relying only on torpedoes and manually operated 4-inch guns, every crewman knew what was in store. Before contact was made, however, the order was given for the destroyers to fire only their torpedoes, concentrating on the enemy transports. Only when all "fish" had been expended were any guns to be used.

"Our orders were clear: make a night attack," recalled Rear Adm. William Mack on board the *Ford*. "We weren't much, but we were full of fight. My men were about to take part in the first American naval engagement in the East since Dewey fought at Manila Bay, and they were proud of it."

Soon after midnight, on Jan. 24, fires at Balikpapan were spotted. The Dutch there were destroying their compounds before the enemy came ashore. The destroyers continued into the Strait, running dark to avoid detection. At approximately 2:45, the silhouettes of the Japanese convoy loomed ahead.

"A whole division of Jap destroyers steamed rapidly across in front of us," Mack continued. "I don't know why they didn't spot us, but possibly several of their own destroyers were patrolling in the vicinity and they mistook us for their own forces. Suddenly we found ourselves in the midst of the Jap transports."

The four destroyers picked their targets and fired their torpedoes without success. Without being spotted, they passed through the enemy ships, turned about and attacked again, striking the transport *Sumanoura Maru*.

Enemy escort destroyers fanned out, looking for the submarines that were firing those torpedoes. Their lookouts were unaware that U.S. warships were in their midst. More torpedoes were fired and another transport went down.

66

The projectile explosions were tremendous. Deck plates and debris flew in all directions. When we last saw her she was on end, slipping slowly under. We had sunk the first ship to be sunk by American gunfire since Manila Bay!

99

— REAR ADM. WILLIAM P. MACK

Again the four U.S. warships turned about and made still another run. Once they had fired their torpedoes, they opened up with their guns, at ranges of 500 to 1,500 yards. "The projectile explosions were tremendous. Deck plates and debris flew in all directions. When we last saw the transport, she was on end, slipping slowly under. We had sunk the first ship to be sunk by American gunfire since Manila Bay!" Mack boasted.

Now under fire, the destroyers quickly turned south for home, before daylight. Miraculously, only a few crewmen had been injured in the fight, and all the four-stackers returned to safe haven. Behind them were four transports and one patrol craft sunk, and an unknown number of Imperial seamen killed or drowned.

Death of a Fleet in the Java Sea

Little more than a month after the unexpected score at Macassar Strait, the tide turned against the tiny U.S. Asiatic Fleet. It found itself engaged in a series of surface-to-surface actions in the waters of what is today Indonesia between Feb. 4 and March 1, 1942.

Oil reserves in the Dutch East Indies were vital to the Japanese, who now planned to attack Java, a strategic Indonesian island. Tokyo believed Java was "protected" by merely a token force of American, British, Dutch and Australian vessels, referred to as the ABDA Command.

ABDA's assortment of ships included one British and one U.S. heavy cruiser; one Australian and two Dutch light cruisers; and three Dutch, three British and five American destroyers, plus an assortment of patrol boats. America's first carrier, the *Langley*, was also part of the U.S. Asiatic Fleet, serving as a seaplane tender.

On Feb. 4, an ABDA force was attacked by Japanese aircraft off Borneo. Lacking air cover, it was forced to retire. USS cruiser *Marblehead* was so seriously damaged that it returned to the U.S. for repairs. Fifteen aboard were killed.

During the Battle of the Badung Strait, Feb. 19–20, six U.S. destroyers were among the ABDA ships that attacked a Japanese invasion force near Bali. *USS Stewart* was damaged. A week later, the *Langley* was sunk by Japanese aircraft while ferrying Army planes to Tjilatjap, Java. She lost 16 men. Escorting destroyers administered the *coup de grace*.

That same evening, the Malay Barrier would be breached in a seven-hour intermittent action fought in the Java Sea. Barrelling toward ABDA were seven Japanese carriers plus a seaplane carrier, 15 heavy cruisers, one battleship, 64 destroyers, seven light cruisers, 97 troop and supply transports, and smaller patrol and mine boats. Instead of intercepting these invasion forces, Allied ships encountered the support force of four cruisers and 13 destroyers.

ABDA commanders were told to hold on for months, but by monitoring the daily teletypes and radio intercepts, they knew defeat could take only a matter of days.

"Still, my men were spoiling for a fight. I didn't have to tell them what

> 66
>
> *The Battle of the Java Sea, viewed strategically, had little impact on the course of the war and yet it has left its scars on history. If ever a battle was fought against hopeless odds it was those naval engagements fought at the end of February and at the beginning of March 1942.*
>
> 99
>
> — F.C. Van Oosten
> author of *The Battle of the Java Sea*

During the Japanese bombing of the U.S. Strike Force Feb. 4, 1942, near Kangean in the Dutch East Indies (on Borneo) the U.S. cruiser *Marblehead* took a hit that killed 15 sailors.
National Archives

to do, just when," recalled Rear Adm. William Mack, then on board the USS Ford.

Early on, Allied doubts turned to optimism as a Japanese transport was torpedoed by a Dutch submarine. A Dutch bomber doomed another supply ship, and U.S. destroyers sank four other enemy vessels.

"We found ourselves right in the midst of the Jap transports," remembered Adm. Mack. "Then came the peculiar combination of a muffled explosion, a whine, a swish, and a splash, that follows the firing of a torpedo. Astern, the *Pope*, *Paul Jones* and *Parrott* were picking targets and firing. Seconds passed. Then came a blinding, ear-shattering explosion. The crippled ships began to list and sink. We reversed course and ran through the convoy again, firing on both sides."

ABDA ships steeled for the fight, but soon after came under air attack. Helpless against enemy pilots, they called in air support but the request was denied. All shipborne spotter planes were ashore to avoid damage. Japanese control of the skies proved fatal.

Their spotters noted every move the ABDA made, whether to converge on the enemy, to parry or to retreat. Night flares silhouetted the Allied ships, while the Japanese welcomed the security of darkness. They had perfected night fighting and Java Sea would be their first chance to test new tactics.

Even smoke screens could not mask ABDA maneuvers. Enemy observers saw every course change and radioed back to the warships, which lobbed shells and fired torpedoes with haphazard results.

In one attack, the Japanese unleashed 43 torpedoes and none found a target. Another time 64 projectiles bore down on the elusive Allies with no success. New long-range torpedoes (Long Lance) allowed the Japanese to strike from a safe distance, but also gave the Allies enough time to evade when the "fish" were spotted soon enough.

> **"**
>
> *The USS S-38 played a very exciting and important part in the Battle of the Java Sea. On Feb. 28, 1942, the bridge reported voices in the water. Twice one of us would swim out to large floats, tie a heaving line to it, and the men in the water would be pulled in alongside the 38 boat.*
>
> *Our final tally of survivors came to 54. As it turned out, they were off the sunken British destroyer HMS Electra. The S-38 had a crew of 44 so we had crowded conditions on board, but we managed for 36 hours until a Dutch boat picked them up. Fifty years later I met up with some of the survivors.*
>
> **"**
>
> — CMDR. JUMBO SECL
> USS S-38

"The Galloping Ghost of Java Coast," the *USS Houston,* sank on Feb. 28, 1942, in the Battle of Sunda Strait, losing 655 of its crew of 1,023. Horribly, many shipmates were strafed while bobbing in the water. Of the 368 who reached safety, many died in prison camps while building the infamous Burma Railroad. U.S. Navy

The U.S. also had new torpedoes, but these cut through the water lower, often passing under enemy ships.

But the Japanese torpedoes that did find their mark proved deadly. The Australian cruiser, *Perth,* lost 352 men. The Allied flagship *De Ruyter* went down with the ABDA commander aboard. Only 54 crewmen from the British destroyer *Electra* were rescued after their ship was sunk.

"At 02:23 on Feb. 28, the bridge [of the submarine *USS S-38*] reported flickering lights and voices in the water," recalled Jumbo Secl. "I went down on the deck with another submariner and we reported that the voices sounded like Limeys, so we started fishing them on board. They were off the British destroyer *Electra.*"

Miscommunications compounded the uncoordinated Allied maneuvers. Radios failed to work; signal flags and lights had to be translated from English to Dutch and back. And none of this was done very well, in the transmission or the interpretation. Also, the Allies were not prepared for night battles.

After nightfall on Feb. 28, some surviving ships from Java Sea engaged in a melee called the Battle of Sunda Strait, which separates Sumatra from Java. The *USS Houston,* dubbed the "Galloping Ghost of the Java Coast," escaped Japanese clutches on numerous occasions. It made a run for safety along with the Australian cruiser *Perth.* "There were many aboard who felt that, like a cat, the *Houston* had expended eight of its nine lives, and that this one last request of fate would be too much," wrote Cmdr. Walter Winslow.

Encountering a Japanese landing in progress in Banten Bay, Java, the two cruisers were put out of action by the covering force. *Houston* ran out of ammunition, hopelessly firing its flares to ward off the closing enemy ships. When the crew had nothing left to fight with, they abandoned ship.

"As much as I loved the *Houston*, I had no desire to join her in a watery grave," wrote Cmdr. Winslow. "Jap destroyers had come in close as they raked her decks with machine-gun fire. Then to my horror I realized that the Japs were coldly and deliberately firing on the men in the water." (Of the 1,023 crewmen aboard the ship the night it was sunk, 655 died and 368 ended up in Japanese POW camps building the notorious Burma Railway.)

The *USS Pope*, along with the British destroyer *Encounter* and British cruiser *Exeter*, also tried to flee but were sunk by Japanese air and surface forces off Surabaja, Java, on March 1. In a separate action, the U.S. destroyer *Edsall* also was sunk. That same day, in yet another surface action, the destroyer *Pillsbury* and gunboat *Asheville* were destroyed off Java's coast.

The U.S. Asiatic Fleet perished in the Java Sea. But ABDA's determination stalled the Japanese juggernaut and forced them to use an excessive amount of fuel and ammunition, which would be evident in future naval encounters.

Japanese Support Force commander, Rear Adm. Takeo Takagi, was highly criticized for his tactics. After his tarnished victory at Java, he was blamed for the heavy Japanese losses in the Battle of the Coral Sea three months later. He was then reassigned to a submarine fleet and was killed at Saipan in 1944, a disgraced commander.

'Most Daring and Spectacular' Raid

After the combined losses in the Java Sea and at Pearl Harbor, America was desperate for good news. Maj. Jimmy Doolittle would soon be the bearer of that news. He was about to explode the 13th century myth about a "divine wind" protecting Japan from invaders. Only Army Air Forces' bombers could reach Tokyo, but they would have to do it via Navy carrier.

In early April 1942, after refitting and practicing short take-offs, 16 B-25 bombers and crews from the 17th Bombardment Group were loaded on the carrier *Hornet* bound for striking range of Japan. Early on April 18, a Japanese patrol boat spotted the American carrier force, and flashed a message back to Tokyo. Still more than 800 miles from Japan, and twice as far as they wanted to be before taking off, the bombers launched immediately. Due to pitching seas it took an hour to get all 16 from the flight deck.

By flying "on the deck" at 75 feet above the water to avoid detection, then skimming the treetops once they crossed over Japan to avoid anti-aircraft fire, 13 bombers struck Tokyo and Yokohama just after noon. Three others headed south for Nagoya, Osaka and Kobe. Just before reaching the target, each plane climbed, delivered its bombs, then ducked back down.

A steel factory, oil refineries, docks, ammo dumps, supply areas and an airplane factory were hit. Only one bomber had to jettison its load. Another bomber, unbeknownst to its pilot, missed an opportunity when it

> The selection of Doolittle to lead this nearly suicidal mission was a natural one. . . . He was fearless, technically brilliant, a leader who not only could be counted upon to do a task himself if it were humanly possible, but could impart his spirit to others.
>
> — GEN. HENRY H. ARNOLD

> They were picked crews. They were the crews that had the most experience with the airplane, and, right from the start, they were absolutely top-flight.
>
> — GEN. JAMES H. DOOLITTLE

Doolittle's Raiders gather around their squadron commander on the _USS Hornet_ just prior to their successful bombing run on Japan's largest city — Tokyo. Most of the Raiders made it safely to friendly territory in China. But nine died — five in crash-landings, one of malnutrition as a POW, and three were captured and executed.
Smithsonian Institution

roared past Tojo, the Japanese prime minister, flying back from an inspection tour.

Japanese broadcasts, at first, tried to reassure the public the raids were just practice drills. As more damage reports came in, however, the propaganda machinery geared up and denounced "the cowardly raiders."

Mission accomplished. Now the bomber crews had to make it to China. Eleven planes ran out of fuel, including Doolittle's, and the crews bailed out over enemy-occupied China. (Japanese press reports claimed the planes had been shot down.) Four of the bombers crash-landed, killing five crewmen. One bomber coasted to Russia where the crew was imprisoned.

Eight crewmen were captured by the Japanese, put on trial and sentenced to death. Three were executed and one died of malnutrition while in captivity.

Of the 80 Doolittle raiders, 71 survived: most had been saved by the Chinese. (Some would later die in other WWII battles.)

For Japan the physical damage was minimal, but the loss of face was devastating. When President Franklin D. Roosevelt proudly announced the raid on Japan, he facetiously said the planes had come from "Shangri-La."

A month after the raid, on May 19, 1942, Doolittle was summoned by the President to receive the Medal of Honor. Brig. Gen. S. L. A. Marshall, noted military historian, put the raid in perspective by calling it "possibly the most daring and spectacular operation in American military history."

Bataan and Corregidor Besieged

After Pearl Harbor, American and Filipino forces braced for an invasion of the Philippines, a U.S. colonial possession since the turn of the century. That invasion began in southern Luzon on Dec. 11, 1941. Less than a month later, the U.S. bastions on Bataan and Corregidor were under siege.

"We knew something was going to happen because contact with the Japanese fleet had been lost weeks before December 7," reported Cpl. Walter Straka, a tanker with the 194th Tank Battalion. The 192nd and 194th had been the first U.S. armor units sent overseas. They provided the primary firepower of the Provisional Tank Force defending the Philippines.

Under the umbrella of the Philippine Defense Force, the two tank battalions joined the 71st Field Artillery, 26th Cavalry Regiment and the 4th Marine Regiment. Filipinos filled the ranks of the 1st Philippine Division (regulars), and the 45th and 57th Philippine Scout regiments. Together with the U.S. 31st Infantry Regiment, they formed the Philippine Division. Other units included the Far East Air Force and remnants of the Asiatic Fleet. Of the 78,100 troops on the Bataan Peninsula, only 11,796, or 15 percent, were American.

Within hours of the attack on Pearl, Japanese bombers rumbled over the "Pearl of the Orient."

"We heard the roar coming, like the deep growl of many powerful beasts — snarling as one. The best of Nippon's pilots must have been in those planes," recalled Army Col. E. B. Miller, commander of the 194th Tank Battalion. "They dropped bombs on installations and grounded airplanes lined up like ducks on a pond."

Under the circumstances, pilots assumed a far different role. "The Provisional Infantry Unit was made up of personnel from these Air Force squadrons that had no airplanes," recalled Wayne B. Lewis of the 31st Infantry Regiment. "From the first day of the war to our bitter end we were at the mercy of the Japanese Zero Fighters and heavy bomber aircraft."

After pounding the defenders from the air and sea, the 50,000-strong 14th Imperial Japanese Army planned to mop up the 20-by-25 mile Bataan Peninsula. But Lt. Gen. Massahura Homma, the task force commander, severely underestimated the "battling bastards of Bataan," who pulled back

At a Roadblock on the Road to Bataan. **On Dec. 26, 1941, the 2nd Platoon of Company C, 194th Tank Battalion, attached to a Filipino army regiment near Lucban, Luzon, engaged the Japanese in a desperate fight at a roadblock. The 192nd and 194th Tank Battalions received three Presidential Unit Citations for their courageous defense of the Philippines.**
National Guard Heritage Painting

66

'Why the dirty bastards!' the man next to me said. ' They're using us as a shield to fire on Corregidor.' It was true. We should have realized then what to expect as their prisoners.

99

— CPL. HUBERT GATER
200th Coast Artillery

A gun crew on Bataan in the spring of 1942 mans a 3-inch anti-aircraft M-2. But all firepower went for naught as the U.S. delaying action broke down and the Japanese overran the peninsula on April 9. U.S. Army

66

The thing that burned itself into my mind for days and days was the imprint of the body in the road that had been run over. I don't know how many times. It was paper thin, but the shape was very clear. It was as if the guy was still pleading for somebody to reach down and pick him up.

99

— SGT. RALPH LEVENBERG
17th Pursuit Squadron

in a bounding overwatch — one unit covering as the others retreated to temporary safety on Mount Rosa.

Americans and their Filipino allies stood their ground for the next three months. From February through March 1942, the Japanese were so badly mauled that they pulled back to regroup and wait for much-needed supplies and reinforcements. Some 50,000 fresh troops finally arrived, allowing the Japanese to launch a final attack: Bataan fell April 9.

"We were defeated not by an overwhelming number of Japanese, but by lack of anything to eat and any medical supplies," remembered Air Force Capt. Arthur Locke. "The majority of our forces were hardly able to stand because of hunger and sickness. Malaria affected nearly everyone of Bataan. Japanese air forces controlled the air, making coordinated defense of the islands impossible."

Next to fall was Corregidor, a fortified island covering two square miles, at the entrance to Manila Bay. It was known as the "Gibraltar of the Pacific."

Some of the Bataan defenders eluded capture and swam the channel to Corregidor, an island two miles off Bataan's tip. There the fight continued, as U.S. artillery counterpunched every enemy barrage. For 27 days, American and Filipino forces held out on the "Rock," enduring constant bombardment.

Among the defenders were U.S. sailors and Army aviators who picked up weapons of fallen soldiers and Marines. They were ably supported by nurses and civilians.

Running short of food and potable water, fighting disease and dehydration, and making sure every round of ammo found an enemy target, Corregidor's defenders, which included the 59th and 60th Coast Artillery regiments, held out for as long as they could.

"We've got about five minutes left and I feel sick at my stomach. I am really low down. They are around smashing rifles. They bring in the wounded every minute. We will be waiting for you guys to help. This is the only thing I guess that can be done. General Wainwright is a right guy, and we are willing to go on for him. But shells were dropping all night, faster than hell. Damage terrific. Too much for guys to take. Everyone is bawling like a baby. They are piling dead and wounded in our tunnel. . . . The jig is up." That's how Sgt. Irving Strobling, U.S. Army radio operator on Corregidor, described the situation in sending his last message before the surrender.

An intricate system of tunnels and emplacements sheltered U.S. and Filipino troops. But intense artillery fire blanketed the "Rock," and a Japanese amphibious assault overran Allied defenses on May 5. Surrender was ordered and Corregidor fell under Japanese control. U.S. casualties totaled 2,000. Some 11,500 troops were taken prisoner.

Many Americans and Filipinos defied the surrender order, fleeing into surrounding jungles where they launched guerrilla attacks until U.S. forces returned to the Philippines in October 1944.

Gen. Douglas MacArthur vividly recalled the valiant warriors of Bataan and Corregidor: "They died hard, those savage men. The vision of grim, gaunt and ghastly men, unafraid, cannot but evoke that tender, at the next instant, admiring, feeling in the hearts of people who value freedom."

This massive 12-inch disappearing gun was used by the 59th and 60th Coast Artillery in the defense of Corregidor during 1941–42.
Courtesy of Walter Collinge

★ ★ ★

Women in the War Zone: 'Angels' and WACs

"The Army nurse is the symbol to the soldier of help and relief in his hour of direst need. Through mud and mire, through the murk of campaign and battle, wherever the fight leads, she patiently — gallantly — seeks the wounded and distressed. Her comfort knows no parallel. In the hearts of all fighting men, she is enshrined forever."
— GEN. DOUGLAS MACARTHUR

When Corregidor finally fell in May 1942, 67 members of the Army Nurse Corps were among the Americans imprisoned at Santo Tomas Internment Camp until liberated in February 1945. These "angels" are honored with a plaque at the Cross of Valor in the Philippines today. (Five Navy nurses, captured on Guam, also experienced imprisonment, in Japan.)

Margery Redding had been one of the first nurses assigned to the 31st Field Hospital on Okinawa during that ferocious battle in 1945. "There was never time to do enough," she remembered. "We did all we could to comfort the patients. Those wounded men gave us

more gratitude than some will see in a lifetime. They also constantly worried about our being there."

Other women served overseas, too. For example, 5,500 Women's Army Corps (WACs) volunteers endured harsh living conditions on New Guinea and in the Philippines. Another 400 WACs were attached to the Army Air Forces in the China-Burma-India Theater, or CBI.

"Tokyo Rose interrupted Armed Forces Radio to say the 25 girls from Hollandia [Dutch New Guinea] wouldn't make it to Tacloban [in the Philippines]," recalled Midge Brubaker, a WAC with the Far East Air Force. "When we landed in Tacloban the airstrip was being strafed. We rolled out of the plane and crawled away on our stomachs."

Moreover, 4,000 U.S. Navy WAVES (Women Accepted for Volunteer Emergency Service), 1,000 women Marines and 200 SPARS — the Coast Guard's unit for women — served in Hawaii and Alaska, then considered overseas..

During the early stages of the war, commanders were concerned that

Jane Cheverton, tending to Bill Wyckoff of Co. F, 2 Bn., 23rd Marines, was the first Navy nurse to arrive on Iwo Jima in February 1945. Marine Corps

servicewomen would not "measure up." Their concerns soon proved groundless. Each WAC "better than replaced a soldier," declared Lt. Gen. George Kenney of the Allied Air Forces. And Gen. Douglas MacArthur rated them "my best soldiers."

Of the 16 Army nurses who died as a result of enemy fire in WWII, six were killed aboard the hospital ship *Comfort* when it was attacked by a *kamikaze* off Leyte Island on April 28, 1945, during the Battle of Okinawa. No WACs lost their lives due to enemy action.

March of Death

"The sun and dust took their toll on the starving and thirst-crazed men. They began falling along the side of the road, as sadistic guards hit and kicked them back into the columns," is how Cornelius Gallegos, a Bataan veteran, remembered the infamous "Death March" to Camp O'Donnell.

Then Pfc. Cletis Overton remembers passing several artesian wells near the roads. "They'd make us sit there looking and listening to those wells for an hour or two. Then they'd move us along without any water." Prisoners too weak to get back in line were clubbed, bayonetted or shot.

Two days into the trek, nearly 400 men from the 91st Division (Philippine Army) were bound together and slaughtered with samurai swords and bayonets. Others were cut down for moving too slowly or asking for water. Japanese truck drivers would run down and crush stragglers who couldn't keep up. All were left along the trails.

"When we saw the trucks carrying infantry, we learned to get as far off the road as we could," recalled former Cpl. Bob Wolfersberger. "The Jap troops would carry bamboo sticks and they'd lean out and swat you as they went by. If they didn't have sticks, they had stones or knotted ropes. They'd just swing whatever they had and see if they could hit you."

At San Fernando, the POWs were crammed into sweltering boxcars. With no room to move, many died standing in place. "Men fainted with no place to fall. Those with dysentery had no control of themselves," remembered then Cpl. Hubert Gater. "As the car swayed, the urine, the sweat and the vomit rolled back and forth."

At Capas, they were unloaded and marched to Camp O'Donnell, a former Filipino compound. "There we were fed a skimpy ration of rice twice a day. To get water you had to stand in line for hours," said Gallegos.

Because of filth and their run-down physical condition, the men were dying at the rate of 50 a day. "I remember one Thanksgiving the guard gave me a strawberry with my rice and I thought that was a real treat," recounted Ed Ziarko, a retired Air Force master sergeant and Bataan survivor. "I almost didn't want to eat that strawberry cause I didn't know if I'd ever get another one."

Many believe that because the Japanese had lost face at Bataan and Corregidor they struck back at the defenseless prisoners.

It would be 3½ years before the POWs were finally free again. "We weren't really liberated," recalls Ziarko. "We woke up one morning and all the guards were gone! The prisoners really went wild — took over everything in the camp until the American liberation forces finally showed up."

Hundreds of American troops line up in surrender and wait for the march to Bataan to begin on April 9, 1942. Many didn't make the trek, while thousands more remained POWs for 3½ years until the U.S. recaptured the Philippines. Mark Wohlfield, among these marchers, said, "An interpreter staged us for the cameraman and said to look dejected. That wasn't hard." National Archives

An estimated 10,000 GIs had begun the Death March: some 650 died along the way. Of the 9,300 Americans who reached Camp O'Donnell, 1,600 were dead from starvation, disease and Japanese brutality within the first six to seven weeks after arriving there.

The destroyer *USS Peary* exploded and sank on Feb. 19, 1942, during a Japanese sneak attack on the bay at Darwin, Australia, taking the lives of 85 of the 120 men aboard.
Signalman Douglas Fraser, *HMAS Deloraine*

Peary Perishes at Darwin Bay

War came to the "Top End" of Australia on Feb. 19, 1942, when some of the same Japanese planes that hit Pearl Harbor struck again at Darwin in the Northern Territory. Moored in the harbor at the time were several U.S. warships of the ill-fated U.S. Asiatic Fleet.

With an armada of four carriers, two battleships and three heavy cruisers, the Japanese were just 200 miles away, easily within striking distance of the Aussie's northern coast. Land-based bombers had also been relocated for an attack on Darwin, deemed unthinkable to the Australians.

At mid-morning, 54 land bombers and 188 carrier planes descended on Darwin, destroying most of the aircraft of U.S. Navy Patrol Wing 10 before they could take off. The few that did make it aloft were quickly pounced on and shot down.

During the attack, all 10 P-40 Kittyhawks of the U.S. 33rd Pursuit Squadron stationed at Darwin took to the air. Four pilots were killed in action in dogfighting, and ultimately every plane was destroyed.

Among the 13 ships sunk in the attack was the destroyer *Peary*, which took two direct hits, followed by three more, turning her into an inferno: 85 men died in action. Only 35 crew members survived. The *Preston*, a seaplane tender, lost 17 sailors in the surprise attack made by more than 200 Japanese planes.

Historian W. G. Winslow in his book, *The Fleet The Gods Forgot*, wrote: "When the smoke cleared, the little four-stack destroyer *USS Peary*, without so much as a 'well-done' for her heroic crew from the Navy Department, was summarily scratched from the lists, to be forgotten by all but a handful of survivors and the loved ones of those who died fighting for their country."

DRAMA ON THE HIGH SEAS

On June 4, 1942, American planes scored devastating direct hits on Japanese warships during the Battle of Midway. Artist Robert G. Smith, U.S. Naval Institute

Open Pacific to 'The Slot'

Carriers in the Coral Sea

> "
>
> *The war in the Pacific was a war of logistics — fought across thousands of miles of blue water. . . .*
>
> "
>
> — NATHAN MILLER
> *The U.S. Navy: A History*

WITH AMERICA's far Pacific and Far East possessions in enemy hands, the nation turned to the sea to swing the tide of battle. On the high seas, while postponing any Allied ground offensive, the Japanese could be defeated in their bid to expand their empire dangerously close to Australia. Some of history's most decisive naval engagements would be waged in the seas to the northeast of this imperiled ally.

The Battle of the Coral Sea — the first sea engagement where opposing naval battle groups never actually came in sight of each other — possibly prevented the invasion of a continent.

Two U.S. carrier groups — the mighty carrier *Lexington* with its escorts, and its sister flattop, the *Yorktown* — carrying more than 140 aircraft, comprised the core of the flotilla sent to engage the Imperial fleet in early May 1942. Attack, fueling, support and search, plus British and Australian combat and support ships, including submarines, proved indispensable to the flotilla.

Aware that enemy forces were somewhere in the vicinity, both Japanese and U.S. commanders launched search aircraft to prevent surprise attacks. On May 7, Japanese pilots radioed back that an American carrier and escort were spotted.

Seventy Japanese planes were quickly launched, sinking the tanker *Neosho* (which had been mistaken for a carrier) and the destroyer *Sims*. Sixty-four sailors who hastily abandoned the *Neosho* were lost; only 14 crewmen from the *Sims* survived. That same day, 93 U.S. fighters over-

whelmed Japan's light carrier *Shoho,* blanketing it with seven torpedoes and 13 bombs.

On May 8, both sides prepared for a battle that would turn the tide of war in the Pacific. Two Japanese carriers with 121 aircraft, six destroyers and four heavy cruisers faced off against the U.S. Navy's two carriers (122 planes), seven destroyers and five heavy cruisers.

Ultimately, however, only the carriers' aircraft fought offensively. All other ships played a defensive role, screening their respective carriers from enemy bombers and torpedo planes. Fighter aircraft on both sides proved vital in protecting the carriers from incoming enemy planes.

By mid-morning May 8, bombers from the *Yorktown* found two of the Japanese carriers. But because of inclement weather, one carrier escaped, disappearing into a rain squall.

Aircraft from the *Lexington* located the other enemy carrier and damaged its flight deck, forcing planes that were launched earlier against U.S. carriers to divert to nearby island airstrips. That carrier — the *Shokaku* — would require months of repairs, forcing her, along with the *Shoho,* to miss the battle at Midway.

Now the *Yorktown* and *Lexington* came under attack. "Our radar had picked up enemy aircraft approaching at about 65 miles away," recalled Walter Hassell, one of the young sailors on board the *USS Lexington.* "This entire group, fresh out of high school and thinking of war as a game, still had the feeling that this was a sporting contest rather than the deadly experience that really lay ahead for us all."

With only 17 protectors overhead to ward off an attacking force of 18 torpedo planes, 18 dive bombers and 24 fighter planes, the *Yorktown* and *Lexington* needed a miracle to escape unscathed. "From my bridge I saw bombers roaring down in steep dives from many points in the sky, and

Duty Down Under

"These bloody Yanks are oversexed, overpaid . . . and over here."

— Australian male's lament

An estimated million American servicemen were stationed on, trained on or transited the continent of Australia during WWII.

The first GIs — members of the 147th and 148th Field Artillery battalions, the 8th Materiel Squadron and 5th AB Group — disembarked from the transport *Republic* at Brisbane on Dec. 22, 1941, only two weeks after the attack on Pearl Harbor. They were part of the "Pensacola Convoy," also known as *Task Force South Pacific*, which delivered 4,500 GIs from seven transports between Dec. 22–28. Most encamped at a place called Eagle Farm.

A flood tide of troops followed. Four Army divisions — the 32nd, 41st, 24th and 1st Cavalry — as well as the 503rd Parachute Infantry Regiment, trained

U.S. troops practice loading into boats by way of cargo nets during training in Australia in the early months of 1942. The nets could accommodate more troops faster than ladders. **U.S. Army**

in Australia for the New Guinea campaign. Air and artillery units went to the Northern Territory and Queensland. Support and service troops arrived in massive numbers.

The U.S. Navy set up shop in Melbourne. Sailors, submariners, Seabees, naval aviators and PT boat crewmen protected the coasts. Australia was the port of call for the Seventh Fleet beginning in November 1942. The 1st Marine Division later recuperated outside Melbourne for six months before returning to combat.

"Submarines operated from bases at Brisbane and Perth-Freemantle, not only early in the war but continued to do so throughout WWII," said Leonard Greenwood, a sub vet.

Seven bases were established at Darwin, Townsville, Brisbane, Melbourne, Perth/Fremantle, Adelaide and Sydney. Camps sprang up in Rockhampton, Logan Village, Jimboomba, Strathpine, Gordonvale, Cairns and Charters Towers.

"Man for man, the GI probably had greater personal impact on Australia than anywhere else in the world between *(continued next page)*

With attack planes on deck, the carrier *Enterprise* leads Task Force 16 near the conclusion of the Battle of the Coral Sea, May 1942, which temporarily thwarted a Japanese plan to extend its invasion to the east. U.S. Navy

torpedo planes coming in on both bows almost simultaneously," related Adm. Frederick Sherman, skipper of the *Lexington*.

"The water in all directions seemed full of torpedo wakes. Bombs were also dropping all around us . . . occasionally the ship shuddered from the explosions of the ones that hit. Enemy planes were being shot down right and left, and the water around us was dotted with towering flames of their burning carcasses."

The *Yorktown*, more maneuverable than the *Lexington*, evaded the torpedoes and sustained only one blast. The bomb penetrated the flight deck and exploded deep in her hull, killing 37 and wounding many more men.

Five bombs and two torpedoes struck the *Lady Lex*. "I could not imagine anything that would take a ship of almost 50,000 tons and shake it like a dog would shake a bone, but that first torpedo did it," said Hassell.

She managed to stay afloat, even though fires below deck were raging. Several hours after combat, the mighty carrier was devastated by an internal explosion from a buildup of leaking gas. Reluctantly, the order to abandon ship was given. Survivors were picked up by escort ships. The *Lexington* was finally put to rest by torpedoes from one of her own destroyer escorts, the *Phelps*. Though 216 *Lexington* sailors were killed in battle, 2,735 crew members were rescued.

An estimated million American airmen, soldiers, sailors and Marines were stationed on, trained on or transited the Australian continent during WWII. (The first units arrived just two weeks after Pearl Harbor, in late December 1941.) The 10,000-strong Fifth Air Force was based at Charters Towers formed there in August 1942. Courtesy of Arch Fraley Collection

1941–1945," wrote John Moore in *Over Sexed, Over Paid and Over Here*. (More than 15,000 GIs married Australian women.)

Americans also played a direct role in Darwin's defense. The U.S. 147th and 148th Field Artillery battalions provided anti-aircraft fire support for the Northern Territory's capital. "The 102nd Coast Artillery Anti-Aircraft Battalion (Separate) also protected Darwin," noted Arthur Telaak. "The unit survived 43 Japanese air raids, losing two KIA and three wounded. Three enemy Zeroes were shot down by its gunners."

The 208th and 197th CAAA were also deployed to the area. "These were the expendable frontline defenses, thrown into the forward areas far from any help had the Japanese landed after Coral Sea in May 1942," noted Charles Schroeder, a member of the 208th. "We knew that had the tide of battle swung in favor of the enemy, our orders were to destroy whatever equipment we had in place, then it was to be every man for himself, and try to get lost in the vast spaces of the interior."

Darwin and its environs served as a base of operations for the U.S. Far East Air Force (later the Fifth Air Force) until April 1942. Thousands of Army engineers and transportation troops were brought in to build airstrips (50

in all) and move materiel. These included the 808th, 43rd and 340th Engineer regiments. Altogether some 60,000 U.S. troops toiled in the Territory's outback.

From March to September 1942, P-40 fighter pilots of the U.S. 49th Fighter Group defended Darwin's skies. They shot down numerous Japanese aircraft, losing seven pilots in combat, and earned the Distinguished Unit Citation. Later on, from Batchelor Field, the U.S. 380th Bombardment Group flew long-range bombing raids against the oil refinery at Balikpapan, Borneo.

Across the Tasman Sea in New Zealand, American servicemen found a sanctuary even more tranquil than Australia. For the thousands of Marines, soldiers and sailors who endured the agony of Pacific campaigns such as Guadalcanal, Bougainville, Tarawa, Munda and Aitape, New Zealand was a paradise.

In many respects, this bit of Britain in the South Seas was home 6,000 miles removed. And it was the average Kiwi who made it feel that way. The people of New Zealand welcomed GIs not only as saviors, but as family and friends — sort of cultural cousins.

"As for the American soldier, he is likely to keep a warm memory of that green and welcoming home away from

GIs stationed in Australia underwent rugged training for eventual combat in the South Pacific, including these medical personnel assigned to a mobile field hospital in November 1942. They are carrying all their equipment on litters. This training would be crucial in future battles. Army Signal Corps

home — known to GIs as 'the land we adored,'" wrote New Zealand author Jock Phillips.

"To a man, I can say we all loved New Zealand and its people. I think they thought the same of us," said Nathan Cook, a member of the 145th Infantry Regiment, 37th Infantry Division, who was selected to be the first off the troopship in June 1942.

Cook was in the vanguard of an estimated 500,000 GIs who saw service in New Zealand by war's end. They included members of the 25th, 37th, and 43rd Infantry divisions; 1st, 2nd, and 3rd Marine divisions; 12 Seabee battalions; Submarine Service; Naval Operating Base and Naval activities; Mobile Operating Bases 4 and 6 (Navy Hospital); and the 39th General Hospital.

Japanese pilots surveyed the damage and cavalierly (and erroneously) reported that three American carriers had been sunk — the tanker sunk earlier that was believed to be either the *Saratoga* or the *Enterprise*, the *Lexington* and the *Yorktown*, which was repaired.

The final toll included the *Lexington*, *Neosho*, *Sims* and 66 aircraft. Some 565 Americans were killed. Japanese losses amounted to two ships, including a light carrier, 77 aircraft and 1,074 casualties.

Coral Sea was clearly a decisive strategic victory for the Allies. It checked Japan's southward expansion, effectively preventing the invasion of Port Moresby, New Guinea, and greatly diminishing the threat to Australia.

Mighty Surprise at Midway

Despite its setback in the Coral Sea, Japan still had a formidable armada, and counted on luring the U.S. Pacific Fleet to its death. Intelligence revealed a trap being set for the remainder of U.S. warships near Midway, an atoll six miles in diameter situated about 1,150 miles west-northwest of Hawaii. That trap would be sprung between June 3 and 6, 1942.

Aware of the impending assault because of de-coded messages, the 3,000 Americans on Midway dug in, laying anti-personnel mines. Marine and Army fighter planes and bombers reached 115, making the atoll an immovable carrier in the middle of the Pacific.

The Japanese Imperial Combined Fleet (divided into five forces) consisted of four carriers, a light carrier and nine battleships, plus a ring of destroyers. More than 5,000 combat troops accompanied the ships. If taken, Midway would serve as a forward base for attacks on Hawaii and the West Coast.

Carriers *Hornet* and *Enterprise*, with 158 aircraft, as well as *Yorktown*, with its 75 planes, also were heading for Midway. *Task Forces 16 and 17* included eight cruisers, 15 destroyers, 19 submarines, auxiliary ships and a fourth "carrier" — Midway Atoll.

Erroneously announcing "no enemy carriers in the waters adjacent to Midway," Vice Adm. Chuichi Nagumo ordered the attack. A contingent of 36 fighters, 36 bombers and 36 dive bombers dropped 30 tons of bombs on Midway — killing 24 Americans and wounding 18. Expecting a counterattack once Midway sent a distress call, the Japanese kept 93 aircraft loaded with torpedoes and armor-piercing bombs, ready to launch against U.S. warships.

With no scout planes reporting U.S. carriers in the area, a second strike on Midway was ordered. This meant the 93 Japanese planes had to be taken below to the hangar deck and refitted with high-explosive bombs.

Unexpectedly, U.S. torpedo bombers from the *Hornet* and *Enterprise* attacked the Japanese fleet without fighter support and were decimated by much faster enemy planes. Ensign George Gay was one of the pilots of Torpedo Squadron 8 who flew against the flagship *Akagi*. His squadron was wiped out in the attack. Gay was pounced on by five Zeroes and ditched after his plane was hit, watching the battle while awaiting rescue in the Pacific.

Early in the morning of June 4, 1942, with battle raging around them, U.S. Marines on Midway still performed their daily ritual of raising the Stars and Stripes. U.S. Naval Institute

"I flew right down the gun barrels, and pulled up on the port side. I could see the little Jap captain up there jumping up and down raising hell and I wished I had a .45 so that I could take a potshot at him. . . . But then I dropped right back down on the deck and flew aft looking at those airplanes. . . . I had a thought right in a split second there, to crash into those planes," remembered Gay.

Meanwhile, Japanese planes that had attacked Midway were now returning. Low on fuel, they had to land immediately, despite the planes sitting on the flight deck. Suddenly, 37 dive bombers from the *Enterprise*, *Hornet* and *Yorktown* swooped down on three enemy carriers, all crammed with aircraft and littered with fuel lines, bombs and torpedoes.

"We dreamed of catching Jap carriers, but none of us had imagined a situation like this where we could dive without a trace of fighter opposition," recalled Lt. Clarence Dickinson, one of the *Enterprise's* dive bomber pilots.

"We were coming from all directions on the carrier. I recognized her as the *Kaga*, and she was enormous. As I was almost at the dropping point I saw a bomb hit. I saw the deck rippling, and curling back in all directions.

"As we went away I could see fires in the middle of the Japanese fleet," wrote Dickinson. "One was a battleship or a big cruiser. But the three biggest fires were the carriers. They were burning fiercely and exploding."

In just six minutes the carriers *Akagi*, *Kaga* and *Soryu* were destroyed. A fourth carrier, the *Hiryu*, had escaped and quickly launched its planes, which found and crippled the *Yorktown* with three bombs and two torpedoes.

At the same time, the *Hiryu* was being attacked by planes from the *Yorktown*. One torpedo bomber pilot from the *Yorktown*, Bill Esders, remembered the attack. "We had between 20 and 25 Zeroes chasing us. All over the sky I could see planes that were on fire, blowing up or spinning out of control."

Still, the American pilots pressed on toward the *Hiryu*. "The plan was to form a semi-circle around the carrier so that when we dropped our torpedoes, there would be a greater chance of not missing the target," explained Esders. "I saw four of our torpedoes launched, and right after, I also saw four of our airplanes go down in a hail of anti-aircraft fire. I was the only one left."

Hiryu was the fourth carrier that had participated in the attack on Pearl Harbor to be sunk that day.

Next day, a Japanese sub penetrated the *Yorktown's* screening ships and fired three torpedoes, sinking the destroyer *Hammann*, and severely damaging *Yorktown*.

All told, the U.S. counted 350 men killed, 147 aircraft lost and the destroyer *Hammann* and carrier *Yorktown* put out of action.

Japanese losses were far greater: 322 aircraft, approximately 3,500 lives (which included many of the pilots who attacked Pearl Harbor), two heavy cruisers, three destroyers and four carriers.

The crew and fliers walk precariously along the sloping deck of the *USS Yorktown*, damaged at Midway as it had been in the Coral Sea. The ship was repaired and sent back into battle, only to receive irreparable damage from an enemy torpedo on June 6, 1942. The next day it listed severely to port and sank. U.S. Navy

66

We took position along with the Enterprise and the Hornet, to the northeast of Midway and waited in ambush. We were hoping the Japanese wouldn't find us before they had launched their attack against Midway. The idea was to wait until Midway was hit — poor Marines! — and then we would launch our air strike against their carriers. Surprise was the major key to victory at Midway, and catching their strike aircraft on their decks sealed their doom.

99

— Lt. (jg) Scott McCuskey
F-3, USS *Yorktown*

Navy fighters peel off after striking a Japanese ship (smoking in center) during the Battle of Midway, June 4–6, 1942. U.S. Navy

The crucial Battle of Midway destroyed all of Tokyo's plans for occupying Hawaii. From this point on, the Japanese Imperial Fleet was forced to fight a defensive sea war. Moreover, the tactics of naval warfare changed, with the mighty aircraft carrier taking center stage.

'Buccaneers' Over the Bismarck Sea

Another epic battle on the high seas occurred nine months after Midway that is unique in the annals of oceanic warfare. In March 1943, the Japanese attempt to reinforce their units on New Guinea was crushed by Allied land-based planes.

B-25s of the U.S. Fifth Air Force — the "Flying Buccaneers" — were effective high-level bombers on land, but had difficulty hitting targets on water. Without firepower of their own to counter anti-aircraft guns, B-25 bombing missions at lower levels were suicidal.

Maj. Gen. George Kenney, commander of Allied Air Forces in the Pacific, asked Maj. Paul "Pappy" Gunn to turn the B-25s of the 90th Squadron, 3rd Attack Group, into flying arsenals. He removed the bombardier position and site, and mounted eight .50-caliber machine guns forward in the nose and alongside the fuselage.

A-20 bombers from the 89th Squadron accompanied the B-25s. "The thought of attacking warships at mast height did not thrill the hell out of us," recalled 1st Lt. Jack Taylor, an A-20 pilot.

Kenney's staff monitored Japanese ship movements and messages. With inclement weather forecast, Kenney felt the enemy would try to cover its advance to Lae and/or Madang on New Guinea. The Fifth Air Force had 37 heavy bombers and 49 medium and light bombers (another 26 were grounded) ready for action. Only 95 of 154 fighters were available to provide air cover.

Because the "Flying Buccaneers" had been hit hard in previous battles, Australians supplemented the crews of the U.S. 90th and 13th squadrons. Also, the heavily armed Beaufighter, used by Royal Australian Air Force squadrons, would play a key role in the coming air battle at sea.

Seven troop transports bearing 6,000 Japanese of the 51st Division, along with artillery and anti-aircraft pieces and vehicles, departed Kabakaul near Rabaul, New Britain, on Feb. 28, escorted by seven destroyers. Next day, despite "pea soup" fog, the convoy was spotted. But the U.S. held off attacking until the following day. Japanese airstrips at Lae, Finschafen and Gasmata were hit instead, to ground some of the enemy fighters.

On March 2, the 63rd Squadron, 43rd Bomb Group, again spotted the convoy and sunk one transport with 1,200 troops aboard. Survivors were rescued by two warships, which sped to Lae to

Maj. Paul "Pappy" Gunn sits in his masterpiece B-25 on New Guinea. In an ingenious strategy, he rigged the B-25s of the Fifth Air Force with machine guns and led the bombers over the Bismarck Sea in March 1943.
Fifth Air Force

drop them off, then returned to protect the convoy.

That night, rather than push on to Lae, the convoy commander decided to circle and delay arrival until the next morning. It would be a fatal decision. Attacking Beaufighters cleared the troopship decks as many wounded and dead Japanese tumbled overboard. Before others could man the anti-aircraft guns, the B-25s roared in, blasting away and releasing their skip-bombs with devastating effect.

A-20s hugged the horizon during their approach, released their bombs, then zoomed directly over the decks. "I thought I had been hit with ack-ack," recalled pilot Capt. Ed Chudoba, "but I had actually clipped the top of the ship's radio mast."

Much higher flew other B-25s from the 38th Bomb Group and B-17s from the 43rd Group. Japanese fighters buzzed in and out of the bomber formations, but were chased off by U.S. P-38s.

Within 15 minutes, every transport had been hit and three of the destroyers were damaged. Remaining ships scattered to avoid the onslaught. Later, warships returned to rescue survivors. Just as quickly as they had appeared, the Allied planes returned to their bases to refuel and reload. Only foul weather prevented another attack that day. "I can recall the ground crews working around the clock and the flight crews flying mission after mission without a break," said Leo Mealey of the 8th Squadron. Most of the bombers completed their runs with little or no damage. But when Lt. Woodrow Moore's B-17 was hit by a Zero and the crew bailed out, enemy fighters strafed their parachutes. None survived.

Over the next two days, each enemy ship in the convoy was attacked. Of the 1,000 Japanese sailors and 6,000 troops bound for Lae, less than 1,000 made it. The Japanese officially recorded 3,664 men lost, with 2,427 survivors making it back to Rabaul on New Britain.

Japan lost six destroyers and light cruisers sunk, and two more crippled; eight transports sunk; 20 planes shot down, and 35 more damaged in the air and on the ground. American and Australian losses: six planes lost or crash-landed, 13 airmen killed and 12 wounded.

Tokyo's attempts to reinforce positions in that sector of New Guinea by transport were permanently abandoned, ending its offensive plans.

A pair of medium bombers attack a Japanese merchant ship at mast height during the Battle of the Bismarck Sea. Allied bombers destroyed a convoy of 22 Japanese ships — 12 troop transports, 10 cruisers — costing the enemy about 15,000 lives and 90,000 tons of shipping. Smithsonian Institution

Slot to Sound: Ships Sunk in the Solomons

Farther southwest in the Solomons, the U.S. Navy had been waging one of the deadliest campaigns in its history in places like "The Slot." That was the American nickname for the body of water — 280 miles long and 30 to 50 miles wide — that runs the length of the Solomons chain between Bougainville and Guadalcanal. The waters between Guadalcanal and the Florida Islands contained so many sunken hulks that they were dubbed

The cruiser **USS Quincy,** along with two other American cruisers, a destroyer and an Australian cruiser were surprised by enemy ships just after midnight on Aug. 9, 1942, with four of the Allied warships sunk and the fifth crippled during the Battle of Savo Island. U.S. Navy

The *Rear Seat Man* of a Douglas SBD Dauntless fighter fends off attacking Zeros in fighting over seas surrounding the eastern Solomons in August 1942. The SBDs flew from the carrier Enterprise on Aug. 23–24, driving off Japanese carriers. Painting by Tom Lea

Ironbottom Sound. Naval battles raged in these waters from August through November 1942.

Savo Island was perhaps the most lethal. U.S. warships were guarding the unloading of troops and supplies on Guadalcanal, when, on the night of Aug. 8–9, Japanese ships slipped past the U.S. sentry cruisers patrolling near the island, just off the northern tip of Guadalcanal. In less than an hour, the intruders sank four Allied cruisers — the *Astoria, Quincy, Vincennes* and Australia's *Canberra* — and damaged the destroyer *Jarvis* in the engagement, dubbed the "Battle of the Five Sitting Ducks."

Marine Col. Warren Baker, a spotter for 1st Marine Division artillery, was on the *Quincy* when she was hit. He jumped overboard then watched as "a tremendous explosion ripped through the *Quincy* as she started down, and capsizing to port, she slipped beneath the sea bow first, her stern reared high in the air with the propellers still churning." One of the *Quincy's* survivors drifted in the water for two weeks before being rescued.

Though officially known as the Battle of Savo Island, this clash was also called "Little Pearl Harbor," due to the loss of so many ships. It was the U.S. Navy's first fleet action since 1898. More than 1,270 Allied personnel were killed (980 Americans) and 709 wounded. Yet the toll could have been much higher if the Japanese warships had attacked the actual offloading operations instead of disappearing into the night.

From Aug. 23 to 25, the Japanese attempted to reinforce their troops at Guadalcanal with 4,500 soldiers. They dispatched three carriers and a full complement of warships to provide cover for the transports. Soon they were engaged in the Battle of the Eastern Solomons.

Task Force 61 — made up of the carriers *Enterprise, Wasp* and *Saratoga* — met them head on. Their planes sank the destroyer *Mutsuki* and the light carrier *Ryujo*, but the *Mighty E* was also crippled by three bombs, though she remained afloat and limped back to Pearl Harbor for repairs.

A third major confrontation occurred just off Guadalcanal's northern tip, at Cape Esperance, on the night of Oct. 11–12. A Japanese force of three heavy cruisers and two destroyers under Rear Adm. Aritomo Goto was sent to escort a troop convoy to Guadalcanal and then bombard the U.S. airstrip at Henderson Field.

A few minutes before midnight, the force was intercepted by Rear Adm. Norman Scott's *Task Force 64.2*, consisting of the heavy cruisers *San Francisco* and *Salt Lake City*, light cruisers *Boise* and *Helena*; and five destroyers.

The Japanese cruiser *Furutake* moved away from the action to sink a few hours later, as did the U.S. destroyer *Duncan*. While Cape Esperance is recognized as a U.S. naval victory — the first victory in a fleet action since 1898, the first victory in a night fleet action and the first surface victory against a Japanese squadron of planes — the Japanese did manage to land reinforcements on Guadalcanal. Ultimately, however, this night fight broke the stalemate in the campaign on Guadalcanal. U.S. casualties were 176 killed in action.

Adm. Chester Nimitz, Pacific forces' commander, reported on Oct. 15: "It now appears that we are unable to control the sea in the Guadalcanal area. Thus our supply of the position will only be done at great expense to us. The situation is not hopeless, but it is certainly critical."

Nimitz tasked Vice Adm. William "Bull" Halsey with taking over command of the South Pacific forces. Astonished, Halsey responded, "Jesus Christ and General Jackson! This is the hottest potato they ever handed me!" Nimitz knew Bull would be his usual aggressive self and somehow turn the tide in the Solomons.

The Japanese, also concerned about the Solomons campaign, transmitted a message to their naval commanders, which was intercepted by Allied code-breakers: ". . . it must be said that the success or failure in recapturing Guadalcanal Island, and the results of the vital naval battle related to it, is the fork in the road which leads to victory for them or for us."

During the Battle of the Santa Cruz Islands, Oct. 26–27, U.S. planes swarmed all over Adm. Yamamoto's Combined Fleet — four carriers, four battleships, 14 cruisers and 44 destroyers — sent to the area in another attempt to destroy the U.S. naval forces supporting the fight for Guadalcanal.

Ships under Halsey consisted of two carriers — the *Hornet* and *Enterprise* — the battleship *South Dakota*, six cruisers and 14 destroyers.

The *Hornet* was lost after punishing blows from enemy bombs and torpedoes. The *Enterprise* withstood three bombs, suffering only minor damage, as did several other vessels, while the submarine *I-22* sank the destroyer *Porter*.

No Japanese ships were lost, but the fleet carrier *Shokaku* and heavy cruiser *Chikuma* were heavily damaged. Though 262 Americans were killed, the battle was considered a U.S. victory because the Japanese failed to secure Guadalcanal and the surrounding waters.

The Japanese continued to send transports down the "Slot" from Bougainville, primarily after nightfall in what became known as the "Tokyo Night Express." And U.S. warships did their best to intercept them: the turning point of this campaign occurred during night runs from Nov. 12–15. It was called the Naval Battle of Guadalcanal.

On board the battleship *Washington*, Capt. Glenn Davis, concerned about the impending actions, addressed his crew: "We are going into an action area. We have no great certainty what forces we will encounter. We might be ambushed. A disaster of some sort may come upon us. But whatever it is we are going into, I hope to bring all of you back alive. Good luck to all of us."

Disaster did strike when Rear Adm. Norman Scott was killed on the bridge of his flagship, the light cruiser *Atlanta*, during the opening salvo. Minutes later, Rear Adm. Dan Callaghan, the task force commander, was

The *Wasp,* at the time the last U.S. carrier remaining operational in the Pacific, goes down in flames on Sept. 14, 1942, from three torpedo hits by a Japanese submarine. Three other shots in the same action in the eastern Solomons sank the destroyer *O'Brien* and damaged the battleship *North Carolina.* National Archives

An F-6F Hellcat takes off from the flight deck of the "Blue Ghost" — the *Lexington* — star of the American carrier fleet, which engaged enemy flat tops for the first time in the Coral Sea, mid-1942. U.S. Army

The *USS South Dakota* during an air defensive in the Battle of Santa Cruz in the Solomon Islands. Adm. Chester Nimitz and Adm. "Bull" Halsey both used the South Dakota as a flagship. Artist Dwight Shepler

Saga of the Sullivans

"Don't worry, Mom. How could anything happen to us if we stick together and protect each other?"

— MATT SULLIVAN
saying goodbye at the Waterloo, Iowa, train station, Jan. 3, 1942

When they heard the news about the Japanese attack on Pearl Harbor, the five Sullivan brothers of Waterloo, Iowa, decided to join the Navy. The two oldest boys — George and Frank — had already served a hitch and knew they would be called back when war broke out. Their younger brothers — Joe, Matt and Al — also decided to enlist.

Navy policy was to put family members on different ships to prevent a tragedy. But the Sullivans insisted on serving together and the Navy agreed to make an exception. Al — who was married and had a child — was exempt from duty.

But it was all the brothers or none: the Navy acquiesced a second time.

The Sullivans were assigned to the newly commissioned light cruiser USS *Juneau*, which had deployed to the South Pacific in mid-1942. By early November, the *Juneau* was in the midst of heavy fighting off Guadalcanal when, on Friday the 13th, a torpedo struck her port side.

Crippled, the *Juneau* and USS *San Francisco* were easy prey a few hours later when the enemy submarine *I-26* spotted them and fired a spread of four torpedoes. One fish found the *Juneau's* magazine.

"*Juneau* didn't sink, she blew up with all the fury of an erupting volcano," recalled Lt. Cmdr. Bruce McCandless in his book *The San Francisco Story*. "When the dark cloud lifted from the water, we could see nothing of this fine 6,000-ton cruiser or the 700 men she carried."

Only 100 crewmen survived the blast. One of those was George Sullivan, who desperately called out for his brothers, who had been below decks when the torpedo hit. After several days, George and most of the other survivors died from shark attacks and the debilitating elements. Just 10 of the *Juneau* crew were rescued: 683 perished.

Two months later, Alleta Sullivan spoke to newsmen about her boys: "If they have gone together, that is the way they would have wanted it. It's hard when you lose even one boy. But I know that they went in of their own free will and they did it together and for their country."

On Sept. 30, 1943, a new destroyer, the USS *The Sullivans*, was commissioned in San Francisco, christened by Alleta Sullivan.

"The Fighting Sullivans." The five Sullivan brothers died when the cruiser *USS Juneau* was attacked and sunk during the battle for Guadalcanal on Nov. 14, 1942. L–R: Joseph, Francis, Albert, Madison and George. Their loss was the greatest ever suffered by one family during WWII. National Archives

killed on the *San Francisco*, marking the first and second flag officers to receive the Medal of Honor posthumously, for a fleet action.

While the toll was heavy for the U.S. — seven destroyers and two light cruisers sunk — the Japanese lost two battleships, three destroyers and seven transports. When the *South Dakota* and *Washington* confronted the *Kirishima* in the Second Naval Battle of Guadalcanal, it was the first time U.S. battleships had fought an enemy battleship at sea.

And when the *South Dakota* was blasted by a shell from the *Kirishima*, it was the first (and possibly last) time a U.S. battleship was hit by guns from an enemy battleship. In the same encounter, the *Washington* sank the *Kirishima*, another first for battleships in naval war. More important, though, thousands of enemy reinforcements were stopped before they could reach Guadalcanal.

Combined, the Naval Battle of Guadalcanal (Parts I and II) cost 1,705 American lives and 707 wounded.

Despite their mounting losses, the Japanese still attempted to relieve and resupply their battle-weary troops on Guadalcanal. On Nov. 30, in the Battle of Tassafaronga, U.S. cruisers and destroyers ambushed eight enemy destroyers, sinking one. The cruiser *Northampton* was lost, though. Three additional ships were damaged, all ripped open by enemy Long Lance torpedoes. They were torn apart "like mechanical ducks in a carnival shooting gallery," wrote historian Samuel Eliot Morison.

Iron Bottom Sound, notorious for the number of warships it claimed, continued to be a final resting place for the Pacific navies. Battles — Vella Gulf, Vella Lavella, Empress Augusta Bay and finally Cape St. George — were waged in the Solomons' waters until Nov. 25, 1943. The latter, off New Ireland and fought by Destroyer Squadron 23, was labeled an "almost perfect naval action" by Adm. Edward D. Kalbfus, past president of the Naval War College.

★ ★ ★

'Silent Service' Beneath the Sea

"Listen, damn it," said Cmdr. Stuart S. Murray to his submarine skippers as he sent them on their first war patrol on Dec. 8, 1941. "Don't try to go out there and win the Congressional Medal of Honor in one day. The submarines are all we have left."

Comprising only 2 percent of the Navy's strength, these undersea warriors nonetheless accounted for 60 percent of Japanese merchant ship losses, as well as 214 of Tokyo's naval vessels. Submarines also surfaced in dangerous waters to rescue downed airmen, carried supplies and ammunition to troops, laid and probed minefields and transported agents on secret missions.

During the Japanese occupation of the Philippines, subs provided guerilla forces with supplies, spirited away civilians hunted by the enemy and, later, liberated prisoners of war.

The *USS Barb* — the first and only submarine to fire rockets in WWII — was typical of the U.S. fleet of submarines. It was 311 feet long and 27 feet wide, with a top surface speed of 20 knots and a submerged speed of 8.75 knots. Crews varied in size from 30 to 84, with the average being about 55 men.

Six torpedo tubes were located in the bow and four in the stern, making them capable of firing a total of 24 "fish." Until the spring of 1943, however, U.S. torpedoes were largely ineffective. They often failed to run or explode, ran too deep, exploded too soon or ran in circles.

Patrols in the Pacific were endurance tests, lasting 30 to 90 days, followed by three weeks leave. Although submarines were famous for their excellent food, by the end of long patrols, supplies were usually depleted, and the crews were forced to eat canned or powdered rations.

U.S. submarines recorded amazing feats — the *USS Batfish* sank three Japanese subs in three days in February 1945; the *USS Wahoo* wiped out an entire four-ship convoy in one day; and the *USS Tang* sank a five-ship convoy in five minutes during the Battle of Leyte Gulf off the Philippines in October 1944.

But the "Silent Service" paid a heavy price: 52 subs went down, 37 with no survivors. Out of a force of about 17,750 men, 3,505 were killed, a rate far greater than among their surface ship counterparts. Some say it was the highest rate among all branches.

Navy skipper Lawson Ramage, aboard the *USS Parche,* under heavy fire during a daring night attack by Task Force 58 against a Japanese convoy off the coast of Formosa in July 1944. Artist Fred Freeman, U.S. Navy Historical Center

SLOGGING THROUGH THE SOLOMONS

Coast Guard First Class Signalman Douglas A. Munro mans a gun aboard his support craft during the landing of Marines on Guadalcanal on Sept. 27, 1942. For his actions in saving the lives of Marines, Munro received the Medal of Honor, posthumously. (Guadalcanal was the first American land offensive of WWII.) Painting by Bernard D'Andrea, Coast Guard Bicentennial Art Collection

Hell in the South Pacific

Guadalcanal: 'Island of Death'

> **"**
>
> *And when he gets to heaven, to St. Peter he will tell: 'One more Marine reporting Sir — I've served my time in Hell.'*
>
> **"**
>
> — Epitaph on the grave of a Marine who died on Guadalcanal, 1942

BY MID-1942, American ground forces were ready to mount a land offensive in the Southwest Pacific. It was time to take the fight to the Japanese on the outer edges of their empire: the Solomons. Divided into the northern (Bougainville, New Georgia) and southern (Guadalcanal) islands, the Solomons were a downright unhealthy place. Indigenous Melanesians were then ruled by the British who had been evicted early in the war. It was left to U.S. troops to take them back, beginning with the "Island of Death."

At dawn, on Aug. 7, 1942, the big guns of *Task Force 61* pounded the Japanese defenses on Guadalcanal, a major island in the southern Solomons. Soon 10,000 Marines from the 1st Division landed virtually unopposed on the island's grey sands, at the mouth of the Tenaru River.

Other elements of the 1st Division landed on a cluster of islands to the northeast, across Iron Bottom Sound. The fighting on Tulagi was especially brutal, with many Japanese killed during desperate suicide charges, while others hid out in deep honeycombed caves. This was the Americans' first experience with routing the Japanese from underground caverns: it cost the Marines 144 dead and 194 missing on these boundary islands. But the Japanese dead totalled 700.

Mockingly referred to as *Operation Shoestring* because the bulk of materiels and men in the United States were earmarked for the fight in Europe, Guadalcanal was fortunately taken with scarcely a shot fired.

Next day, after frightened Japanese fled, Leathernecks seized their objective — a nearly completed airstrip hacked out of tall grass along Guadalcanal's north coast. The airstrip was renamed Henderson Field, in honor of Marine dive-bomber squadron leader Maj. Lofton Henderson who perished with his plane at the Battle of Midway.

The Japanese garrison had abandoned their food stores, ammunition, heavy construction equipment and even an ice-making machine, which made up for any equipment the Marines didn't have. This booty was a lifesaver, because Allied transports unloading what little supplies were available at Red Beach halted operations when enemy planes from Rabaul on New Britain roared down the Slot to harass them.

That night, Japanese destroyers and cruisers slipped into the strait and torpedoed six Allied ships. Remaining ships had to curtail off-loading operations and head for open waters and out of harm's way, despite pleas from Marine commanders ashore. This left the Marines with only a few days' supply of rations and ammunition — plus a few tons of rice the Japanese left behind.

(Half of all supplies and ammunition required for sustained combat on Guadalcanal remained in ships' holds. Precious 155mm howitzers and coastal defense guns were also left on board.)

Marine MPs display a Japanese flag captured on Guadalcanal in September 1942. U.S. Naval Institute

35th Infantry Troops leave the line after 21 days of fighting to capture the Gifu. Tense nerves and weariness are apparent in the first two men of the returning column.

Three American carriers left Guadalcanal with little air support. Another two weeks passed before Henderson Field was ready to receive fighter aircraft, dubbed the "Cactus Air Force."

Despite its uneventful beginnings, the Guadalcanal campaign quickly escalated. It ended six months later with Japan's advance into the South Pacific stopped.

Besides battling the Japanese, U.S. ground troops also fought an incredibly inhospitable environment. Marine scout private and author Robert Leckie described it: "She was a mass of slops and stinks and pestilence; of scum-crested lagoons and vile swamps inhabited by giant crocodiles; a place of spiders as big as your fist and wasps as long as your finger, or lizards, tree-leeches, scorpions, and centipedes whose foul scurrying across human skin leaves a track of inflamed flesh.

"By night, mosquitoes come in clouds, bringing malaria, dengue or any one of a dozen filthy exotic fevers. And Guadalcanal stank. She was sour with the odor of her own decay, her breath so hot and humid, so sullen and so still, that the Marines cursed and swore to feel the vitality oozing from them in a steady stream of enervating sweat."

Before the campaign was over, the emaciated men of the 1st Marine Division were pulled out and replaced by fresh troops, who quickly learned how unforgiving Guadalcanal could be.

On D-Day plus 11, Japan's first reinforcements secretly landed east of the airfield on Guadalcanal. More than 900 troops commanded by Col. Kiyono Ichiki slipped through the coconut groves to the mouth of Ilu River, hoping to surprise U.S. defenders.

But the Americans were tipped off by a native named Jacob Vouza, whom the Japanese had interrogated to no avail, beaten, bayoneted and left for dead. Miraculously, he crawled back to American lines to warn them of the enemy presence.

When the Japanese charged across the Ilu River, Marines waiting on the opposite bank returned a blistering fire. Then five U.S. tanks crossed the stream and mowed down survivors. The Ichiki offensive was crushed. Two others followed with similar results.

Almost daily, Japanese planes from Rabaul appeared overhead to harass the Americans. Fred Beilfus, Jr., 3rd Marine Defense Battalion, from Stanwood, Wash., recalled the bombing raids. "They would come out of the sun within five minutes of noon every day. It was like a milk run. They didn't deviate at all." John Stevenson, 1st Marine Division, from Everett, Wash., remembered, "They didn't do much damage. They made some holes in the airstrip, but those were filled right away."

Desperate to reinforce his decimated ranks at Guadalcanal, Adm. Yamamoto dispatched more transports accompanied by an armada of warships. These too ran into a buzz saw — U.S. torpedo bombers and warships thwarted almost every attempt to navigate the Slot. Yet in mid-September, the enemy managed to land another 6,000 men.

Both of Japan's land offensives on Guadalcanal came from the mountains, where a grassy ridge drops within half a mile of the runway. The September and October battles of Bloody Ridge produced the most frightful combat of the campaign.

U.S. Marine and Army units fought off night attacks and *banzai* charges that almost pushed them back. Beilfus, positioned at the base of the ridge, remembers Japanese breaking through to his position. "We got a look at them," he said. The desperate fight produced "a terrible noise."

Though driven back, the 1st Marine Raider Battalion, under Lt. Col. Merritt Edson, toughed it out and refused to relinquish the ridge. "This is it. There is only us between the airfield and the Japs," Edson told his men during a lull in the fighting at Bloody Ridge. "If we don't hold, we will lose Guadalcanal."

With artillery and P-39 fighter support, the Marine Raiders held their ground and chewed up the Japanese.

Bloody Ridge was not the last battle. In October, the Japanese 17th Army landed, but so, too, had the U.S. 2nd Marine Division, and the Army's American and 25th divisions. The 164th Infantry Regiment, American Division, arrived on Guadalcanal Oct. 13 and 11 days later defended Henderson Field against a major counterattack. Then between Nov. 5–11, it participated in the battle at Koli Point and Gavaga Creek.

One by one the GIs took Mt. Austen, now called Grassy Knoll, then Gifu Hill, Skyline, Sea Horse and Galloping Horse Ridges. The Japanese again hid in caves and dugouts, requiring grenades and mortars to blast them out or seal them in.

Ken Sarff of Corvallie, Ore., served with the Army's 25th Infantry Division toward the end of the campaign. "Most of the action was down in the jungle between those bare ridge tops," he recalled. "We didn't face any *banzai* charges like the Marines had earlier." On Christmas Day, Americans captured Hill 27 near what is now Honiara. It was one of the last battles.

After that, Sarff said, "It was a game of tag. The Japs were trying to slow us down so they could reach Cape Esperance and get out of there."

Enemy transports loaded with supplies and reinforcements were either sunk or forced to turn back during numerous naval battles. The last starving Japanese — some 13,000, mostly diseased and wounded — deserted Guadalcanal on Feb. 3, 1943. Fittingly, the Japanese, who sacrificed 24,000 lives there, referred to it as the "Island of Death."

"The Japanese have a mistaken notion that they must die for their emperor and our job is to help them do that just as fast as we possibly can," Lt. Col. Scheyer, commander of the 9th Defense Battalion, said as his unit departed Guadalcanal bound for Rendova in June.

U.S. Casualties on Guadalcanal

	Killed	Wounded
1st Marine Division	774	1,962
Americal Division	334	850
2nd Marine Division	268	932
25th Infantry Division	216	439
TOTALS	**1,592**	**4,183**
U.S. Navy	**4,900**	

Source: *The Second World War: Asia and the Pacific.* West Point, 1984, p. 279. *Guadalcanal* by Richard B. Frank, p. 614.

From the *New York Herald Tribune*, Friday, July 9, 1943: "Grinning through heavy beards raised during their stay on Guadalcanal, the husky Madden brothers, Al, John and Walt, bear their rifles on their last day on the island before returning to their Glendale, Calif., home. They wear old-style campaign hats."
After furlough, they returned to the 1st Marine Div. for another 16 months.
U.S. Marine Corps

With Japanese forces deeply entrenched in fortified emplacements near Munda Field on New Georgia in September 1943, a soldier from the 43rd Infantry Division's Chemical Warfare unit fires a gas canister to rout the enemy. U.S. Army

Nailing Down New Georgia

Once the southern Solomons were secure, U.S. strategy called for GIs to capture other links in the island chain. Some 10,000 Japanese occupied the central Solomon island of New Georgia in June 1943, and 4,000 more were on the way.

On June 21, 1943, the 4th Marine Raider Battalion followed by a detachment of the 103rd Infantry, 43rd Division, seized Segi Point on the island's southern tip to prevent it from falling into Japanese hands. Then men of the 70th Coast Artillery and 47th Naval Construction Battalion quickly landed. The Navy Seabees went to work laying a vital airstrip.

Ten days later, on June 30, *Operation Toenails* — the main invasion of New Georgia — was launched. Viru Harbor, northwest of Segi Point, was a key enemy supply port. The 4th Marine Raider Battalion marched overland and took the harbor. It was a "nightmarish" experience. "Crouching under our ponchos, we ate scraps of cheese from our C rations. A few minutes later I was asleep . . . I was dead tired, and I didn't give a damn if my throat was slit as I lay sleeping," recalled Sgt. Anthony P. Coulis of the 4th Battalion.

"I heard men curse the jungle. We cursed in hoarse, hysterical whispers" . . . those "snake-like roots that reached out to trip us; the damnable mud that sucked us down; the million and one vines and creepers which clawed at a man and threw him off balance." That night, his unit's members "flopped in the goo and slept like dead men."

Farther south on Vangunu Island it took the 4th Battalion and the 103rd Infantry four days to root the enemy from Wickham Anchorage. "Vangunu was the base for Major Donald Kennedy, the renowned New Zealand coast watcher and his small 30-man militia of Solomons' natives," said Joe Finnegan, then a first lieutenant with E Battery, 70th Coast Artillery. "Once, they came back with six sets of Japanese clothing and equipment and severed heads, which they procured with their ever-present machetes."

Rendova Island, west across the Blanche Channel, was taken by the 172nd Infantry Regiment. Rain and fog delayed the landing on June 30, but the 120-man Japanese garrison rapidly fell to the regiment. Seabees followed closely behind, laboring to build a road from the landing site to another beach. "The men ceased to look like men," Seabee Commander H. Roy Whittaker recalled. "They looked like slimy frogs working in some prehistoric ooze."

Enemy planes from Rabaul harassed the Rendova beachhead, in one attack killing 30 and wounding 200 Americans when fuel dumps exploded. Japanese aircraft also managed to damage the flagship *McCawley*; it was later sunk accidentally by a U.S. PT boat. On July 4, U.S. anti-aircraft fire and fighters brought down 16 unescorted Japanese bombers when they appeared over Rendova. "Jap planes bombed and destroyed the guns and

Yamamoto Shoot-Down

On April 4, 1943, Adm. Isoroku Yamamoto, the architect of the attack on Pearl Harbor, was on Rabaul, New Britain, encouraging pilots from the 204th Air Group, 11th Air Fleet, to swoop down on the U.S. fleet investing Guadalcanal in the Solomons.

Nine days later, a detailed and coded itinerary for Yamamoto's visit to the Shortlands was sent to all units involved. This message was intercepted and forwarded to code-breakers in Hawaii, where it was quickly deciphered.

President Roosevelt gave the green light to take out Yamamoto.

On April 18, two Japanese "Betty" bombers with fighter escorts took off for Ballale Island near Bougainville. Yamamoto was in one bomber; Vice Adm. Matome Ugaki, second-in-command, was in the other.

At 7:30 p.m., just as the formation arrived over Bougainville, 18 P-38 fighters from the 339th, 70th and 12th Fighter squadrons pounced on the enemy planes, downing both bombers. Yamamoto's plane crashed along the west coast of Bougainville, killing the admiral; the second bomber ditched at sea. Ugaki survived and made it to shore.

Capt. Thomas G. Lanphier, Jr., and Lt. Rex T. Barber were given credit for the actual kill of Yamamoto's plane. One American plane was shot down during the mission.

In his book, *Get Yamamoto*, Burke Davis wrote, "In both Tokyo and Washington it was felt that the course of the war had changed with the death of Yamamoto. His loss dealt an almost unbearable blow to the morale of Japan's military forces."

Adm. Isaruko Yamamoto, commander-in-chief of the Japanese navy, was traveling in a Betty bomber over Kahili, Bougainville, in the Solomons on April 18, 1943, when Rex Barber and Thomas Lanphier — P-38 pilots from the 339th Fighter Squadron at Guadalcanal — pumped .50-calibre bursts into the enemy bomber, killing Yamamoto. Sgt. Vaugn A. Bass, 4th Air Force Historical Section, U.S. Air Force

ammo, though, and killed all of the boys on this firing battery," noted Master Sgt. Waclow Pieczynski, G-2, Headquarters, 14th Corps.

On the northwest shore at Rice Anchorage, another 2,200 Marines and GIs of the Northern Landing Group, composed of the 1st Marine Raiders, and the Army's 3rd Bn., 145th Inf. and 3rd Bn., 148th Inf., 37th Inf. Div., landed on July 5 and made an unsuccessful attempt to cut off Japanese supply lines from Bairoko to Munda. The effort lasted a full 15 days, causing considerable casualties.

USS *Helena*, after being torpedoed off New Georgia on July 5, was forced to leave 275 survivors in the water. About 200 of them attempted to reach Kolombaranga by life raft, but were carried by wind and current into enemy waters. Some 165 sailors finally made it to Vella Lavella where they hid in the jungle until rescued on July 16. Of *Helena's* nearly 900 men, 168 had perished.

Between July 2–6, the Western Landing Force got fully ashore at Zanana, northeast of Munda Point. Though only three miles from their objective, men of the 169th and 172nd Inf., 43rd Div., encountered dense jungle as they inched their way along the Munda Trail, a narrow footpath where visibility was measured in yards. Third Battalion, 169th Infantry, especially experienced jungle brutality: it recorded 700 cases of "combat neuroses" by the end of July.

"The imagination of the tired and inexperienced American soldiers began to work. . . . In their minds, the phosphorescence of rotten logs became Japanese signals. The smell of the jungle became poison gas. . . . Men of the

Above: GIs of the 43rd Infantry Division find protection in the dense jungle of Arundel Island. Starting a new phase of the Solomons campaign, they invaded on Aug. 27, 1943, and were joined by the 27th Infantry Regiment on Sept. 11. The Japanese put up heavy resistance, but finally evacuated on Sept. 27. U.S. Army

Opposite: Troops go over the side of a Coast Guard combat transport and enter the landing barges at Empress Augusta Bay to start the invasion of Bougainville, November 1943. U.S. Coast Guard

169th are reported to have told each other that Japanese nocturnal raiders wore long black robes, and that some came with hooks and ropes to drag Americans from their foxholes," according to the Army's official history.

With the 43rd Division "about to fold up" — battle fatigue and tropical diseases wracked its ranks — the 37th Division was called in as reinforcements. Resuming the offensive, regiments engaged in vicious small unit actions. Finally, by July 29, the Japanese withdrew to a final defensive line in front of Munda airfield. That same day, 1st Lt. Robert S. Scott of the 172nd Infantry and Pfc. Frank J. Petrarca, a medic with the 145th, earned the Medal of Honor, the latter posthumously. Still another GI, Pvt. Rodger W. Young of the 148th Infantry, sacrificed his life in receiving the same honor, two days later.

On Aug. 3, the airfield's perimeter was encircled. Over the next two days, Bibilo Hill fell and the 43rd Division overran Munda. Within two weeks the airfield was operational; its 6,000-foot runway became the busiest in the Solomons.

But the campaign for New Georgia was not over. It took two weeks, until Aug. 25, to eliminate Japanese forces around Bairoko. Two regiments spent 10 days mopping up Baanga Island.

Arundel Island proved to be a tough nut to crack because of its terrain — possibly the worst of the campaign. The 172nd Infantry landed Aug. 27, followed by the 169th Infantry, two battalions of the 27th Infantry Regiment, 25th Infantry Division, a mortar company and Marine tanks.

Fighting on Arundel — which proved to be "the most bitter combat of the New Georgia campaign" according to one battalion commander of the 43rd Division — lasted through the first three weeks of September when the Japanese again fled, this time to the stronghold of Kolombangara Island. Instead of assaulting the heavily fortified island, it was bypassed in favor of Vella Lavella, which was taken by the 35th RCT, 25th Division, in mid-August. Later, 9,000 Japanese troops evacuated Kolombangara to southern Bougainville, essentially ending the New Georgia campaign.

It had been a costly lesson in jungle warfare for the Army. American casualties climbed to 1,094 killed in action and 3,873 wounded in action. Greater losses due to disease, combat fatigue and neuropsychiatric disorders accentuated the toll.

Battered Bougainville

On Oct. 27, 1943, Allied forces launched a two-pronged attack from New Georgia against the Japanese on the Treasury Islands south of Bougainville, and a feint against Choiseul, to the southeast. Members of the 2nd Marine Parachute Battalion harassed the Japanese for 12 days before withdrawing from Choiseul. Bougainville, largest island in the northern Solomons, was the primary target.

'We Build. We Fight.'

"They're a rough, tough bunch of men who don't give a damn for anything but getting the job done, the war won and going home," is how one Pacific commander categorized the famous Seabees. He was right.

The famed "Bees for the Seven Seas," nicknamed from their formal unit designation — Naval Mobile Construction Battalion (CBs) — were highly skilled construction workers. Their average age was 34, giving rise to the Marine line: "Be kind to a Seabee, he might be your father."

Commanded by officers of the Civil Engineer Corps, 326,000 men joined the Seabees, peaking at a quarter million by August 1945. They were organized into 12 brigades, 54 regiments, 150 battalions, 39 special battalions and numerous maintenance units and detachments.

Formed March 5, 1942, they first entered the combat zone the following Sept. 1 when the 6th Naval Construction Battalion landed on Guadalcanal to construct Henderson Field. Seabees participated in every Pacific invasion from then on. In living up to their motto — "We build. We fight" — 297 'bees were killed in action during World War II.

Seabees of the 36th Construction Battalion take a breather from the day's job of repairing an airstrip on Bougainville where they spent Halloween in 1943. U.S. Navy

The importance of the impending battle was emphasized by Japan's commander of Destroyer Division Three at Rabaul, New Britain. Rear Adm. Miatsuki Injuin said, "If Bougainville falls, Japan will topple." With Bougainville captured, Japan's air and naval fortress at Rabaul would come within easy striking distance of U.S. planes.

More than 25,000 Japanese troops waited along Bougainville's southern coast and the Shortland Islands. Mid-island at Empress Augusta Bay were 3,200 soldiers and sailors. The northern portion of the island and Buka Island, to the north, held 5,000 more troops and two vital airstrips.

The "soft spot" was at Cape Torokina, north point of Empress Augusta Bay. Terrain there was swampy; the least likely place for an invasion, or so the Japanese assumed. On Nov. 1, only 270 Japanese troops were at the cape to face the 14,000 men of the 3rd Marine Division, a Figi infantry regiment and Australian and New Zealand units transported by *Task Force 31*. TF 39 provided fire support, while *TF 38*, with the carriers *Saratoga* and *Princeton*, hit from the west and launched planes against airfields to the north.

Despite a naval barrage, the dug-in enemy troops caught the invaders in a cross-fire. Still, the transports forged on through a heavy hail of lead.

Once ashore, Sgt. Robert Owens of Co. A, 3rd Marines, took his squad to silence an enemy 75mm gun. Snipers picked off his men and wounded Owens, but he still charged the bunker, killing the crew. Owens stumbled out and died. For his actions at Cape

Torokina, Owens received the Medal of Honor, posthumously.

"During 53 days of consecutive combat, the 3rd Marine Regiment defeated the Japanese at Cape Torokina, Puruata Island and the Numa Numa Trail," according to Gerald Dunn, H & S Co., 3rd Regt., 3rd Div.

Enemy bombers and fighters, pulled from carriers in the Pacific, flew out of Rabaul and descended on transports off-loading at Cape Torokina. Most of the transports moved off quickly, but the destroyer *Wadsworth* was damaged.

U.S. and British fighters of the Air Command Solomons — the "AirSols" — provided a protective umbrella for the invasion forces. AirSols' bomber groups also pounded enemy bases at Rabaul and northern Bougainville almost daily. Bombers and fighters from the Fifth Air Force on New Guinea hit Rabaul, too.

Marine Raiders and their dogs patrol the jungles on Bougainville in November and December 1943. The dogs scouted and carried messages.
T.Sgt. J. Sarno, Marine Corps

"The 1st Marine Air Wing, AirNolSol, Marine Air Group 24, Service Squadron 24 and 27 and associated squadrons flew sorties off Torokina and Piva airstrips, destroying shipping and aircraft at Rabaul," noted George Innes, a veteran of MAG-24.

Allied planes hugged the earth to avoid detection. But as 1st Lt. Marion Kirby of the 431st Fighter Squadron remembered: "When you arrived at the target, you were pretty damned close to their guns. They had much greater accuracy at 1,500 feet than at 25,000."

With the beach secured, patrols scoured the jungles for the remaining 3,000 enemy troops in the area. War dogs sniffed out Japanese waiting in ambush. Jungle fighting on the island "had to be the meanest, darkest, and most treacherous battleground in the world," according to Sidney Altman, then commander of E Co., 2nd Bn., 21st Marines.

Meanwhile, the naval Battle of Empress Augusta Bay unfolded. Two heavy cruisers, a light cruiser and seven destroyers, plus three carriers from Japan's southern task force, headed for Bougainville. *Task Force 39*, with nine destroyers and four cruisers equipped with radar, honed in on the enemy without visual contact.

Navy Capt. Arleigh Burke led four destroyers at high speed through the night to hit the Japanese. The cruiser *Sendai* lost 320 men, and two enemy destroyers collided and withdrew from the fight. Another enemy cruiser was rammed by an escort ship, and went down without survivors. The Japanese lost 880 men.

In less than 30 minutes, the Americans sank one cruiser while the enemy crippled three ships — *three of their own*. A U.S. cruiser and destroyer were damaged, with 19 killed and 26 wounded.

Marine Raiders gather in front of an enemy dugout at Cape Torokina on Bougainville in the Solomons, which they overran in January 1944, adding to their reputation as skilled jungle fighters. U.S. Navy

U.S. ships pursued the enemy fleeing for Rabaul, and pilots from the carriers *Saratoga* and *Princeton* knocked off eight Japanese cruisers and destroyers. Utilizing "hit and run" tactics, PT boats from Motor Torpedo Boat Squadron 23 joined the action. Burke's "little beavers" detected enemy ships on radar and fired their torpedoes, sinking three battleships.

Despite wildly exaggerated claims, enemy torpedoes struck only the cruiser *Denver*, killing 20 men and wounding 11, and the transport destroyer *McKean*, which lost 52 Marines and 64 sailors.

But the Imperial Command had no idea how many warships, especially carriers, the U.S. really had. They did know their own navy no longer had the strength to blunt the landings at Cape Torokina, and soon abandoned reinforcing Bougainville.

That left the 23rd Imperial Regiment, 2,500-strong, hacking through jungles from the south to link up with 880 commandos landing near the Allied beachhead. They arrived at night and set up machine gun and mortar positions.

The 3rd Marine Division tried to repel them, but got pinned down. Sgt. Herb Thomas of Co. B, 3rd Marines, led his squad against one Japanese gun emplacement. When an errant grenade fell among the Marines, he blanketed it, saving his men but sacrificing his own life. Thomas was awarded the Medal of Honor, posthumously, for his actions that Nov. 7, 1943.

Two days later, another Marine, Pfc. Henry Gurke of the 3rd Marine Raiders Battalion, also was recognized for saving a buddy in his foxhole in the same manner as Thomas. His family accepted his Medal of Honor.

Because the 3rd Marine Division drove the enemy into the interior of Bougainville, the remaining Japanese reinforcements — some 2,500 — were not committed to the fray.

By Nov. 13, soldiers from the Army's 37th Inf. Div.'s 145th Inf. Regt., and the 21st Marines, were deployed on Bougainville to secure enough space for the Seabees of the 36th Battalion to lay an airstrip. Within days, Allied planes from Bougainville attacked and destroyed 190 enemy aircraft at Rabaul. The rest pulled out. The once mighty Japanese fortress on New Britain was no longer a threat.

Attempting to cut Bougainville in half, the 21st Marines ran into the Japanese 23rd Infantry. Lines shifted so much that eventually Japanese anti-tank guns caused havoc *behind* U.S. lines. Once again, the war dogs proved invaluable in finding the enemy.

Most of the East-West Trail cutting the island in two was under American control by mid-December. The only enemy stronghold left was a natural fortress referred to as Hellzapoppin Ridge, where the Japanese 23rd Infantry Regiment held out.

Over the next five days, utilizing air strikes and artillery barrages, the 1st and 3rd battalions of the 21st Marines inched up the ridge. Hill 600A, a final Japanese bastion, was secured by Christmas eve. Central Bougainville was now in U.S. hands, but both ends of the island were held by well-entrenched Japanese. Fighting had cost them 2,000 casualties.

By March 1944, the Japanese assembled a counterattack force. U.S. XIV Corps manned the perimeter around Empress Augusta Bay with 62,000 men, including the Americal and 37th Infantry divisions. Ground forces were backed by the destroyers of the "Bougainville Navy."

Six veteran Army infantry regiments held the line against up to 19,000 Japanese attackers. At Hill 700 and Hill 260, bitter contests were fought. A final, futile attack was made on the perimeter on March 23. The failed offensive had cost the Japanese 5,000 dead versus 263 Americans killed and several hundred wounded. (In addition, the Marines had already sustained 732 KIA on Bougainville.) Sporadic fighting continued for a few weeks to follow.

In December 1944, Australian II Corps, augmented by Fiji scouts, replaced the Americans and continued the assault on the battle-weary Japanese well into the summer of 1945.

Standing rear guard duty on Jan. 9, 1944, Pvt. R. Dennis of the 182nd Infantry, Americal Division, uses the heavy jungle growth of Hill 260 for camouflage for his position on Bougainville in the Solomon Islands. After a surprise U.S. assault on the island the previous Nov. 1, fighting continued until the end of April at a cost to the Japanese of about 7-to-1 in KIAs. U.S. Army

The 112th Cavalry Regimental Combat Team moves through a coconut plantation on Arawe, New Britain. The independent 112th landed on Dec. 15, 1943, at Arawe, 80 miles away from Cape Gloucester, to confuse the enemy during the main assault on New Britain. U.S. Army

New Britain: 'Green Hell'

U.S. forces next drove northwest of Bougainville toward the last stepping stone in the path to isolating the Japanese stronghold at Rabaul — that base's home island of New Britain in the Bismarck Archipelago. To Marines it was a "green hell" and "the slimy sewer." One Leatherneck said it was "one of the evil spots of this world." Whatever it was called, New Britain would host "the most perfect amphibious assault in World War II," according to Marine historian Frank Hough. Officially, it was known as *Operation Dexterity*.

Supported by gunfire from the cruisers *Phoenix* and *Nashville* of *Task Force 74*, a handful of destroyers and bombers from the 1st Air Task Force of the Fifth Air Force, the 1st Marine Division landed at Cape Gloucester on the island's western tip on Dec. 26, 1943.

But they were not the first Americans on New Britain's shores. "Eleven days before, on Dec. 15, the 112th Cavalry Regiment arrived at New Britain. Along with the 148th Field Artillery Battalion, it formed a regimental combat team which conducted a diversionary operation on Arawe Island, on the southwest end of New Britain," wrote 112th veteran Henry Grim. Cape Merkus, along with small offshore islands, was captured. The intent of the operation was to seize territory for an air and PT base.

To break the stalemate that ensued on Arawe, a company from the 1st Marine Light Tank Battalion and two companies from the 158th RCT were landed to reinforce the cavalrymen. By Jan. 16, 1944, the Japanese had been driven from their trenches outside the peninsula's perimeter. Actions on Arawe claimed 118 Americans KIA, 352 WIA and four MIA.

Invading Marines faced not only 10,788 Japanese troops, but a horrendous environment. "Because of the rugged terrain and swamp areas along the shore," said the division action report, "progress was difficult and the front was finally reduced to one company."

Pfc. John M. Smith, of the 7th Marines, remembered: "It was damp up to our neck. Time and again members of our column would fall into waist-high sink holes and have to be pulled out. A slip meant a broken or wrenched leg." Drenching rains, coupled with strong winds and felled trees, which in turn caused injuries and even deaths among the Americans, made moving a feat in itself.

Though fighting was initially relatively light, the torrential downpours and resultant sea of mud made life unbearable. Lt. Col. R.M. Wismer later wrote: "On at least one occasion, I had six to eight inches of water collected in the lowest portion of my hammock while attempting to sleep."

Japanese troops took advantage of the weather by withdrawing inland. When the enemy was encountered, such as at "Hell's Point," fighting was fierce. Three days after landing, Marines swarmed across Gloucester airfield. By the next night, the airdrome was in American hands.

"The objective of the 1913th Engineer Aviation Battalion was to rebuild the airstrip at Cape Gloucester and the Japs at Rabaul were determined to keep us from it as every night they came over the mountain and bombed our progress," recalled Sgt. Melvin Rudy of Company B.

Action then shifted south to Tauali where the isolated 2nd Bn., 1st Marines, waged the "Battle of Coffin Corner." An intense, confused firefight ensued. Gunnery Sgt. Guiseppe Guilano of Company H gallantly supplied mobile firepower with his light machine gun — firing from the hip. Guilano's heroics became an apocryphal story for the Marine Corps.

Coffin Corner ended resistance in the region. After 10 days of patrolling, the 2nd Battalion linked up with the main body at Gloucester.

In the weeks ahead, Marines fought a series of battles — Suicide Creek, Hill 150, Aogiri Ridge and Hill 660 — in the Borgen Bay area that proved vital. With the capture of Hill 660 on Jan. 16, 1944, the western phase of the New Britain campaign was over.

But it had come hard. "The boys were tired, wet to the skin, and going on nerve alone. Not even Colonel Buse could explain it, but spontaneously those bedraggled and bedeviled Marines rose and charged that vertical face of rock and clay. . . . That night we camped on the crest of Hill 660," wrote two combat correspondents.

Navajo Code-Talkers

They developed the only code in World War II never to be broken by the enemy, and utilized it in the Solomons, the Marianas, Iwo Jima and Okinawa. They served primarily in the Marine Corps, but some were in the Army. And occasionally they were mistaken for Japanese soldiers. They were the Navajo code-talkers.

Ironically, the idea for a secret code based on the Navajo language came from a white man. Staff Sgt. Philip Johnston, the son of a missionary and fluent in the language, read about Indians in an armored division who communicated in their own language while on maneuvers. He presented his plan to the area signal officer at Camp Elliott north of San Diego. The officer was skeptical until Johnston gave him a sample.

Navajo code-talkers Cpl. Henry Bake Jr. and Pfc. H. Kirk send messages on Bougainville in December 1943.

"If I had lighted a string of firecrackers and laid them on the desk, the effect could not have been more startling," Johnston recalled years later.

The pilot project received approval by Marine brass, and after training at Camp Elliott in April 1942, the original 29 Navajo code-talkers became the 382nd Platoon of the 4th Marine Division.

American Indians had been used in WWI to send messages in their native tongue, but the experiment met with mixed results. The Navajos, however, devised a sophisticated code, and because they spoke in their ancient language, the scrambled information was indecipherable to the Japanese. This system proved invaluable in the South Pacific.

"Were it not for the Navajos, the Marines would never have taken Iwo Jima," said Maj. Howard M. Conner, signal officer of the 5th Division at the time.

Of the 540 Navajos who served in the Marines during WWII, 420 were code-talkers.

Back on the carrier *Saratoga*, a wounded air crewman receives assistance. He has returned from an attack on Rabaul, Nov. 5, 1943.

Operation Dexterity officially ended Feb. 10, 1944. In the next few months, the Marines continued east, and later that spring, the largest Marine patrol — known as the "Gilnit Patrol" (384 men) — of WWII was conducted to bisect the island.

Rabaul was simply bypassed and reduced as part of *Operation Cartwheel*. An air offensive neutralized it. Some 29,354 sorties dropped 20,967 tons of bombs on the base, which was protected by 367 antiaircraft guns. Approximately 91,000 Japanese troops based in the area surrendered Sept. 6, 1945, four days after the peace treaty was signed.

That, however, does not lessen American achievements on New Britain. Tortured by tropical insects, torrential rains and never-ending sniper fire, the 1st Marine Division slashed through dense jungle and struggled in mud which mired artillery pieces and prevented movement. Yet it managed a striking tactical success at the cost of 310 KIA and 1,083 WIA.

The 1st Marine Division was relieved on April 28, 1944, by the Army's 40th Infantry Division. This was to be the Marine Corps' last *jungle* operation of World War II.

★   ★   ★

Members of the 2nd Bn., 1st Marines, pay their respects to dead comrades at Cape Gloucester, New Britain, Dec. 29, 1943.
MacArthur Memorial Museum

FIGHT FOR NORTH AMERICA

Defense of the Aleutians by Domenick D'Andrea. Gunners of the 206th Coast Artillery Regiment (Arkansas National Guard) ward off Japanese aircraft in Dutch Harbor, Aleutians, on June 3, 1942. National Guard Heritage painting

Frozen and Forgotten in the Aleutians

Death at Dutch Harbor

"

The Aleutian theater might well be called the 'Theater of Military Frustration.' Both sides would have done well to leave the Aleutians to the Aleuts.

"

— LT. CMDR. SAMUEL ELIOT MORISON
Naval Historian

On the high ground of an icy inlet in Alaska, U.S. Marines man a machine gun at a lookout post. U.S. Marine Corps

AT THE NORTHERNMOST FRONT of the Pacific Theater was Alaska. When WWII erupted, it was considered an overseas outpost. Duty there was difficult under the best of circumstances. But when Japan zeroed in on the territory as part of its conquest of the Pacific, the Army was put on a war footing that made life even more strenuous. Despite extensive preparation, GIs were still surprised at the audacity of the attack that came.

On June 3–4, 1942 — a full six months after Pearl Harbor — Japanese forces again hit U.S. turf, shocking the nation. Their carrier-based bombers and fighters struck Dutch Harbor Naval Base and nearby Fort Mears in the eastern Aleutians, which stretched west from mainland Alaska.

Twenty-five Americans were killed at Ft. Mears that first day, and on the 4th a four-man 20mm coast artillery crew was lost. All told, 43 Americans (33 soldiers) were killed, 64 wounded and 11 planes lost. Tokyo was minus 10 planes and only 15 men in the raids.

Subsequent capture of Kiska and Attu caused a degree of consternation among the West Coast public. But the military was confident. Maj. Gen. Simon Bolivar Buckner, Jr., the Army's top officer in Alaska, remarked: "They might make it, but it would be their grandchildren who finally got there; and by then they would all be American citizens anyway."

Wresting control of the vast, 1,000-mile-long Aleutian Island chain was a formidable task. (Kiska was captured June 6, 1942, by the Japanese. This was the first time U.S. territory was occupied by a foreign power since the war of 1812.) Holding it was equally challenging. Both objectives required almost three separate and distinct campaigns: land, sea and air. The most extended battle, by far, was waged by the Army Air Forces — the 11th Air Force — created especially for that theater.

Braced for an attack by Japanese bombers on June 4, 1942, the defenders at Dutch Harbor in the Aleutians had cleared the area of Navy ships, except for the barracks ship _Northwestern_, hit in the second attack. U.S. Navy

Aleutians by Air: The 11th Air Force

It was the smallest U.S. air force. At the height of its strength, it consisted only of bomber and fighter commands, 343rd Fighter Group and the 28th Composite Group. The 11th Air Force was activated in early 1942 as part of a major build up of forces in Alaska following Pearl Harbor.

Fighter and bomber squadrons were deployed to Cold Bay on the Alaskan Peninsula and Umnak Island in the western Aleutian Islands during May 1942. "The 151st Combat Engineer Regiment built three runways and the roads at Cold Bay," remembered veteran Donald Miller.

Air duels were first fought over Dutch Harbor that June. Then the air arena shifted to Japanese-occupied Attu and Kiska. Patrol bomber flying boats (PBYs) from Patrol Air Wing 4 along with planes from the 11th Air Force attempted to drive the Japanese from Kiska.

One squadron, the 54th Fighter, was equipped with P-38s. It scored the first P-38 aerial victory against an enemy aircraft on Aug. 4, 1942. Of the squadron's 30 pilots who went north, 17 were dead a year later. There was no rotation in the 11th. "The only way to get home is in a box," observed one pilot.

The 1,200-mile round trip from Otter Point on Umnak Island to Kiska limited the effectiveness of the B-17s and B-24s and prevented the employment of medium bombers as well as fighters. So an airfield was constructed on Adak, 250 miles closer to Kiska, placing aircraft within range. A typical bombing mission in the Aleutians seldom exceeded 10 bombers and a like number of fighters.

During the campaign to retake Aleutians, which officially closed Aug. 24, 1943, the 11th flew 297 missions and dropped 3,662 tons of bombs. It

ALCAN: 'Engineering Marvel of the 20th Century'

For eight months and 12 days in 1942, averaging eight miles a day, some 11,000 soldiers fought mud, muskeg and mosquitoes, endured bitter cold, ice and snow and bridged raging rivers to construct the Pioneer Alcan Military Highway, better known as the Alaska Highway.

Seven U.S. Army engineer regiments — known as "machines of 1,000 men each" — helped build the highway: the 18th, 35th, 93rd, 95th, 97th, 340th and 341st. Combined, they formed a provisional engineer brigade, along with the 73rd and 74th Engineer companies, and companies from the 29th and 648th Engineer Topographic battalions. Three regiments (93rd, 95th, 97th) were all-black with white officers. "Hell, we stayed out in the damn woods, freezing our you know what," says veteran Richard Trent.

"The 74th Engineer Company ran supplies — gas, diesel fuel and food — to the big outfits," added Richard Casey. "We got just as cold and miserable as they did." The 428th Engineer Company (DT) and Co. A, 648th Engineer

At work along the Kluane River. Approximately 11,000 soldiers and 16,000 civilians constucted 1,520 miles of the ALCAN Highway at a cost of $140 million. Army Signal Corps

Topographic Battalion, were among the advance units. "Company A's members led the effort through frozen obstacles and bitter cold," said veteran John Fisher.

A construction project so vast was not without casualties, from road accidents and explosives mishaps to cold

weather injuries. Eleven members of the 341st drowned in Charlie Lake when their pontoon raft was swamped and it capsized. "The pontoon ferry belonged to the 74th Engineer Company (Light Ponton)," recalled veteran Frank Hunter. "There was only one survivor and a trapper in a canoe had rescued him from the icy water."

Bulldozers of the 97th and 18th Engineers ceremoniously touched blades at Beaver Creek, a few miles shy of the Alaska border, on Oct. 25. At Soldiers' Summit, Kluane Lake, Yukon Territory, on Nov. 20, the highway was officially opened to Army traffic. Two days later, cargo moved by truck over the full length (1,685 miles) of the highway from Dawson Creek to Fairbanks, Alaska. Cpl. Otto Gronke and Pfc. Robert Rowe became the first to drive the entire length of the highway.

The original Alaska-Canada or ALCAN (it was officially renamed the Alaska Highway by the Canadian government in July 1943) cost approximately $140 million to build. It's construction, called "the engineering marvel of the 20th century," was one of the war's greatest feats.

> **"**
>
> *We hauled supplies and gasoline in trucks without heaters or defrosters in weather 35 to 70 degrees below zero along the ALCAN Highway.*
>
> *We lived in tents and slept on the ground because there were no cots available. Finally, summer arrived, but it was muddy, with big mosquitos and forest fires.*
>
> **"**
>
> — FRANK HUNTER
> 74th Engineer Company
> (Light Ponton), Peace River

accounted for approximately 60 Japanese aircraft, one destroyer, one submarine and seven transports. But in the process, 239 men were KIA and 46 died as a result of accidents. Also, the Navy's Fleet Air Wing 4 sustained 10 KIA and 16 MIA, as well as 34 killed in accidents.

Thirty-five AAF aircraft were lost in combat (about half to flak) and another 150 to operational accidents. This was the highest U.S. combat-to-operational loss ratio of the war. Weather was the prime culprit.

For the remainder of the war, the 11th flew bombing and reconnaissance missions 650 miles in length against Japanese military installations in the northern Kurile Islands. Airmen endured mind-numbing boredom at air bases on Attu and Shemya, which supported the operations.

"I was a crew member on a B-25 of the 77th Bomb Squadron flying from Attu," wrote Art Pallan. "The B-24 high altitude bombers of the 404th Bomb Squadron flew from Shemya. We bombed and fought off Japanese fighters over the northern Japanese islands of Paramushiro and Onekotan and other spots in the Kurile Islands, which included confrontation with the Japanese northern Pacific fleet."

The Kurile missions were some of the war's longest. The first successful one was flown July 18, 1943, by B-24s of the 21st, 36th and 404th Liberator squadrons. It was the first land-based air attack against the Japanese home islands and the second air attack on Japan of the war. During a mission on Aug. 11, 13 enemy fighters were downed.

On Sept. 11, 1943, the 11th suffered its greatest loss amidst a 50-minute dogfight over Paramushiro. Attacked by 60 Japanese planes, three American aircraft were shot down and another seven had to crash-land at Petropavlovsk on the Soviet Kamchatka Peninsula. "When our planes couldn't make it back to Attu, they landed in Russia," recalled J. P. Bloom, a veteran of the 77th Bomb Squadron "The planes were turned over to Russia and the airmen were interned there for the duration of the war."

B-24s of the 404th Bomb Squadron made the 2,700-mile round trip flight from Shemya to Kruppu on June 19, 1945: the longest Kurile mission of the war. Crews were aloft for 15½ hours. The last bombing mission against Paramushiro was completed Aug. 13, just prior to the armistice. All told, the 11th flew 1,500 sorties against the Kuriles, holding down 10 percent of Japan's air defense forces — 500 planes and 41,000 ground troops.

One of the air crews of the 406th Bombardment Squadron, which flew missions during the Aleutians Campaign of 1942–43. Staff Sgt. John Karlheim, flight engineer; Master Sgt. Ralph Davis, radio operator; Staff Sgt. Louie Tyrone, armorer-gunner; Maj. Russell Redman, pilot; Lt. Jack Roberts, bombardier; Capt. John Mullican, navigator; and Lt. H.R. Resnor, co-pilot.
406th Bombardment Squadron

Komandorskis: Naval Duel in the North Pacific

By early 1943, the Japanese position in the Aleutians had become untenable. Rear Adm. Thomas Kinkaid's surface warships and submarines prowled the North Pacific. And the crews of Fleet Air Wing 4 and the 11th Air Force continued to harry Japanese resupply efforts.

Between Nov. 1, 1942 and Feb. 11, 1943, Japan dispatched 33 shiploads of men and materiel to Attu and Kiska. Fourteen failed to reach their destinations. In desperation, the Japanese switched to sending in high-speed transports with warship escorts.

However, Kinkaid added to their difficulties by dispatching Rear Adm. Charles "Soc" McMorris and his small force of cruisers and destroyers to cover the approaches to the western Aleutians. But the Japanese succeeded in getting a convoy through on March 9, 1943.

Several weeks later, Tokyo dispatched another convoy consisting of three transports escorted by a powerful force of two heavy and three light cruisers and four destroyers — virtually the entire North Pacific Japanese fleet. The transports carried troops, equipment, ammunition and supplies intended for Attu.

On March 26, the Japanese convoy ran into *Task Group 16.6*, consisting of the heavy cruiser *Salt Lake City*, the light cruiser *Richmond* and four destroyers — *Bailey, Coghlan, Dale* and *Monaghan* — 180 miles due west of Attu and 100 miles south of the Komandorski Islands.

Despite being outnumbered two-to-one by the newer and faster Japanese warships, McMorris stood his ground. While the transports retired to

During the Battle of the Komandorskis, the cruiser *USS Salt Lake City* — "old Swayback" — lobbed shells at the enemy cruiser *Nachi,* scoring direct hits on the morning of March 26, 1943. But "Swayback" also was hit and eventually floated dead in the water. Three U.S. destroyers provided a smoke screen and covering fire for the *Salt Lake City* until she could resume power. U.S. Navy

safer waters, Rear Adm. Boshiro Hosagaya, commander of the Japanese force, pressed the attack.

Beginning at 8 a.m., the two opposing forces slugged it out for 3½ hours before Hosagaya, running low on ammunition and fuel and fearing a bomber attack, withdrew his force from the scene of battle.

During the fighting, the *Salt Lake City* went dead in the water after the engine room flooded, boilers lost power and sea water doused the ship's remaining oil burners.

The damage inflicted on both sides was minimal. The heavy cruiser *Salt Lake City,* which had just joined McMorris' force, was hit four times and the destroyer *Bailey* twice. Seven men were killed and 20 wounded, 13 of whom did not require hospitalization. The Japanese heavy cruiser *Nachi* was damaged. Enemy casualties totaled 14 killed in action and 27 wounded in action.

Though outnumbered and outgunned, *Task Group 16.6* had achieved a strategic victory in the last and longest daylight surface naval battle of fleet warfare. It also had the distinction of engaging in the longest continuous gunnery duel in modern naval warfare.

"And yet it was a strange, illogical victory," wrote war correspondent John Bishop, who was aboard the *Salt Lake City,* "a victory won by three hours and a half of bitter defensive retirement against nearly two-to-one odds; a victory won in the moment of despair when six ships and many hundreds of men reeled helplessly on the crumbling verge of defeat and death."

Adm. Hosogaya, who had failed to take advantage of his superior force, was placed on the retirement list. The Japanese on Attu and Kiska were left hopelessly isolated. The American air and naval blockade was complete. Only submarines could now reach the Aleutians.

The Japanese garrison on Attu waited for the inevitable arrival of the Americans. Had the Japanese convoy gotten through, the May battle to retake Attu would have been far more bloody. Many owed their lives to a small naval force and the courage of its leader.

Attack on Attu

The Battle of Attu was the U.S. Army's first island amphibious operation of World War II. The 7th Infantry "Hourglass" Division, garrisoned at Fort Ord on the Monterey coast of California, and equipped and trained for desert warfare in North Africa as a mechanized force, made the assault. It was then the only division in the Western Defense Command in a state of readiness for combat.

Task Force 16, comprising the battleships *Mississippi, Pennsylvania, Nevada* and *Idaho,* provided naval gunfire support. The carrier *Nassau* (CVE-16) was assigned to provide close air support for the impending attack on remote Attu, the westernmost island in the Aleutian chain.

The Attu assault force *(Task Force 51)* dropped anchor in Cold Bay on

May 1, 1943. The place lived up to its name: bleak, with snow-covered mountains. Marine Capt. John Elliott noted in his diary, "The ships look out of place in a world that belongs so little to man."

By early morning May 11, all three forces stood poised for America's third amphibious operation of the war. Men of the 7th Infantry Division would experience their first assault of an island from the sea. They also would have the honor of reclaiming the first enemy-occupied American soil since the War of 1812. Four months before, however, some preliminary reconnaissance already had been performed.

During the Battle of Attu, which began May 11, 1943, soldiers from the Southern Force, including two battalions of the 17th Infantry Regiment, 7th Infantry Division, struggled to advance over the spongy tundra in Massacre Valley. Enemy snipers overlooking the approach directed mortar and machine gun fire on the GIs. U.S. Navy

"The first amphibious assault in the Aleutians was made by the 2nd Battalion, 37th Infantry Regiment (Separate), with support groups, against Amchitka Island on Jan. 12, 1943," wrote John Young, a veteran of the operation. "Scouts from G Company sighted Japanese soldiers, but had orders not to fire unless fired upon."

The 2,000-man Southern Force consisted of the 2nd and 3rd battalions of the 17th Inf. Regt. and the 2nd Bn. of the 32nd Inf. Regt., reinforced by three 105mm artillery batteries. The Northern Force included 1,500 soldiers of the 1st Bn., 17th Inf. Regt. and a 105mm artillery battery. A third, smaller force of 500 men was composed of reconnaissance units, including the Provisional Scout Battalion.

Troops waited in their landing barges until late afternoon when the order came to head for the beaches. Fog still hung heavily in the air, hiding the landing beaches ahead, as the coxswains aboard the landing craft slowly made their way toward the undefended shores.

Southern Force landed on a "beach in fog so thick that a man 10 feet ahead was invisible. . . .Within 75 yards of the beach, the tractors pulling the 105mm howitzers were hopelessly mired, spinning their treads in the tundra. The guns had to be emplaced where they stood, and their crews hurried about scrounging around for steel matting and whatever solid detritus they could find to keep the howitzers from sinking too deep to be trained on any target," wrote Simon Rigge in War in the Outposts.

Contact with the enemy finally came 12 hours later. Southern Force had advanced 2,500 yards up Massacre Bay Valley when it ran into determined opposition. Northern Force had managed to move as far as Hill X overlooking the West Arm of Holtz Bay before being bogged down. Recon units, lost and out of the action, continued to grope their way toward the Japanese rear positions at Holtz Bay.

"The soldiers, the infantry, will have to go in there with corkscrews to dig out the Japs," predicted Gen. Simon B. Buckner, Jr., commander of the Army's Alaska Defense Command, who knew his men were not ready for what awaited them.

"Gen. Buckner had pleaded with the high command in San Francisco to properly equip those of us going to Attu with cold weather gear, but to no avail," said Arthur Hopper, who served with the 7th Division's 53rd

Above: A gun emplacement is set up at Massacre Bay on Attu during May 1943. National Archives

Top: Soldiers at Massacre Bay, Attu, load an 81mm mortar to lob projectiles over the ridge into the Japanese-held valley below in May 1943. The GI manning the phone is receiving firing directions from a forward observation post. National Archives

Infantry Regiment. "This oversight cost the limbs of many who survived the Japs but became victims of the weather."

Philip Arcuri of U.S. Navy Battery No. 417 remembered especially the willowaws (violent squalls) — severe winds up to 100 miles an hour that blew snow so hard "you could get lost trying to find the chow hall." But GIs would have more to contend with than just the weather.

Lt. Frank Jarmin led his platoon up the mountain slope at Massacre Bay to within 200 yards of his objective. The Japanese poured down a wall of fire, killing Jarmin and driving his platoon back. The pass separating Holtz Bay from Massacre Valley, key to the Japanese defeat, was later named after the young lieutenant.

The turning point of the battle occurred when the Japanese evacuated the Holtz Bay area and transferred their forces to Chichagof Harbor on May 15.

Next day, an assault was launched to take Moore Ridge separating the west and east arms of Holtz Bay. Moore Ridge was in U.S. hands by day's end. Two days later, patrols from the Northern and Southern forces met at Jarmin Pass.

A series of hard-fought battles took the ridges behind Massacre Valley and Holtz Bay, opening the way to the last Japanese stronghold in Chichagof Harbor.

The separate 4th Infantry Regiment landed on May 17 to join in the fight and take some of the pressure off the 7th Division. Within four days, Point Able on Gilbert Ridge overlooking Massacre Valley was taken, clearing the area of the last vestiges of Japanese control.

Infantrymen of the 7th Division and 4th Regiment then began the tough push across Sarana Nose, Prendergast Ridge, Buffalo Ridge and Fish Hood Ridge toward their final objective — the Japanese camp at Chichagof Harbor.

Lt. Gen. Simon Bolivar Buckner, commander of the Alaska Defense Force, looks up at the American flag over a former Japanese headquarters bunker in the Chichagof area of Attu in May 1943. U.S. Army

Gen. Eugene M. Landrum, Buckner's chief of staff, wrote: "I know this country and my heart bled for the boys I had to send up there. I knew how cold and bitter it was on the mountains. But I knew death was more bitter.

"I gave them a terrible task. I believed it not kind to send them into the mountains to whip the Japs than to hold them in the valley where Jap snipers could cut them down."

One by one the ridges fell until only Fish Hook and Buffalo remained. Attacks to gain the high ground overlooking Chichagof Harbor faltered and then failed in the face of fierce Japanese resistance.

Fish Hook Ridge, recalled one pilot, "looked terrifically steep, like a wall in fact, to which the receding snow still clung." Nonetheless, GIs clawed their way over the open, snow-streaked slopes of the ridge.

One soldier, frustrated with the slow progress, stood up and moved forward against the withering Japanese fire. Pvt. Joe P. Martinez, 23, from Taos, N.M., was a BAR (Browning Automatic Rifle) man with Co. K, 3rd Bn., 32nd Inf. Regt. With the rest of his company pinned down by machine gun fire, he climbed alone up the steep slope. Reaching the top, he moved from position to position, firing a burst from his BAR into each hole until he was finally cut down.

This single-handed assault by a lone man stunned the Japanese defenders. The rest of the 3rd Bn., inspired by his feat of arms, advanced. By early evening of the 26th, Fish Hook Ridge, except for isolated pockets of resistance, had been secured. Martinez died the next day from his wounds. He earned the distinction of being the only Medal of Honor recipient during the Aleutian campaign.

The Japanese now had three choices: surrender, evacuate or attack. The

GIs display some of the spoils of war. After 18 days of bitter fighting on Attu — from May 11 to May 29, 1943 — Japanese forces were cleared from the westernmost island of the Aleutians. U.S. Air Force

latter was their only recourse under the code of *Bushido*. So rather than wait for the final assault on their beach position, they took the initiative.

Paul Nobuo Tatsoguchi, a Seventh Day Adventist medical missionary and a 1932 graduate of Pacific Union College who had been inducted into the Japanese Army on his return to Japan, recorded in his diary: "The last assault is to be carried out. All the patients in the hospital were made to commit suicide. Only 33 years of living and I am to die here. I have no regrets. *Banzai* to the Emperor."

On May 29, approximately 700 Japanese, moving in close order formation, tore through the American front lines at the head of Lake Cories. They continued across Sarana Valley, overrunning two command posts and a medical installation. Capt. William Willoughby of the Scout Battalion was there: "I got a machine-gun bullet across my face and then a hand grenade put hunks of heavy metal in me, tore up my chest and arm."

Then they smashed into a hastily organized defense erected by the 50th Combat Engineers, artillerymen and rear area troops dug into the crest of Engineer Hill. Japanese troops repeatedly attacked the position, only to be mowed down. "Within rock-throwing distance of the top of Engineer Hill, the *banzai* charge finally slowed and stopped, brought to heel by a withering point-blank concentration of bullets and grenades from the hasty, improvised American line.

"The Japanese faltered, fell back a few yards, then gathered themselves and charged with a frenzy that propelled them to the top," wrote Brian Garfield in *The Thousand-Mile War*.

By that evening, all effective enemy opposition ceased. Grotesque heaps of Japanese bodies covered a two-mile stretch of bloody ground on the slopes of Engineer Hill. Many bodies were horribly disfigured by self-inflicted grenade wounds — an estimated 500 had committed mass suicide.

For the next two days, patrols hunted down and killed the few remaining Japanese on the island. Mopping up lasted three months, but Attu was largely silent within several days of the battle.

U.S. casualties totaled 549 dead, 1,148 wounded and another 2,100 taken out of action by accidents, disease, exhaustion and the effects of harsh weather and terrain. Approximately 2,350 Japanese were killed. Only 29 survived to be taken prisoner.

The official Army history, in summing up the battle, noted "that in terms of numbers engaged, Attu ranked as one of the most costly assaults in the Pacific; and in terms of Japanese killed, the cost of taking Attu was second only to Iwo Jima. For every 100 of the enemy on the island, about 71 Americans were killed or wounded."

Operation Cottage: Kiska

One more island in the Aleutians remained to be retaken, or so American strategists believed.

On Aug. 15, 1943, the U.S. launched an operation to recapture Kiska Island from the Japanese. The invasion force totaled 34,426 combat troops: 4th, 17th, 53rd, 159th and 184th Infantry regiments, 87th Mountain Combat Team, 13th Royal Canadian Infantry Brigade and the 1st Special Service Force. Some 100 U.S. Navy warships supported the transports while the 11th Air Force flew cover and bombing missions over the Aleutians.

Unknown to the invaders, the Japanese had secretly completed evacuation of the island on July 29. Nevertheless, *Operation Cottage* caused casualties on the island: 17 deaths in accidental shootings, four men lost to booby-traps and mines, 50 wounded by booby-traps or in accidental shootings and 71 men put out of action by sickness. After eight days, the island search ended.

As part of *Task Force 16*, destroyer *Abner Read* pounded Kiska. Three days after the invasion, on Aug. 18, the ship's stern was ripped open by a floating Japanese mine. "The concussion tore a huge hole in her stern and ruptured her smoke tanks," according to an official account. "Men sleeping in aft compartments suffered from smoke inhalation. In the darkness, a few men fell through holes in the deck into fuel oil tanks below. Soon the stern broke away and sank." Seventy-one men were killed, either from the blast or succumbing to Arctic waters. Another 47 were injured. This was the largest number of casualties sustained in a single incident in the Aleutian campaign. *Abner Read* was towed away and eventually repaired.

"Although interest in the theater waned, it was in the Aleutians that the United States won its first theater-wide victory in World War II, ending Japan's only campaign in the Western Hemisphere," concluded the official Army history.

★ ★ ★

U.S. and Canadian forces — including the 17th Infantry Regiment, 53rd Infantry, 87th Mountain Infantry, 184th Infantry, 13th Royal Canadian Infantry Brigade and the 1st Special Service Force — stormed ashore at Red Beach on Kiska on Aug. 15, 1943, as part of *Operation Cottage*. Two weeks before the landing, the 5,183 Japanese defenders of Kiska had clandestinely departed the island at night via transports. U.S. Army

"

The outcome was satisfactory, but nothing could disguise the fact that for more than two weeks the Allies had bombarded an abandoned island, and that for a week thereafter they had deployed 35,000 combat soldiers — 313 of whom became casualties — across a deserted island.

"

— BRIAN GARFIELD
author of *The Thousand-Mile War*

NEW GUINEA NIGHTMARE

Red Arrow At War: The 32nd Infantry Division At Buna. Regiments of the 32nd entered combat at Buna on New Guinea's southeast coast on Nov. 16, 1942, fighting there until Jan. 2, 1943. Their participation led to the Japanese army's first defeat in modern history. But the price was steep, foreshadowing a bitter campaign to come. National Guard Heritage painting by Michael Gnatek Jr.

'Poor Man's War' of Attrition

**War in Miniature:
Bloody Buna**

"

*Men fought, lived and slept in
mud and slime amid swarms of
malaria-bearing mosquitoes.
They broke out with horrible
skin diseases and ulcers.*

"

—SAMUEL MORISON
Historian

AT THE opposite extreme of Alaska — below the equator — the world's second largest island presented a far different yet arguably even more horrendous environment in which to wage a war. Papua New Guinea was described as a "... primitive, almost unknown wilderness of towering mountains and steaming coastal jungles, burned by the equatorial sun and drenched by tropical downpours." Shaped like a prehistoric monster, it contains primeval swamps and dank, dark bush which was then inhabited by Stone Age natives only half-weaned from cannibalism.

The few mountain trails cut "through a fetid forest grotesque with moss and glowing phosphorescent fungi." Dizzying heights (rising to 13,000 feet) alternate with plunging gorges carved by turbulent rivers. A 1943 report on New Guinea concluded: "The conditions confronting them [GIs] were difficult and cruel beyond expectations."

New Guinea, "a poor man's war" of attrition, taxed the limits of endurance like few other campaigns. Wrote historian Samuel Morison: "Men fought, lived and slept in mud and slime amid swarms of malaria-bearing mosquitoes. They broke out with horrible skin diseases and ulcers."

GIs "were loaded down with up to 70 pounds of gear in the steaming heat of the low-lying jungle and swamps or the chilling cold of the higher mountain passes, plagued by malaria, dysentery, and a particularly virulent form of typhus; they were usually short of food, always near exhaustion," he wrote.

Then ruled by the Australians and Dutch, the island was the only buffer

between Australia and the Japanese juggernaut sweeping south. Consequently, in 1942, this strange land became the centerpiece of Allied strategy in the Southwest Pacific. Protecting Port Moresby, located on Papua's southern coast, was the primary task at hand. To ensure its safety, the Australians and Americans would have to evict the Japanese from their coastal toeholds on Papua's northern coast. For GIs that meant combat at obscure Buna — the U.S. Army's first large-scale taste of jungle warfare in WWII. (Two Army divisions had fought on Guadalcanal, but not in jungle.)

On Dec. 28, 1942, while describing the struggle for Buna to news reporters, Gen. Douglas MacArthur said: "Nowhere in the world today are American soldiers engaged in fighting so desperate, so merciless, so bitter, or so bloody."

While other battles like Guadalcanal gained fame in the annals of military history, the Battle of Buna, which Gen. Robert L. Eichelberger termed a "miniature war," did not. It was neither a headline-making event nor an overwhelming success. Nonetheless, this drawn out, high-casualty battle was the first Allied ground victory in the Pacific.

On the nights of July 21–22, 1942, the Japanese landed 4,400 troops on the north shore of Papua New Guinea and immediately captured Buna. A few days later, they started their push south along the treacherous Kokoda Trail over the Owen Stanley Mountains toward their strategic goal at Port Moresby.

Control of this port by the Japanese would sever the Allies supply line between Australia and the U.S. To prevent this, the Allies went on the offensive by pitting the Australian 7th Division against the advancing Japanese. Unfortunately, by Sept. 16, after a month of fierce mountain battles, the enemy was 16 miles from Port Moresby.

To assist the Australians, the Americans deployed to New Guinea the inexperienced 32nd Infantry "Red Arrow" Division in what was then the biggest airlift in U.S. military history.

"While we were naturally inexperienced at combat, we also were poorly equipped, inadequately fed and denied reasonable medical supplies," stressed 32nd Division veteran Frederick Neises. "Moreover, the 32nd had little or no support — either air or artillery."

The Fifth Air Force also joined the campaign and, in the latter stages of the battle, so did the 163rd Infantry Regiment, 41st Infantry Division. This brought U.S. troops ultimately committed to the battle to 14,464.

"As a member of the 163rd, I fought under the fine 7th Australian Division," noted Buna veteran Clarence Johnson. "Men of the 41st Division were highly trained and properly led."

While the Australians forced the enemy back over the mountains, the 32nd was flown to the northern airstrips to envelop the Japanese. Because they withdrew to the northern coast, Buna became the central battleground.

Crossing the mountains took its toll on both the enemy and the Allies. Capt. Alfred Mendendrop, commander of Co. C, 2nd Bn., 126th Inf. Regt., described the ruggedness of the Owen Stanley divide: "Here the track was so narrow that the troops had to walk in single file and in places was so rough that they had to crawl on their hands and knees."

GIs "climbed, scrambled, clawed and suffered" across the hostile mountain barrier, wrote Jay Luvaas in *America's First Battles*. "It was one green hell at Jaure," one sergeant later recalled. "We went up and down continuously. . . . It would take five or six hours to go a mile, edging along cliff walls, hanging on to vines, up and down, up and down." In his diary, he despaired: "God, will it never end?"

Obstacles included swamps surrounding Buna and a dug-in and determined enemy. Eichelberger described the situation at Buna as a "Leavenworth Nightmare." "At Guadalcanal, the Americans were in the coconut groves and on dry land," he said. "They had the breeze, and the Japanese were in the jungle.

"At Buna, the situation was reversed. We were in the jungle, and the trails by which we could advance splayed down from the sea through otherwise impenetrable territory. It was easy for the Japanese, secure in the buried log bunkers, to command our approaches with heavy automatic weapons."

Two Allied task forces — *Warren* and *Urbana* — formed in the channeling of forces, first by the mountains and then by the marshy terrain. Capt. John Murphy, of the 32nd, recalled: "Although only two or three miles apart by air, the fronts were separated on the ground by impassable swamps and thick jungles . . . the distance between [forces] was more a matter of hours than of miles. It took six hours to walk from one flank to the other."

An Australian war correspondent described the Japanese defenses he inspected: "Every weapon pit is a fortress in miniature. From every trench or pit or pillbox all approaches are covered by wide fields of sweeping fire along fixed line. . . .

"[The] wily enemy . . . has established concrete gunpits and dug grenade-proof and mortar-proof nests beneath the roots of giant jungle trees. He has put keen-eyed snipers in hundreds of treetops. These pockets cannot be bypassed because of neck-deep swamps of black, sucking mud. They must be assaulted at whatever cost, and destroyed one by one."

On Nov. 19, both task forces launched attacks preceded by air bombardments. Because the lines were so indistinct, Allied bombs fell on members of the *Warren Force*, causing extensive casualties.

After the war, an official military historian explained that units were so juggled that some were mixed in among both task forces. *Urbana Force* comprised 2nd Bn., 128th Inf. Regt.; 2nd Bn., 126th Infantry; and 3rd Bn., 127th Infantry. *Warren Force* consisted of the 1st Bn., 128th Inf.; 3rd Bn., 128th Inf.; and the 1st Bn., 126th Inf. This hodgepodge task organization made it nearly impossible for commanders to control their forces.

The fighting for Buna Village was savage, according to an Australian newspaperman: "It's the same old picture of trench fighting, or dugouts and pillboxes, of stomach-twisting bayonet charges behind lifting artillery barrages, of nerve-wracking night patrols . . . of deadly sniping and awful moments of suspense waiting for the zero hour."

For the remainder of November 1942, both sides remained in a near deadlock, with Allied morale deteriorating. Lt. Charles Kepple of the *Warren Task Force* recalled: "The leaders had an over-sympathetic attitude toward the hardships their men had experienced in the jungle. No steps to counteract the myth of the invincibility of the Japanese forces were taken, and the leaders became permeated with the tendency toward lethargy brought on by the tropics."

After hearing of the poor morale and lack of unity of command, MacArthur ordered Eichelberger to "remove all officers who won't fight. Relieve regimental and battalion commanders. . . ." "Tell them to take Buna, or not come back alive."

Eichelberger quickly regrouped, reorganized and appointed new commanders for each task force on the front.

No sooner had he done so than, on Dec. 4, a platoon from Co. G, 2nd Bn., 126th Inf., finally penetrated enemy lines and advanced through to

Paddling down the Girau River on New Year's Eve 1942, these men of the 127th Service Co., 32nd Div., haul supplies to the Buna front.
National Archives

Soldiers from Co. A, 1st Bn., 128th Inf., 32nd Div., comb the jungle where a Japanese position had just been captured during the battle for the Buna Mission on Jan. 3, 1943.
National Archives

the sea. Then on Dec. 13, the 3rd Bn., 127th Inf., relieved the 2nd Bn., 126th Inf. In one hour, the freshly committed troops captured a portion of the objective designated Buna Village, only to find it deserted by the Japanese.

However, the capture of Buna Village was like a shot in the arm for the Allies. Five days later, Eichelberger ordered forward seven Australian Stuart tanks to cover the infantry movement across Simeni Creek. For weeks, it had been a formidable obstacle just yards inside the enemy's final protective fire.

Tanks in the swamps were "like race horses harnessed to heavy ploughs." Yet properly guided by infantrymen, they could destroy machine-gun nests that beforehand had cut down advancing infantrymen with ease. By Dec. 23, 1st Bn., 126th Inf., had crossed the creek. Japanese forces, impenetrable for more than a month, finally cracked.

William King, a member of the 126th Infantry, fought alongside the Australians, recalling, "Those Aussies are the only ones that could stop a war for a cup of tea! Two of them would carry a large pole with a bucket of tea, accompanied by two guards."

Once inside the Japanese perimeter, both task forces conducted slow and tedious "bunker-busting" tactics. They belly-crawled from bunker to bunker, routing the enemy with grenades. By Dec. 28, the *Warren* and *Urbana Forces* were poised to attack the lone remaining objective located on the coast — Buna Mission.

The next three days proved difficult for the Allies. Reinforced with fresh troops and more armor on the first day of 1943, the *Warren Force* attacked and reached the coastline in one hour. In spite of stiff enemy resistance to the west, the *Urbana Force's* G and H companies of the 127th Infantry drove northeast. On Jan. 3, they linked up with the *Warren Force*, ending the battle for Buna.

Fighting on Papua New Guinea continued until Jan. 22, with the hard-won victory at Buna as the campaign's centerpiece. MacArthur resolved never again to force "a head-on collision of the bloody, grinding type" as Buna had been.

Compared to Guadalcanal, which ended in victory on Feb. 9, 1943, Buna had been the bloodier. Of some 60,000 Americans committed to Guadalcanal, 1,592 were killed and another 4,183 wounded in ground fighting. Between Nov. 19 and Jan. 3, 40,000 Australians and Americans (14,464) fought at Buna; 3,095 were killed in action and 5,451 were wounded. The precise breakdown for the Americans was: 32nd Infantry Division — 690 KIA and 1,680 WIA and 163rd Infantry Regiment, 41st Infantry Division — 97 KIA and 238 WIA. These figures cover the entire Papua Campaign.

Eichelberger wrote: "To see those boys with their bellies out of the mud and their eyes in the sun, closing in unafraid on prepared positions, made

"Tonight the battalion under Captain Baba will annihilate the enemy who have landed. This is not a delaying action. Be resolute to sacrifice your life for the Emperor and commit suicide in case capture is imminent. We must carry out our mission and annihilate the enemy on the spot. I am highly indignant about the enemy's arrogant attitude. Remember to kill or capture all ranking officers for intelligence purposes," ordered Col. Yoshio Ezaki, commander of Japanese troops on Los Negros Island. The enemy had 3,650 troops to make good its threat.

On Feb. 29, 1944, *Operation Brewer* — the invasion of the Admiralty Islands in the Bismarck Archipelago — was spearheaded by the 2nd Sqdn., 5th Cavalry Regt., 1st Cavalry Div. It landed at Hyane Harbor near Momote Plantation airfield. This was the first combat action for the "First Team." Two days later, the remainder of the 5th Cav was ashore along with the 99th Artillery Battalion and the 40th Naval Construction Battalion.

The most critical fighting of the campaign occurred the night of March 3. "On this night, the Japanese advanced in the open in frontal assault with a good deal of talking, shouting, and even singing. Artillery and mortars opened fire at once. As they approached, the leading enemy waves hurled grenades, but they fell short of the cavalry lines. The Japanese pushed through the mine fields, taking casualties but not stopping, and drove into the interlocking bands of fire from machine guns, which promptly cut them down. More kept coming; the cavalry lines held, but some Japanese managed to infiltrate," according to an account in *Cartwheel: The Reduction of Rabaul*.

Along the American perimeter, the 2nd Sqdn., 5th Cav, bore the brunt of the attack. Bravery was common, as exhibited by Sgt. Troy McGill of G Troop, who earned the Medal of Honor, posthumously. At daybreak, 750 dead enemy soldiers were counted, having "committed suicide." Some 61 men of the 5th Cav were KIA. The 2nd Squadron received the Distinguished Unit Citation for its work on the line.

With a solid foothold on Los Negros, the 2nd Brigade moved to capture Manus, the other principal island in the Admiralties. On March 15, the 8th Cav assaulted Lugos Mission. The nearby airfield was well-fortified, but it was secured by the 8th and 7th Cav regiments. From March 19 to 25, the Japanese put up stiff resistance at a village called Old Rossum.

Mopping up operations were unique in one respect: On April 1, cavalrymen in native dugout canoes assaulted the islands of Koruniat and Ndrilo. This was the only time during the entire Pacific campaign that such craft were used to attack an island.

Operations continued until the last isolated pockets of resistance were eliminated by May 18, 1944. Clearing the Admiralties of enemy troops cost the 1st Cavalry Division 396 KIA and 1,977 WIA.

me choke, and then I spent a moment looking over the American cemetery which my orders of necessity have filled from nothing. Not large, perhaps, but you can understand."

Moreover, many more troops died of illnesses. Most GIs at one time or another contracted malaria (5,358 cases in the 32nd alone), dysentery or dengue fever. Also, more than 200 soldiers succumbed to the deadly scrub typhus. Of the 10,825 men in the 32nd Division, 7,125 or 66 percent, ended up on sick call.

Placing the long-awaited victory into proportion, Col. J. Sladen Bradley, chief of staff of the 32nd Division, said, "The successful conclusion of the Buna campaign was brought about by the mere fact that the American and Australian troops were able to 'exist' longer than the Japanese. We lived the longest and therefore took our objective."

Neutralizing New Guinea

After Buna, U.S. combat units in Papua required six months to reconstitute. From February through June 1943, a stalemate occurred — a war of attrition. But by the end of June, U.S. forces began to move from Papua up the coast into Northeast New Guinea. As part of *Operation Cartwheel*, the

A Japanese naval gun captured during the Admiralty Islands campaign — Feb. 29 to May 18, 1944 — is fired by American artillerymen. The two principal islands of the group — Los Negros and Manus — were largely secured in March of that year.
U.S. Army

GIs of I Corps, helmeted and packs strapped on, transported by Task Force 77, await their landing on the beach at Aitape, New Guinea, April 22, 1944. U.S. Coast Guard

U.S. Sixth Army/Alamo Force went on the offensive. Nassau Bay was taken first by the 162nd Inf. Regt., 41st Inf. Div. In operations between Salamaua and Lae between June and mid-September, 81 GIs were killed and 396 wounded.

Early in September, the first coordinated airborne and amphibious assault in the Pacific was launched. The 3,200-man VII Amphibious Force and 2nd Engineer Special Brigade transported Australian troops to the Lae area. Meantime, 20 miles west of Lae, the 503rd Parachute Infantry Regiment was dropped on Nadzab on Sept. 5. No opposition was encountered.

At Finschhafen, on Oct. 17, Pvt. Nathan Van Noy, Jr., of the 532nd Engineer Boat and Shore Regiment, displayed the courage that became the hallmark of the American fighting man. While manning a machine gun near the shoreline, exposed and grievously wounded, he stayed at his post until out of ammo. Found in front of his position were 30 dead Japanese. His Medal of Honor citation read: "His heroic tenacity at the price of his own life not only saved the lives of many of his comrades, but enabled them to annihilate the attacking detachment."

Several months later, on Jan. 2, 1944, the 126th RCT, 32nd Division, made an unopposed landing at Saidor. GIs would soon be in the position to leapfrog around the coast to the heart of Japanese troop concentrations in Northeast and Dutch New Guinea. Strategists planned for the next move.

The U.S. plan fulfilled three objectives: encirclement of the Japanese fortress at Rabaul, control of enemy movement throughout the Bismarck Archipelago, and, most important of all, setting up the return to the Philippines. Japan would be separated from its South Seas conquests and the Allies would gain control of the strongest and longest sector of the Southwest Pacific front.

Objective No. 1 was the capture of Hollandia. Loss of this main crossroads would isolate much of the Japanese Eighteenth Army: 16,000 men at Madang, 35,000 at Hansa Bay and 55,000 at Wewak.

Fifth Air Force bombers and planes of the fast-moving *Task Force 58* softened up Hollandia before the invasion. About 200 enemy planes were destroyed by D-Day, April 22, 1944, ensuring complete control of the air and allowing the landings to take place without an effective counterattack by enemy aircraft.

Some 79,800 troops of U.S. I Corps, including the 41st Division, headed for Humboldt Bay, largest naval anchorage on New Guinea's north coast,

and Aitape, 120 miles east of Hollandia; and the 24th Division, assigned to capture Tanahmerah Bay, another large anchorage 22 miles west of Hollandia.

Assault forces aimed to employ a pincers movement and capture an important complex of roads and Japanese barracks, supply depots and airfields near Lake Sentani, 12 miles from Humboldt Bay and inland of Hollandia. Equidistant from Humboldt and Tanahmerah bays and shielded by the Cyclops Mountains, Sentani was defended by 11,000 enemy troops.

The invasion armada of 217 ships of the VII Amphibious Force was then the largest naval force ever assembled in the Southwest Pacific. The Japanese did not learn of the fleet's approach until, as one enemy officer said, the Americans were "already in the harbor with their transports and battleships."

Though protected by 1,000 Japanese, Aitape was secured within 24 hours by the 163rd Regt., 41st Div. Enemy survivors fled into the mountains. With its two airfields, Aitape was quickly turned into a bulwark against Japanese counterattack from the east.

In other action, the 24th Division and the balance of the 41st Division came ashore at Humboldt and Tanahmerah bays. Naval and air bombardment drove off most defenders, and assault troops landed largely unopposed. By evening, strong U.S. forces had advanced six miles past Hollandia into the mountains and were converging on Sentani.

"I belonged to the 41st Division Recon Troop and we were very involved in locating enemy camps behind the front lines," noted veteran David Herbst. As Japanese resistance stiffened, however, fighting became fierce. Combat raged four days before the last pocket of enemy troops broke up. Including the mopping-up phase, which lasted until June 6, Hollandia cost a total of 159 U.S. dead and 1,067 WIA.

To secure their rear for a northward turn toward the Philippines, U.S.

66

Sept. 5, 1943, marked the first major parachute jump of the Pacific war. That morning 86 planes of the 54th Troop Carrier Wing dropped about 1,500 men of the 503rd Regiment at Nadzab in the Markham Valley of New Guinea in a classic and totally successful mission. The paratroopers leaped at the lowest altitude attempted — perhaps as low as 300 to 350 feet. General MacArthur observed the whole operation from the gun turret of a B-17.

99

— JOHN A. GLAROS
Radio Operator
C-47 Honeymoon Express

93rd Breaks New Ground in Southwest Pacific

Men of the 93rd Infantry Division — the only all-black division in the Pacific — saw service in the Northern Solomons, Bismarck Archipelago and New Guinea campaigns from 1944–45.

On Bougainville, the 1st Bn., 24th Inf. Regt., became the first black U.S. infantry unit to engage in combat during World War II. Later, the 25th Infantry Regiment's 1st Battalion was ambushed while escorting wounded from Hill 500: four men were KIA.

The 2nd Battalion was part of a task force assigned to secure a trail junction near the mouth of the Jaba River. Pvt. Wade Fogge of Company F received the division's first Bronze Star by knocking out three enemy pillboxes.

On April 6, 1944, Company K was setting up a blockade east of Hill 250, when it encountered an enemy unit and also took "friendly fire." Ten men died and 20 were wounded. "This has resulted in many instances in jungle warfare when troops were committed without proper seasoning," said Col. Everett Yon, commander of the 25th Regiment.

Throughout 1944, elements of the 369th Regiment were parceled out among the St. Matthias Islands, Biak Island and Morotai Island, protecting beaches from Japanese troops who had retreated to the interior mountains.

In April 1945, division elements were at Sansopar, New Guinea. "We didn't have any artillery support," said Staff Sgt. Clarence Ross, Service Co., 2nd Bn., 369th Regt. "The Japs dropped mortars on us at night and probed our lines for weak spots. We only had three reinforced companies, and they could have come down and wiped us out any time they wanted to."

Within a week, the 369th was reunited on Morotai, where it stayed for the duration of the war.

Black soldiers of the 25th Regiment, 93rd Infantry Division, conducted patrols on Bougainville beginning in mid-April 1944. The 93rd — the only all-black division in the Pacific — served in the Northern Solomons, Bismarck Archipelago and New Guinea campaigns. U.S. Army

forces moved to isolate the strategic Vogelkop Peninsula. On May 17, a task force made up mainly of the 163rd Infantry and code-named *Tornado* landed in the Maffin Bay area.

Part of the force landed on Wakde, a tiny island in Maffin Bay, only 3,000 yards wide and 1,000 yards long. Wakde's 800-man garrison holed up in coral caves and held out four days before it was annihilated by May 21.

Remainder of *Tornado* landed at Toem on a swampy coastal plain bordering Maffin Bay, 20 miles east of a major Japanese base at Sarmi. Toem was defended by 10,000 Japanese troops dug into the jungle-covered mountains overlooking the plain.

Securing the Maffin Bay area embroiled *Tornado* elements and parts of the 31st and 33rd divisions in nonstop battle for three months. By Sept. 1, 418 Americans were dead and 1,510 WIA.

U.S. forces almost simultaneously leaped some 200 miles northwest against the strategic island fortress of Biak. Troops of I Corps, primarily the 41st Division, landed May 27 and suffered terribly. "Biak was a redoubtable natural fortress. It was virtually all coral, but unlike other coral islands of the Pacific, with their low-lying terrain and visibility unhampered except by scattered palm trees. Biak was hilly and densely covered by tropical rain forest and jungle undergrowth. In many places the coral had formed ridges and terraces, and these were honeycombed by hundreds of huge caves with connecting galleries," is how Rafael Steinberg aptly described it in *Island Fighting*.

Biak's stubborn garrison of 11,000 fought tenaciously until Aug. 20. "Huge amounts of gasoline were poured into caves and bunkers and set afire, incinerating the Japanese holed up there. Burned and mutilated Japanese corpses were strewn everywhere, and the stench on the island was sickening. Still, the Japanese fought on," wrote William Breuer in *Geronimo!*

Biak cost 471 American lives and 2,433 WIA. In addition, more than 7,000 GIs were rendered ineffective by disease.

To achieve control of New Guinea, forces under MacArthur surged ahead of schedule and seized the island of Noemfoor, 60 miles west of Biak and halfway to the Vogelkop. The 158th Regiment ("Bushmasters") assaulted Noemfoor on July 2 preceded by a stupendous air bombardment.

Fifth Air Force commander Gen. George C. Kenney reported that when U.S. troops went ashore the Japanese who were behind the beaches and still alive were "so stunned . . . that they sat by their machine guns staring straight ahead, numb with shock, while our infantry gathered them in."

When reinforcements were needed to eliminate 3,000 Japanese die-hards, the 503rd Parachute Infantry Regiment (1,400 men) was dropped July 3, in only the second Allied airborne operation of the Pacific war so far. Noemfoor was secured two days later with U.S. losses of 70 KIA and 348 WIA.

To complete the chokehold on the Vogelkop Peninsula, 7,500 men of the 6th Infantry Division (Task Force *Typhoon*) landed July 30 at Sansapor

Above: A GI on Biak Island, off the coast of New Guinea, guides his companion from the QM War Dog Platoon at an abandoned Japanese outpost, July 18, 1944. National Archives

Right: Invasion troops from an LCI (Landing Craft, Infantry) pick their way across a Japanese jetty mauled by bombing, arriving on Biak Island in the Schouten Group in June 1944. MacArthur Memorial Museum

on the peninsula's western end, trapping 18,000 troops of the Japanese Second Army by the end of August. From September through December 1944, the U.S. 6th Infantry Division occupied the Vogelkop Peninsula.

Meanwhile, throughout the middle phase of the campaign, the costliest of all the New Guinea fighting had been under way. On July 10, elements of the battered, but jungle-wise Japanese Eighteenth Army, 35,000-strong, launched a surprise counterattack, striking the U.S.-held Driniumor River line only 10 miles east of Aitape.

"The night of July 10, 1944, 10,000 howling Japanese troops burst across the shallow Driniumor River and charged through the center of the badly outnumbered and undermanned covering force. GIs fired their machine guns and automatic rifles until the barrels turned red hot, but the Japanese, eerily visible under the light of the flares, surged forward.

"American artillery fell in clusters on the Japanese infantrymen, killing and maiming hundreds or crushing others beneath the tall trees that snapped apart in the unceasing explosions. Japanese numbers proved irresistible. Their breakthrough precipitated a month-long battle of attrition in the New Guinea wilds," recorded the official U.S. Army history of the campaign.

The line was held by the U.S. XI Corps, including the 32nd Division; 124th Regt., 31st Div.; and the independent 112th Cavalry Regiment. Just before midnight, massed Japanese artillery opened fire, stunning the most exposed U.S. units and creating a gap through which elements of two Japanese divisions poured across the river.

Savage fighting raged back and forth until Aug. 9, when the Japanese began withdrawing. For weeks thereafter, U.S. forces pursued the enemy along muddy, sniper-infested jungle trails leading to Wewak, which was hopelessly cut off by converging U.S. and Australian forces.

'Bushmasters' Master the Bush

Gen. MacArthur said that "no greater combat team ever deployed for battle." The Bushmasters, more than a match for the Bushido warriors, were reviled as "bloody butchers" by Tokyo Rose. To the Japanese, they possessed the lethality of the deadly pit viper for which they were nicknamed: the Panamanian bushmaster. At the same time, they were a tightknit outfit that lived up to their motto — *Cuidado* or "Take Care."

Originating in Arizona as a National Guard outfit, the 158th Infantry Regiment's ranks were filled primarily with American Indians (from 22 different tribes) and men of Mexican descent. However, when the unit was expanded in Panama, recruits from all parts of the U.S. joined.

Arriving in combat for the first time at Arawe, New Britain, on Jan. 6, 1944, they were formed into a regimental combat team in March at Finschhafen, Dutch New Guinea. They fought at

Members of the 158th Regimental Combat Team — the famed "Bushmasters — land on Arawe, New Britain in January 1944. MacArthur Memorial photo

Wakde-Sarmi and Noemfoor Island later that summer. In late May, they engaged in the fierce battle for Lone Tree Hill along the Tor River.

By January 1945, the 158th RCT found itself on Luzon in the Philippines, engaging the Japanese at Damortis-Rosario, Batangas, Legaspi, Sorsogon, Camalig and Mt. Isarog. During the

Bicol Peninsula campaign in April, the unit fought daily battles to open the Visayan passages for Allied ships in the region. This merciless operation lasted two months in terrain laced with tank traps, wire, mines and bamboo thickets. By war's end, the unit counted 293 KIA, 20 MIA and 1,344 WIA, based on what can be gleaned from *Bushmasters: America's Jungle Warriors of World War II* by Anthony Arthur.

After five more months in the archipelago, in October, the Bushmasters moved on to Yokohoma for occupation duty. On Jan. 17, 1946, the proud 158th was deactivated and its remaining members sent home from Japan.

But that did not end the fighting for the 158th's veterans, who for years went unrecognized for their exploits. According to Lt. Hal Braun, B Company's commanding officer, their "standards were so very high that more was expected" of them and their "outstanding actions were taken for granted."

"Cuidado [Take Care], Bushmasters!" depicts the 158th Regimental Combat Team, consisting largely of minorities from Arizona, in close-fire battle during the Bicol campaign on Luzon, Philippines, April 3–4, 1945. The 158th RCT fought across the Pacific, earning a well-deserved reputation for courage in combat. U.S. Army painting

Above: About 1,400 paratroopers of the 503rd PRCT drop on Kamiri, one of three airstrips taken July 2–6, 1944, on Noemfoor Island in New Guinea. This was the second Allied airborne operation of the Pacific war. U.S. Army

Top: Command Post on July 2, 1944, the day the Army landed near Kamiri airstrip on Noemfoor Island, Dutch New Guinea. Troops went ashore on sharp reefs and other hazardous obstacles. National Archives

For the remainder of the war, the encircled Japanese survivors were kept neutralized by shelling and bombing. Nonetheless, the enemy's unexpected lunge at Aitape exacted a terrible toll: 440 U.S. dead and 2,500 WIA. GIs wracked up a body count of 10,000 Japanese.

In the brutal, nearly year-long Dutch New Guinea campaign — one of the war's most complex and costly — U.S. forces suffered 2,151 KIA on the ground. All American wounded numbered 7,486. Often overlooked, however, is the fact that the Fifth Air Force lost even more men — 2,533 — killed in providing tactical air support.

(The Fifth Air Force supported the Allied advance on New Guinea. It bombed strongpoints and airstrips, and flew troops and supplies from Australia to Port Moresby, then across the Owen Stanley Mountains to combat areas. The "Flying Buccaneers" also hit Japanese convoys attempting to reinforce their garrisons on the island.)

The astonishing triumphs of Allied arms on New Guinea added up to a decisive defeat for Japan, which squandered 43,000 men and had two field armies destroyed there.

★ ★ ★

American troops of the 6th Infantry Division board the *USS Ward* at Maffin Bay, New Guinea, to head for the invasion of Cape Sansapor elsewhere on the massive island on July 30–31, 1944. National Archives

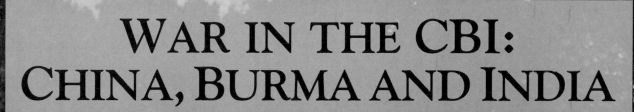

WAR IN THE CBI: CHINA, BURMA AND INDIA

Famed "Merrill's Marauders" — officially known by the unwieldy designation 5307th Composite Unit (Provisional Regiment) — ford a stream to penetrate the treacherous terrain that characterized Burma. Code-named Galahad, their behind-the-lines exploits in Southeast Asia between 1944-45 proved tremendously costly in casualties yet vital to disrupting Japanese operations. By Jim Dietz

Confused Beyond Imagination

I F NEW GUINEA had a rival in terms of almost unbearable climate and terrain, it was surely Burma. Yet the campaign to roll back Japan's expansion into Southeast Asia remains the least-known of U.S. efforts in World War II. In fact, more than 250,000 GIs served in the China, Burma and India (CBI) Theater. And although U.S. combat troops were few in number, the CBI arguably produced the most unique set of units in the war.

To the American servicemen — "Flying Tigers," "Hump" pilots, "Pick's" engineers, OSS agents, Merrill's Marauders, SACO personnel and Mars men — the CBI rated various epithets, none of which were complimentary. Bill Sinclair, of the wartime *CBI Roundup*, said the initials stood for "Confusion Beyond Imagination." Other GIs had a different view of the initials, seeing themselves as "confused bastards in India." As for the formal sounding South East Asia Command (SEAC), it really stood for "Save England's Asiatic Colonies," in many men's minds.

As a theater of operations, the CBI had no equals. "It ranged from the borders of Mongolia, Manchuria and China on the northeast, nearly 4,000 miles southwest to the southern tip of India. From the coast of China on the east it stretched nearly 3,500 miles to India's western shore on the Arabian Sea," wrote William B. Sinclair in *Confusion Beyond Imagination*. It also had "the longest lines of supply across high mountains, rice paddies, swamps and heavily jungled terrain."

Flying the Himalayan 'Hump'

Inaugurated in April 1942, the "Hump" — the 550-mile air route between the Brahmaputra Valley across the towering Himalayas to Kunming in Yunnan Province, China — was a treacherous path. (The actual Hump was the 15,000-foot Satsung Range between the Salween and Mekong rivers.) It was also called the "Aluminum Trail" because of the crashed planes along the way that served as guideposts.

"Few areas on earth posed more terrifying challenges to air transportation than the alternating steaming jungle, deep gorges, and snow-capped peaks between Assam and Kunming," wrote Leslie Anders in *The Ledo Road*. "Weather created special hazards for aerial navigation. On some days during the monsoons, the icing level was beneath the summits of the Hump. There were times when even the C-87 could not 'get on top,' and flight schedules were disrupted.

"During the winter, violent winds up to one hundred miles an hour in velocity created sudden dangers to the air line. In the first week of January 1945, winds gusting to 248 miles an hour wrecked nine transports and many buildings at the Hump fields. Updrafts sometimes forced planes upward at a rate of one mile a minute; downdrafts, equally unpredictable, were certainly more dangerous.

Above: C-46s flew across the picturesque Himalayas to and from China with everything from trucks to hand grenades to K-rations. By 1945, the Air Transport Command was delivering 45,000 tons of supplies a month to the besieged Chinese forces.
Smithsonian Institution

Top: Ox-drawn carts carry supplies to a C-46 transport that will fly the Chinese 22nd Division over "The Hump" to Chanyi, China. U.S. Army

"Extreme summer heat [up to 130 degrees F.] often caused vapor lock and doomed plane and cargo if not the crew. Floods could close airfields with little or no warning. One day in September 1943, fog compelled two dozen transports to 'stack up' [wait in the air] over Kunming."

Yet the India-China Division of the U.S. Air Transport Command (ATC) defied the odds and successfully supplied Chaing Kai-Shek's Nationalist Chinese armies with war materiel for three years. But at a heavy price: By Nov. 1, 1945, the division had lost 594 planes along with 910 crewmen killed in action or in accidental crashes.

U.S. Tenth Air Force fighters protected the Air Transport Command units flying the Hump. It also achieved air supremacy in Burma. Raids destroyed shipping, supply dumps, convoys and oil refineries. Cooperation with ground troops was important in stopping Japanese advances into India and China, and allowing the Allies to succeed at Myitkyina. As airman Michael Demos said, "The 503rd Squadron, 311th Fighter Group, for

As I came in for a landing at the Chabua base, far up the Brahmaputra River in Upper Assam, that day in early August 1944, I could hardly fail to see the huge black blotches at the end of the runway. I knew too well what they were. Each was a lasting memorial to a group of American airmen, the crew of the plane that had crashed and burned at the spot.

Like all other planes flying the Hump, the C-46s were being used hard, flown without adequate maintenance, and always loaded to the maximum. This was a cumbersome beast that could cause anguish when it lost an engine and you were calling upon it to give all it had to get your extra-heavy plane off the ground.

If you were already starting to make your turn, and were making it just a little too sharply, even full power on the remaining engine couldn't save you. The ship would stall, and a black spot at the end of the runway would be your memorial.

— LT. GEN. WILLIAM H. TUNNER
Air Transport Command

Col. David "Tex" Hill, a combat air ace of the Flying Tigers, boards his P-51 for a mission over China. U.S. Air Force

instance, dive-bombed and strafed all of the major targets in Burma, 'softening' them up for ground troops before they made their assaults."

In China proper, the U.S. Fourteenth Air Force — successor of the American Volunteer Group ("Flying Tigers") — led by Gen. Claire L. Chennault, attempted to sever Japanese supply lines. But many air bases were overrun. When the Japanese began retreating in May 1945 toward the coast, the Fourteenth harassed them, destroying 600 locomotives, 900 railroad cars and 2,000 sampans and barges. Many P-40 Warhawk pilots attributed their success to common sense. "Chennault had a ditty he used to repeat: 'It's better to shoot and run away and live to shoot another day,'" said fighter ace Maj. John Alison.

Chennault's famed "Flying Tigers" were not the only Americans to serve in China. Other unusual and unknown units served in the theater, too. "The U.S. 988th Special Operations Group — later Signal Company — was a liaison unit for the Nationalist Chinese," pointed out veteran James D. Gill. "I served with the Chinese 50th Division from Myitkyina to Lashio. The Group reached a peak of 30 Americans. We operated totally undercover. Our unit was decorated with the Chinese Breast Order of Yun Hui, as well as a Presidential Unit Citation."

Veteran John B. Morland served with the 464th Coast Artillery Battalion (Automatic Weapons Anti-Aircraft). "Ours was the only U.S. ground unit stationed in China during World War II," he wrote. "Known as the 'Burma Roadsters,' this separate battalion was situated along the Salween River near Yunan. There it defended a crucial bridge used to reopen the Burma Road and fought off Japanese Zeros until the war ended."

'Pick's Pike: Toughest Road in the World'

With enemy forces controlling China and Indochina, the only overland supply routes for transporting Lend-Lease aid to Allied Chinese forces — the old Burma Road and the railway to Yunnan Province — were in Japanese hands.

U.S. Army engineers plotted an alternate route through jungle-covered mountains and swampy lowlands, from Ledo in India to Bhamo in northern Burma. (The Ledo Road link combined with the Burma Road to make a 1,044-mile supply line to Kunming, China.) Monsoon rains from May to October, malaria-carrying mosquitoes, giant leeches and typhus-plagued mites compounded the problems.

"It is almost as if Mother Nature uses this country as a proving ground to try out new models of pests with which to plague humankind," wrote Lt. Col. Ingvald Madsen, one of the engineer officers in Burma.

Overall responsibility for the Ledo Road fell to Lt. Gen. Joseph Stillwell and his Service of Supply (SOS), with the first units arriving in India in July 1942. After building warehouses, barracks and hospitals, the engineer units started clearing the trace on Dec. 16, 1942.

Among the many Army units involved with completing the Ledo Road were five general service regiments; five engineer aviation battalions; two engineer combat battalions; a special service battalion; a topographical battalion; and numerous support companies. All told, 17,000 American engineers toiled on the road.

The onsite commander, Lt. Col. Lewis Pick, drove his crews hard, but the engineers completed the first leg of the route, into Burma, on Feb. 28, 1943 and erected a sign stating: "Welcome to Burma, this way to Tokyo."

Monsoon rains and the hectic pace were taking a toll on the equipment, until maintenance crews arrived to keep the trucks and bulldozers running. Still, less than five miles of roadway were completed from May to August 1943.

Once the monsoon rains stopped,

Col. Robert F. Seedlock (right), commander of the Burma Road engineers, shakes hands with C.C. Kung, director-general of the Yunnan-Burma Highway Engineering Administration, in ceremonies on Jan. 29, 1945, commemorating the joining of their road-construction projects at the China-Burma border.
U.S. Army

progress proceeded at one mile a day. On Jan. 1, 1944, the 117-mile route — from Ledo to Shingbwiyang—was open.

It would take another year to complete the entire route, at a total cost of nearly $150 million to the U.S. and its allies.

Then, on Jan. 12, 1945, a ceremonial "first convoy" — comprised of jeeps, weapon carriers, ambulances and heavy cargo trucks pulling artillery pieces, all driven by engineers who worked on the project — left Ledo for the 1,100-mile

A survey party, travelling atop elephants, passes a bulldozer along the Ledo Road, built by U.S. engineers from Dec. 16, 1942 to May 20, 1945. "Pick's Pike," as it was known, stretched from Ledo, India, to Bhamo, Burma.
Army Corps of Engineers

trek to Kunming, China where it arrived Feb. 4.

It would be May 20, 1945, before all roadwork along the entire route — dubbed "Pick's Pike" — was completed. "Pick the man with the stick," was determined to build the road — "rain, mud and malaria be damned."

A total of 1,133 Americans died during construction of the road. "Of this number, 261 were from Engineer units," wrote Leslie Anders in his book, *The Ledo Road*. "Among the 624 Americans killed in combat were 130 Engineer soldiers; among the 63 dead of typhus, 8 were Engineers. Road accidents claimed 44 lives, drownings 53, and malaria only 11 (including 7 Engineers). Finally, 173 Americans lost their lives in aircraft accidents."

Mountain-climbing medium tanks manned by Chinese and American crews use the Burma Road for the first time after the combined Allied offensive in 1945 broke the two-year Japanese control of the only overland supply route to China. Note the switchbacks on the road.

An "Orange" Combat Team mortar crew from the 5307th Composite Unit (Provisional) — "Merrill's Marauders" — lobs rounds at nearby Japanese positions during combat from March 28 to April 8, 1944, at Nhpum Ga, Burma. The Marauders sustained 59 killed and 314 wounded in the Nhpum Ga actions, while Japanese suffered 2,000 casualties. U.S. Army

Not to be outdone in terms of elite units, the U.S. Naval Group China, the American component of the Sino-American Cooperative Organization (SACO), fielded 250 men to assist Chinese guerrillas. Capt. Milton E. Miles', SACO's deputy director, orders were clear: "You are to go to China and set up some bases as soon as you can . . . to prepare the China coast in any way you can for U.S. Navy landings in three or four years. In the meantime, do whatever you can to help the Navy and heckle the Japanese."

For this top-secret operation, Miles recruited scouts and raiders — the forerunners of today's SEALs. Among those recruited was Julius W. Ulaneck. "We did undercover or clandestine operations in the interior of China throughout our stay. They covered all the way from Kunming to the Gobi Desert then to Chikiang and Shanghai. I was evacuated from Shangahai in December 1945 and was hospitalized on the hospital ship *Repose*."

Burma or Bust

The campaign — code-named *Operation Capital* — to reopen northern Burma aimed at Myitkyina, terminus of the Rangoon railroad and the key to the Japanese stranglehold on China. With this vital hub in hand, the Ledo Road could connect with existing trails. And air crews flying supplies over the Hump could use a shorter, safer route.

Taking Myitkyina was a tall order. It was surrounded by some of the world's most difficult terrain: towering, jungle-covered mountains, steep gorges, flooded streams, swamps and disease-infested valleys dominated by thick underbrush, impenetrable bamboo and knife-edged elephant grass.

Northern Burma was held by 20,000 Japanese. The Allies had only one Chinese corps and the first U.S. ground combat unit in the CBI: the 5307th Provisional Regiment, an all-volunteer commando unit code-named *Galahad*. Besides the 1st, 2nd and 3rd battalions, the 31st and 33rd Quartermaster Pack Troops, a detachment of the 835th Signal Service Battalion and a platoon of the 502nd Military Police Battalion comprised the Galahad Force. The 5307th — called "Merrill's Marauders" after their commander, Brig. Gen. Frank D. Merrill — became the U.S. spearhead in the CBI.

Detachment 101 of the top-secret Office of Strategic Services (OSS) supported ground operations by organizing and training Kachin Rangers, warlike tribesmen, to serve as pathfinders and scouts.

Initially, it screened the advance of the Ledo Road into Burma. But later it expanded its duties to encompass a variety of highly effective tasks. OSS Detachment 101 — 566 Americans at the head of 10,000 Kachin Rangers at its peak in December 1944 — inflicted 5,500 Japanese casualties and rescued 200 Allied airmen behind the lines in Burma. Only 15 U.S. and 200 Kachin were killed in action. Det. 101 was deactivated July 12, 1945, but not before earning the Distinguished Unit Citation.

By February 1944, the enemy had been forced on the defensive, but was fighting a stubborn delaying action against the Allies. To block their withdrawal, the 5307th struck 100 miles behind enemy lines in the Hukawng Valley. Despite nonstop rain and endless jungle, its members averaged 20 miles a day and lived on rations dropped by the Tenth Air Force.

GIs dug in along the Nampyek Nha River, east of Walawbun, and for three days beat off human-wave assaults by an entire Japanese division. When the battle ended March 7, about 800 enemy soldiers had been killed at a cost of seven U.S. dead and 37 WIA. The surprising U.S. victory at Walawbun secured undisputed Allied control of the Hukawng Valley. As a consequence, the Japanese withdrew farther than they had in the preceding three months of fighting combined.

Merrill's Marauders raised such havoc behind lines that the enemy attempted an envelopment attack of their own. The 5307th barely had time to dig in at Nhpum Ga when the Japanese came at them in force on March 28. An entire division encircled the unit, razed the village with artillery and mortar fire and captured the only source of drinking water in the area.

Troops of the 5307th Composite Unit (Provisional) — Merrill's Marauders — cross a foot bridge over the Chindwin River in northern Burma in March 1944. Signal Corps/National Archives

"At Nhpum Ga, the Japanese attacks persisted on every section of the perimeter and came either in succession or in coordinated simultaneous attacks. From their position near Kauri at a range of 1,000 yards there was little time to take cover for the shells arrived almost simultaneously with the sound of the gun firing," remembered Marauder veteran Alan Baker.

However, the Tenth Air Force parachuted enough supplies to them to hold on for 12 days. Before abandoning their attacks on April 8, Japanese losses mounted to 2,000 men versus 59 KIA and 314 WIA for the Americans.

Now at half-strength, the Marauders resumed spearhead duty in the final phase of the northern Burma campaign: the capture of Myitkyina. The airfield was seized May 17, but then an intense battle ensued for the town, which lasted until Aug. 3. *Yank* correspondent Dave Richardson described the 5307th's epic struggle:

"Merrill's Marauders climbed a range of mountains 6,000 feet high and sneaked southeast into the Sumprabum Valley, leading Chinese columns in the surprise capture of Myitkyina airfield. There gliders and transports rushed in more troops, and the battle for the city of Myitkyina began. From then on, the war in Burma became much more like the war in Europe and less like the one in New Guinea.

"Myitkyina, the third city in northern Burma, contained wood-frame and stone buildings, a railroad station, a hospital, a movie theater and warehouses. It was surrounded by flat, open country — as flat as Normandy.

Brig. Gen. Frank D. Merrill receives the Legion of Merit from Lt. Gen. Joseph Stilwell on April 18, 1944, beside Merrill's tent in a Burma jungle clearing. Witnessing are Maj. Alvin Larson, Col. Ernest Easterbrook and Col. Joseph W. Stilwell Jr.
Signal Corps

❝

We walked through the jungles and over the mountain ranges for several months . . . flew over the Hump [twice] . . . routed the Japs from the Ledo Road . . . drove convoys for the Chinese front over the famous China '21-Step Road.' We were the Mars Task Force.

❞

— CALVERT E. BOSLEY
Weapons Squad, Co. L, 3rd Bn.
475th Infantry Regiment

Jungle-fighting tactics were useless in most sectors of the city, under siege for 78 days. The Chinese and Americans hauled out their bazookas to blast down buildings.

"They fought from street corner to street corner, from house to house. The place became the Cassino of Burma — a fiercely defended city that had to be reduced to rubble by artillery barrages and daily dive-bombing attacks. Myitkyina was finally taken, in the middle of the monsoon season, by infantrymen who waded through waist-high flooded areas and slogged through knee-deep mud."

Any American who could carry a rifle was thrown into the battle. Casualties were flown out at the rate of 75 to 100 per day. In one U.S. company, "hardly a man could walk for fatigue, sores and skin diseases," according to one report.

Enter the combat engineers. To reinforce the Marauders at Myitkyina in May, Stilwell sent in the 209th and 236th Engineer Combat battalions. In early June, the two battalions were formed into a provisional regiment and brigaded with the Marauders. The engineers helped fight off enemy counterattacks until the end of July when they returned to Ledo. The 209th had lost 71 KIA and 179 WIA; the 236th counted 56 KIA and 112 WIA. Both battalions received the Presidential Unit Citation for their actions at Myitkyina.

The Myitkyina fighting — as bitter, uncompromising and costly as anywhere in the war — raged for three rain-soaked months until the town fell Aug. 3. In the last 2½ months of hole-to-hole, hand-to-hand combat, the Japanese lost more than 3,000 dead. Allied casualties included 272 U.S. KIA, 955 WIA and 980 sick.

Now the way for the Ledo Road was clear. Additionally, in a few months, Hump flights using the new airstrip at Myitkyina increased the monthly rate of supplies being flown into China to as much as 46,000 tons.

Air Commandos — specially organized U.S. and Chinese composite air groups — used gliders and small liaison planes to land long-range penetration groups hundreds of miles behind the lines. By dropping troops and equipment deep into enemy territory, and then quickly constructing secret airstrips, they kept large enemy forces tied down.

The 1st Air Commando Group, a component of the U.S. Army Air Forces, supported British Gen. Orde Wingate's *Chindits* as well as U.S. forces in Burma. Its most famous action, *Operation Thursday* — transport and resupply of troops attempting to push back the Japanese — was conducted in March 1944. This effort proved that air power could effectively bolster unconventional warfare.

After the war, the Japanese army paid the unit the ultimate tribute:

"Penetration of the airborne force into northern Burma caused the failure of the Army plan to complete the Imphal [India] operation . . . the airborne raiding force . . . eventually became one of the reasons for the total abandonment of northern Burma."

As the weakened Marauders withdrew, a second U.S. ground combat unit arrived in northern Burma in autumn 1944. The 5332nd Provisional Brigade — another *Galahad*-type commando unit code-named *Mars Task Force* — was made up of the jungle-wise 124th Cavalry and 475th Infantry regiments. Aided by the 612th and 613th Field Artillery battalions, *Mars Force* went to work battling the Japanese along the Ledo Road. In long, overland marches across mountains and through jungle, the brigade became the new U.S. spearhead in the CBI.

"Many of the men in [the *Mars Task Force*] had arrived in the theater during the siege of Myitkyina. Some had been taken from ships at Bombay, hurried to waiting transport planes, and flown into the thick of the fight. Mars artillery, which packed its big guns on Missouri mules, went into action as the first completely American artillery unit in Burma.

"At Mo-Hlaing it bore the brunt of a Japanese attack. During a bayonet charge an American was stabbed in the abdomen; he jumped up, ran down the Japanese who had bayoneted him, and killed him with bare hands. The American lived," related Edward Fischer in *The Chancy War*.

In another display of bravery, 1st Lt. Jack L. Knight of the 124th Cavalry Regiment, earned the Medal of Honor on Feb. 2, 1945, at Loi-Kang, for single-handedly taking out several enemy pillboxes. He was mortally wounded.

By suddenly showing up behind the lines and cleaning out enemy concentrations and supply centers, *Mars Force* convinced the Japanese that a full-fledged army was in the field. Successful though they were, however, *Mars Force* casualties totaled 122 KIA, 573 WIA and about a thousand non-battle injured and sick by the time the outfit was pulled from the field in mid-summer 1945.

By the time Tokyo agreed to a truce on Aug. 15, U.S. casualties in the CBI numbered 3,590 killed in action — 1,075 on the ground and 2,515 shot from the sky. Wounded totalled 2,183 from both the Army's air and ground forces. Most American losses were sustained in Burma — 3,349 KIA and 2,020 WIA. A relatively few GIs — virtually all airmen — became casualties in China: 241 KIA and 163 WIA.

Army Chief of Staff Gen. George C. Marshall paid tribute to the GI in Southeast Asia when he said the soldier there "had a most difficult physical problem of great distances, almost impassable terrain, widespread disease and unfavorable climate; he faced an extremely difficult political problem and his purely military problem of opposing large numbers of enemy with few resources was unmatched in any theater."

Above: Infantrymen and K-9 dogs of the Mars Task Force ferry across a river into Burma in late 1944.
Signal Corps

Top: A mortar crew of the Marauders' 2nd Battalion waits for orders to resume firing during the battle for Myitkyina, a vicious engagement waged from May 17 to Aug. 3, 1944. U.S. casualties mounted to 272 KIA and 955 WIA. *AP/Wide World*

★ ★ ★

Tarawa Landing by Tom Lovell. Members of the 2nd Marine Regiment pour off their Higgins boat into the waters surrounding Betio in the face of raking machine-gun fire and explosions. Marine Corps Art Collection

Cracking the Oceanic Perimeter

Terror on Tarawa

66

Life was boring, rugged, and stereotyped. Its formula was rigid and simple: rigorous training, followed by another invasion of another island. Unlike Europe, where Americans liberated cities and countries and enjoyed the rewards of conquering heroes, the Pacific was a sad and different story.

99

— BILL D. ROSS
Iwo Jima: Legacy of Valor

MOVING FROM mainland Asia to the Central Pacific, the entire character of the war changed. By capturing strategic island chains that formed a trail north to Tokyo, the Allies would be able to compel Japanese troops to capitulate. The bases left behind along their outer ring of defense were within striking distance of the home or other heavily fortified islands. By fall 1943, these stepping stones began to fall, starting with the Gilbert Islands as part of *Operation Galvanic*.

For four days in November 1943, the Fifth Amphibious Corps' (*Task Force 53*) 2nd Marine Division took part in the smallest yet bloodiest of the great battles of World War II.

On and in the waters around Betio, the citadel of the Tarawa Atoll in the Gilbert Islands, U.S. Marines waded ashore from their blue Higgins boats into raking machine gun fire coming from the formidable beachhead 500 yards to their front.

"No military historian who viewed Betio's defenses," wrote American WWII chronicler Samuel Eliot Morison as he watched the assault from the sea, "could recall an instance of a small island having been so well prepared for an attack. Corregidor was an open town by comparison."

Some 5,000 Japanese held positions honeycombed with underground shelters and 400 concrete pillboxes, bunkers and strong points. Surrounding the three-mile-long, 1,000-yard-wide island were minefields and a double fence of tangled barbed wire. Adding to the assaulting forces difficulties was a coral shelf 500 yards from shore, which made the tiny island

Marines descend toggle ropes to waiting transports for the landing on Tarawa in November 1944. Marine Corps photo contributed by Donald A. Eunice

> ❝
>
> *The USS Clamp [ARS-33] arrived within sight of Tarawa on the afternoon of Nov. 19, 1943, a few hours before the arrival of the battle fleet [because of a mistake] and fell under torpedo attack by a Jap Betty bomber plane. Our executive officer, 'Cool Head' Smith, ran to his cabin and returned with a Thompson, but no ammo. He ran again to his cabin and returned with ammo, but no Thompson.*
>
> *The plane had made one run and was two miles off the port bow banking for a return run. 'Cool Head' Smith pulled out his trusty .45 and blazed away at a two-mile range, only to be ordered by the 'Old Man' to 'put that thing away before you shoot someone!'*
>
> ❞
>
> — ROBERT M. CONNER
> *USS Clamp*

insurmountable by landing ship from the sea. Gun and man per square foot, Betio was the most heavily fortified island in the world.

"About two days prior to the Nov. 20 landing, Cruiser Division Five, using the USS *Salt Lake City, Chester, Pensacola, Oakland* and a submarine, hit Betio. The ships bombarded the island — while facing 6" Japanese naval guns — relentlessly," remembered Francis G. Ward, who was aboard the *USS Chester* at the time.

On Nov. 20, battleships *Maryland* and *Colorado* began a 3½-hour bombardment of the island with their powerful 16-inch guns. A few hours later, minesweepers *Pursuit* and *Requisite* led destroyers *Ringgold, Sigsbee* and *Dashiell* into position, adding to the Navy's firepower. Aviation squadrons from *Task Force 50* supplemented the ships' punch.

Soon the island became a smoldering ruin — but only on the surface. Beneath the steel, log and sand strongpoints, the enemy was ready.

Some amphibious tractors reached the shore, but most grounded on the inner reef. Marines had to wade several hundred yards, with 75-pound packs on their backs and no place to hide. "It was like being in the middle of a pool table with no pockets" is how Sgt. Welles Grey of the 2nd Marines later described the assault.

The 3rd Bn., 2nd Marines, hit Tarawa's north side at Beach Red 1, suffering heavy casualties while struggling to reach land. Many men were wounded and hundreds drowned as they fell into 25-foot bomb craters at the bottom of the shallow lagoon leading up to the beach.

Observing the assault from a Kingfish float plane flying above the island, Lt. Cmdr. Robert MacPherson recalled that "the water never seemed clear of tiny men, their rifles held over their heads, slowly wading beachward. I wanted to cry."

Above: Marines pull maintenance on an armored battle wagon, which served with distinction.

Marine Corps photo contributed by Donald A. Eunice

Top: A Marine tosses a grenade at a pillbox through the thick smoke of battle. During Nov. 20–23, 1943, the 2nd Marine Division endured 76 hours of the fiercest combat in Marine Corps history, wiping out more than 4,000 Japanese entrenched on tiny Betio Island.

Marine Corps

But progress was made. Some 34 handpicked men of the 2nd Scout-Sniper Platoon led by Lt. William Hawkins seized a critical objective. In the middle of the beachhead, Hawkins' unit grabbed a 750-yard-long pier, used later to unload essential supplies to support the attack. Killed in doing so, Hawkins was awarded the first of four Medals of Honor presented to 2nd Division Marines.

Beach Red 3, the far western part of the island, was assaulted by the 2nd Bn., 8th Marines, seven minutes after the first battalion arrived. The third assault unit — 2nd Bn., 2nd Marines — went ashore five minutes later on the island's center at Beach Red 2.

"No sooner had we hit the water than the Japanese machine guns really opened up on us," *Time* magazine correspondent Robert Sherrod reported after landing at Betio on D-day with the landing team of the 2nd Bn., 2nd Marines. "It was painfully slow, wading in such deep water. And we had seven hundred yards to walk slowly into that machine-gun fire, looming into larger targets as we rose onto higher ground. I was scared, as I had never been scared before. Those who were not hit would always remember how the machine gun bullets hissed into the water, inches to the right, inches to the left."

Moving inland against bitter resistance, units became badly scrambled and confusion reigned. Marines, nevertheless, held together by the common determination to move forward.

Division Chief of Staff Col. Merrit Edson, after the battle, said, ". . . The reason we won was the ability of junior officers and non-coms to take command of small groups regardless of where those men came from, and lead them as a fighting team."

With the situation desperate, the reserves — 1st Bn., 2nd Marines — came ashore at Beach Red 2, followed by the 3rd Bn., 8th Marines on Beach Red 3. For the remainder of the first day, Marines were unable to maneuver.

Yet some gains were made with the assistance of tanks from Co. C, Corps Tank Bn. and artillery from the 1st Bn., 10th Marines, which made it ashore before noon. Still, riflemen fought mostly with nothing more than their light individual weapons.

When darkness fell, the 2nd Marines held two small beachheads on Betio. The bulk of the forces (four battalions) manned a perimeter on Beach Red 2 barely 700 yards long and 300 yards deep. Farther west, 3rd Bn., defended the island's northwest corner at Beach Red 1 and along Beach Green.

Nov. 21 began with the commitment of 1st Bn., 8th Marines, to Beach

Red 2. When it made contact with the 3rd Bn. at Beach Red 1 later that day the tide began to turn for the Americans.

By day's end, Marines advanced to Betio's south coast, or Beach Black. Later that afternoon, 1st Bn., 6th Marines, landed at Beach Green while that regiment's 2nd Battalion secured adjacent Baikiri Island.

Next day, 1st Bn., 6th Marines, attacked east along the south coast; 2nd Bn., 8th Marines on Beach Red 3 went the same direction up north. Japanese soldiers who had, in many instances, thrust bayonets into their own bellies, choosing suicide as a last desperate means of avoiding disgrace, were found on both coasts.

During the night of Nov. 22-23, the surviving Japanese launched a series of piecemeal, uncoordinated attacks, which caused some casualties, but did not crack the Marine's eastern line. When the sun rose, Marines overran the exhausted enemy on Betio's eastern tail.

The 3rd Bn., 2nd Marines and 1st Bn., 8th Marines, with the support of 75mm self-propelled guns, flamethrowers and demolition teams from Co. C, 8th Marines, attacked from Beach Green and Beach Red 2 and crushed the final Japanese pocket in the west.

Betio was declared secure five days later on Nov. 28. (Mopping up, though, continued until Dec. 8, 1943.). Pfc. James Williams stepped forward and lifted his bugle to sound the colors for the first time on Tarawa as the U.S. flag was hoisted.

Tarawa proved to be the most bitter and concentrated battle of WWII.

A column of troops advance on Japanese forces, which retreated to a far end of Makin in November 1943. In the background, a Japanese seaplane is submerged in the lagoon after a strafing. **U.S. Coast Guard**

In four days, the Marines lost 1,085 KIA and 2,292 WIA. The Navy counted an additional 727 dead with the loss of the USS Liscome Bay.

"Adm. Richard Turner vowed that never again would American forces be trapped in the waters of an invasion beach approach," wrote Marvin Cooper of UDT 13. "Thereafter, every invasion beach was reconnoitered and cleared by underwater demolition teams [UDTs] days before the invasion took place, and never again did assault troops flounder and die in the approach waters."

Before the battle, Japanese Rear Adm. Keiji Shibasaki boasted, "A million men cannot take Tarawa in a hundred years." But 5,600 U.S. Marines took the islet in just four days, and only 17 Japanese survived and 4,836 died.

Time magazine memorialized the men best: "Last week some 5,000 U.S. Marines, most of them now dead or wounded, gave the nation a name to stand beside those of Concord Bridge, the *Bon Homme Richard*, the Alamo, Little Big Horn and Belleau Wood. The name was Tarawa."

Makin Taken

Another island in the Gilberts was taken at the same time the battle for Tarawa raged. Makin Atoll, dominated by Butaritari Island, was attacked by *Task Force 52* on Nov. 20.

"The spectacular trade-wind clouds scurrying to leeward, the flash and rumble of great ordnance seemed more appropriate to the harsh crags of Morven than to this soft Micronesian dream world," recalled naval historian Samuel Eliot Morison as he watched the pre-invasion bombardment of Butaritari Island. "There is nothing more beautiful in war than an amphibious operation when it clicks; and this one did."

Some 6,500 men of the 165th Regimental Combat Team and the 105th Infantry Regiment of the 27th Infantry Division, landed on Red and Yellow Beaches. Clearing and occupying the entire atoll took four days. Casualties totalled 66 killed in action and 152 wounded. "It is often overlooked in history," wrote Bruno Chiesa, a veteran of the 152nd Combat Engineers, 27th Division, "but we went up against the same crack Imperial Japanese Marines as did the Leathernecks on Tarawa."

Mastering the Marshalls

Rear Adm. Raymond Spruance, commander in the Central Pacific and of the U.S. Fifth Fleet, was reluctant to attack along his front because of the recent Tarawa experience. Yet an invasion of the Marshall Islands made possible a three-part scenario: isolation of enemy bastions at Truk and Rabaul, descent upon the Mariana Islands and raids by fast carrier forces as far west as the Palau Islands.

Moreover, Japan already had 20,000 soldiers and crack Imperial marines and 150 planes in the Marshalls, and was rushing in more men and aircraft to meet the expected U.S. attack. Since there appeared more to gain by striking sooner rather than later, the U.S. invasion of the Marshalls was launched as planned — just 10 weeks after the fall of the Gilberts.

The first softening-up blows against the Marshalls came on Dec. 4, 1943, by the soon-famous U.S. fast carrier force designated *Task Force 58*. In raids on airfields and anchorages, the carriers accounted for a large number of Japanese planes and ships, including seven ships sunk and three damaged.

Thereafter, U.S. Seventh Air Force bombers — flying from the Ellice and Gilbert islands — kept enemy airfields in the Marshalls under constant attack until the landings moved into high gear. By D-Day, U.S. air power had won complete mastery of the skies over the Marshalls, and the assault phase of the invasion went through without a single strike by enemy aircraft.

Operation Flintlock, code-name for the invasion, consisted of three attack forces — Northern, Southern and Majuro — totaling 85,000 assault and garrison troops. Principal units included:

- Marine — 4th Marine Division; the independent 22nd Marine Regiment; V Amphibious Corps Reconnaissance Company; 4th, 10th and 11th Amphibian Tractor battalions; 1st Armored Amphibian Battalion; and various Defense battalions.

- Army — 7th Infantry Division; 106th Regiment, 27th Infantry Division; 767th Tank Battalion; 708th Amphibian Tank Battalion; and 145th Field Artillery Battalion.

Their joint aim was to capture undefended Majuro Atoll and Kwajalein, the world's largest atoll. Each atoll consisted of a string of 20 to 50 sandy,

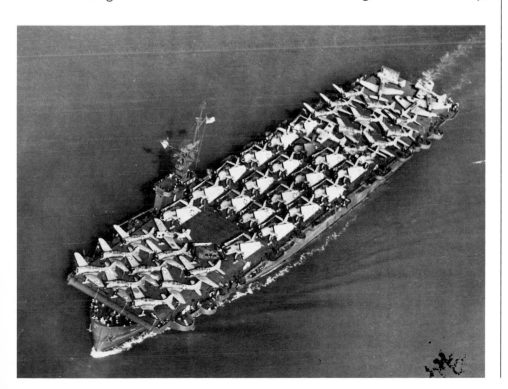

The *USS Liscome Bay*, loaded with SBD Dauntless dive-bombers and TFBs in September 1943. It suffered a torpedo blast and sank on Nov. 24, 1944, with 646 men, including Rear Adm. H.M. Mullinix, during the battle for the Gilbert Islands. National Archives

Liscome Bay's Last Combat

The first battle mission of the *USS Liscome Bay* was its last. The escort carrier was part of Carrier Division 24 supporting *Task Force 52 (Northern)* near the Gilbert Islands in November 1943.

Liscome Bay was near Butaritari Island on Nov. 24 when a lookout spotted a torpedo closing fast just before dawn. The deadly "fish" caught the carrier broadside. A second torpedo from the enemy sub *I-175* exploded seconds later.

Within minutes, the ship listed to starboard and went down, taking 55 officers, including Adm. H. M. Mullinix, and 591 seamen. Only 272 sailors survived of the original complement of 918. Loss of the *Liscome Bay*'s complement added to the deadly cost of the Gilberts campaign.

Here's how the *Dictionary of American Navy Fighting Ships* wrapped up its fate: "There was no warning of a submarine in the area until about 0510 when a lookout shouted: . . . here comes a torpedo!

"The missile struck aft the after engine room an instant later with a shattering roar. A second major detonation closely followed the first: the entire interior burst into flames. At 0533 *Liscome Bay* listed to starboard and sank. Gallantly her men had served; gallantly they died in the victorious campaign."

After swimming ashore, under enemy fire, an Underwater Demolition Team (UDT) platoon attaches primacord and a small explosive charge to an enemy's shore defenses.

UDTs in the Pacific were first sent into action at Kwajalein on Feb. 1, 1944. From there the famed "frogmen" went on to Guam, Saipan, Peleliu, the Philippines, Iwo Jima, Okinawa and Borneo. Their operations substantially cut down the number of fatalities during these invasions.

A total of 3,500 men in 30 commissioned UDTs served during WWII: 81 were killed in action. U.S. Navy

reef-encircled islands — some only a few hundred yards in diameter. Sixty-six miles long, 20 miles wide, and made up of no fewer than 93 small and low-lying islets, Kwajalein Atoll was the center of Japanese resistance in the Marshalls.

The invasion fleet of 373 ships that departed for the Marshalls Jan. 22, 1944, was at the time the largest naval force ever assembled under the Stars and Stripes. The Japanese avoided engaging this massive armada, allowing U.S. forces to arrive in the Marshalls unopposed.

Pre-invasion naval and air bombardment commenced Jan. 29 with warships and carrier planes pounding all the islands targeted for capture. Marine Gen. H.M. ("Howlin' Mad") Smith, commander of *Flintlock* ground forces, said the bombardment — the destructive power of which was unprecedented — was never again equalled, and enabled assault troops "to go in standing up" at the various objectives.

Landings began on Majuro, 300 miles southeast of Kwajalein. It was secured in a few hours without the loss of a man by Marine scouts and the 2nd Bn., 106th Regt. With its large lagoon, Majuro promptly became a supply depot and served as an advance base for the remainder of the war.

In other D-Day action, the 25th Marine Regiment and 1st and 2nd battalions, 17th Regt., 7th Div., seized islets adjacent to the main objectives at Kwajalein Atoll at a cost of 26 KIA and 42 WIA. Artillery was then set up to support the next day's principal landings on Kwajalein's southern part and Roi-Namur in the north — separated by 50 miles.

Shortly after sunrise Feb. 1, Navy underwater demolition teams (the famous UDTs) made their first appearance in the Pacific at Roi-Namur — 2,600 yards long, 900 yards wide and defended by 3,500 enemy troops. After the frogmen confirmed that reefs would not hold up landing craft, the 23rd and 24th Marine regiments hit the shores.

While planning *Flintlock*, Rear Adm. Kelly Turner, commander of supporting naval forces, predicted "Roi-Namur will be a tougher nut to crack than Tarawa." Fighting on Namur was furious. "At one point in this swirling maelstrom of action, I was kneeling behind a palm tree stump with my carbine on the deck, as I fished for a fresh clip of bullets in my belt," recalled 2nd Lt. John C. Chapin, platoon leader with the 24th Marines on Namur on Feb. 1.

"Something made me look up and there, not 10 feet away, was a Jap charging me with his bayonet. My hands were empty. I was helpless. The thought that 'this is it' flashed through my brain. Then shots chattered

A crushes
volved.
Tokyo

LE nvade
KI kazes.
a ty-
Wi
Mi kazes o

ny
n Mike
Da Total

19 0 Japa
De 044-mi
ning,

Army:
De orces
ask
ers,
ttles.
De n.
U.S.:
De
shoot
De destroy
De
De drops
De itter
KIA; 67
De
31 KIA;
19
Ja IR, 11t
Ja
Ja r III

B-29s o
ese
Ja
Fe s.

Fe s.

Fe ps

n kami-
Fe
U.S.:

Ma by 77t

Ap rmy
days.
S. KIA:

681.
Ap battle-

res afte
Ap aged:

Ap hth

Ap s.
Ma
Navy
asions a
Ma pan.

Ma l U.S.
Ju 6 Amer

Ju). U.S.

Ju and
staining

Ju
Ju

Above: GIs fire a 37mm anti-tank gun (M-1A1) at an enemy pillbox on Jan. 31, 1944, as the landing operations begin at Kwajalein, the world's largest atoll, located in the Marshalls. U.S. Army

Left: An enemy soldier surrenders after Marines blew apart his bunker during the Marshalls campaign of February 1944. Adm. Nimitz Museum

from all sides of me. My men hit the running Jap in a dozen places. He fell dead three feet from me." Overall, casualties were surprisingly light. The two-day battle cost 190 KIA and 547 WIA. Four Medal of Honor recipients were among the U.S. casualties. Only 51 Japanese surrendered.

Meanwhile, the Army's 32nd and 184th regiments, 7th Inf. Div., assaulted Kwajalein in the south. UDTs scouted the beach beforehand and naval gunfire razed the island, but the Japanese did not cave in as quickly as at Roi-Namur. Enemy defenses and the size of both the garrison (5,100 troops) and island (2½ miles long, 800 yards wide) delayed victory.

Fierce fighting raged four days before GIs eliminated the last Japanese pocket and overran the island. Gen. Charles Corlett, commander of the 7th Infantry Division, recalled, "Only in a few instances, and largely at night, did the Japanese leave the shelter of pillboxes and dugouts and attempt to delay the advance by fighting in the open."

Stubbornly defended, the island fortress exacted a toll: 144 U.S. dead and 845 WIA. The Japanese fought until only 49 were left to be taken alive.

With Majuro and Kwajalein in the bag, the U.S. could leap forward and invade Eniwetok Atoll, 380 miles west of Kwajalein. The 22nd Marines and 106th Infantry assaulted Eniwetok on Feb. 17 in a hastily organized operation code-named *Catchpole*. "The 708th Amphibian Tank Battalion also made beachhead landings on both Kwajalein and Eniwetok," wrote Vincent Sulpizio of the 708th's Company A.

To cover the landings, *Task Force 58* carriers struck simultaneously at Truk — Japan's "Gilbraltar of the Pacific" — 770 miles west of Eniwetok. In a two-day raid, Feb. 17–18, U.S. planes set a record for a single action

UDTs — Team One at Kwajalein and Team Two at Roi-Namur — demonstrated a major lesson in the Marshalls:

66

The task of destroying enemy underwater defenses and other obstacles would have to be done by men, not by push-button warfare.

99

— ORR KELLY
Author, *Brave Men-Dark Waters: The Untold Story of the Navy Seals*

Above: A burly, bare-chested Seabee depresses the handle of a detonator to blast coral into bits, which then could be used to surface an airstrip on Eniwetok in the Marshall Islands, February 1944. U.S. Navy

Right: A coast artillery crew of the Marine 51st Defense Battalion displays its mighty 90mm gun called "Lena Horne," on Eniwetok. U.S. Marine Corps

66

We came to the island after it was mostly secured. Our engineers went in to repair the pipelines and get the fuel tanks set up. We came upon these cliffs one day and when you looked over the side there was a sickening sight. Instead of surrendering to us, the Japanese jumped off the cliffs and plummeted down onto the rocks below. There were literally thousands of bodies sprawled out over the beach.

99

— 2ND LT. DAN DICKINSON
1398th Engineer Construction
Battalion

during the war by destroying some 200 enemy aircraft and sinking 41 ships totaling more than 200,000 tons.

By Feb. 24, tiny Engebi, Eniwetok and Parry islands, as well as other islets of the Eniwetok Atoll, had fallen after sharp combat. U.S. losses numbered 339 dead and 757 WIA. Of Eniwetok's 3,400 defenders, only 66 were taken prisoner. "It was a terrible place of destruction and death," recalled Robert Reichling, 22nd Marine Regiment. "We slept among the dead and the smell was something else. To eat we had to brush thousands of flies from our food."

Except for four heavily defended atolls — Mili, Jaluit, Maloelap and Wotje — that were isolated and ignored, the rest of the Marshalls were mopped up at leisure by U.S. occupation forces. Such bypassed Japanese-held islands were kept neutralized by bombing and naval gunfire.

"The Marshalls fight was a lot easier than what came later, but we still took enough casualties to make it bloody," recalled Gunnery Sgt. Keith Renstrom in the book *Semper Fi, Mac* written by Henry Berry. U.S. losses totalled 673 dead and 2,149 WIA.

Foraging Through the Marianas

Three pivotal and closely interwoven clashes in the western Pacific in the summer of 1944 cleared the Mariana Islands: Guam, Saipan and Tinian. Guam, a pre-war U.S. territory with excellent airfields and a good harbor, was the main target. Next in importance was Tinian, from which Japan itself could be bombed. However, since Tinian was within reach of artillery on Saipan, the latter island had to fall first.

The Marianas invasion force consisted of an army of 127,000 assault and 30,000 garrison troops, more than 600 U.S. Fifth Fleet ships, and a thousand carrier-based and U.S. Seventh Air Force aircraft. For sheer size, *Operation Forager* was unprecedented among Pacific amphibious operations. Main battle units included:

• For Saipan-Tinian, V Amphibious Corps: *Marines* — 2nd and 4th divisions; 1st Bn., 29th Regt.; V Amphibious Corps Reconnaissance Battalion; 2nd, 5th and 10th Amphibious Tractor battalions. *Army* — 27th Infantry Division; 762nd and 766th Tank battalions; 145th and 225th Field Artillery battalions, XXIV Corps; 534th, 715th and 773rd Amphibian Tractor battalions; and 708th Amphibian Tank Battalion.

• For Guam, III Amphibious Corps: *Marines* — 3rd Division; 1st Provisional Brigade; 3rd and 4th Amphibious Tractor battalions; 1st Armored Amphibian (Tank) Battalion; 1st and 7th 155mm Artillery battalions. *Army* — 77th Infantry Division; and 706th Tank Battalion.

Often overlooked are the parts played by the Navy's specialized units — both pre-and post-invasion. "There were five underwater demolition teams that played an active role in *Operation Forager*," said William Donath, a veteran of UDT 7 at Saipan. "These teams did recon and destroyed beach and reef obstacles, much of it done in broad daylight under enemy fire."

According to Seabee vet Harmond Littlefield, "Seabees also were prominent in the Marianas operations. The 121st and 18th Naval Construction battalions were on Saipan; the 25th and 53rd on Guam; and 13th Battalion on Tinian. The 5th Naval Construction Brigade assumed responsibility for development of base facilities on Guam."

A GI of the 27th Infantry Division at the base of a cliff on the Nafutan Peninsula on the east coast of Saipan in June 1944. Two regiments of the division — the 105th and 165th — assaulted Nafutan Point. It would take nine days to clear the ridge.
U.S. Army

Suicide on Saipan

Forager commenced June 12, 1944. Fast carrier force *Task Force 58* moved in and destroyed hundreds of Japanese aircraft, securing air supremacy over the Marianas.

At the same time, battleships and cruisers pounded Saipan's invasion beaches. The battle promised to be long and difficult: Saipan was the fulcrum of Japanese defenses in the western Pacific. It covered some 72 square miles of jungle and mountainous terrain, and was defended by about 25,000 men of the Japanese 32nd Army and 6,000 naval personnel.

V Amphibious Corps landings began June 15 on a six-mile front in the face of fierce Japanese fire. By evening, 20,000 2nd and 4th Division Marines were ashore, but their losses were a harrowing 2,500 killed and wounded in action.

During the night, Japanese infantry, with strong tank support, made

Above: A Marine on patrol on Saipan came across this Japanese family hiding in a hillside cave. The mother, four children and a dog hid from the fierce fighting in the area. All such civilian captives — including Koreans and Chamorros — went to safe havens in the beach area. U.S. Marine Corps

Top: Soldiers of the 27th Infantry Division scour the cliffs for enemy soldiers still hiding in caves that dotted the Nafutan Peninsula. During mop-up operations, 200 dead Japanese were found in five caves. U.S. Army

heavy suicide attacks against the U.S. beachhead. The Marines beat off the charges and inflicted severe losses on the enemy, including more than 700 men killed and 30 tanks destroyed.

"I was with H Company, 165th Regiment, 27th Division, and we came in on June 16 then pushed south and immediately captured Aslito Airfield," said Edward Britton. "Soon a Jap plane landed there and we captured the pilot, too."

The 121st Seabees had stormed ashore with the 4th Marine Division, while the 18th Seabees accompanied the 2nd Division. "Despite severe fighting, Aslito Airfield was in our hands by June 19 and the Seabees set out repairing the battle-damaged runway," added Littlefield.

Within a few days, the 27th Infantry Division had landed and cleared southern Saipan. From that point, the V Amphibious Corps' 77,400 Marines, soldiers and attached seamen advanced line abreast up the length of the island, resisted furiously at every turn by the dug-in Japanese.

Unexpected resistance was encountered on Nafutan Peninsula. Fighting focused on three areas: "Hell's Pocket," "Purple Heart Ridge" and "Death Valley." Not until the end of June was the 27th Division able to eliminate the last of the enemy strongpoints on the peninsula. Next, 3,000 remaining Japanese were taken out in the sweep to Marpi Point at places like Tanapag Village.

Mount Tapotchau, from which the Japanese looked down on the U.S. invasion forces, fell on June 27 to the 2nd Marine Division. The main line of enemy resistance collapsed on June 30. The island's capital, Garapan, fell two days later after costly street-fighting.

As Japanese strength waned and they became hemmed in on the island's northern end, the enemy concentrated their surviving forces for one final effort to drive the Americans back into the sea. That push came July 7, with the full weight of the *banzai* charge crashing into the 1st and 2nd battalions, 105th Infantry, 27th Division, near Makunsha.

1st Sgt. Norman Olsen recalled: "The first thing I saw was a long thin glistening object waving back and forth in the half-darkness, then another one glistened over by the beach. Then I saw one in the bushes toward the

Above: Cpl. Oscar B. Iithma, Pfc. Jack Nez and Pfc. Carl C. Gorman were among the first Marines to assault Saipan. U.S. Marine Corps

Left: After days of artillery bombardment and naval shelling, Garapan, Saipan's capital, was reduced to rubble. Men of the 2nd Marine Division entered the city on July 2, 1944, engaging in fierce street fighting. U.S. Marine Corps

cliffs. In a second it seemed as if there were hundreds of them all over the area, waving wildly back and forth. As they came closer, you could see they were sabers, and around every one was a little squad of Japs."

Another account recorded the results. "When they hit us there were so many of them we couldn't shoot fast enough," recalled Tech. Sgt. Frederick Stiltz of the 1st Battalion, 105th Infantry. "We were shooting them at 15 or 20 yards. [Our perimeter] was about 50 yards deep and 100 yards across. Artillery was breaking them up, but some of the artillery fell short and hit among us. We must have killed 300 or 400 Japs; they were piled around us."

But the Americans held tenaciously, displaying courage in the face of fanaticism. Lt. Col. William J. O'Brien rallied his men along the perimeter and Sgt. Thomas A. Baker was severely wounded yet refused evacuation. Both men fought until killed, each earning the Medal of Honor.

It was the most devastating such counterattack of the entire war. Between 2,000 and 3,000 Japanese, amply fueled with *sake*, started out. When the attack was broken up two days later, more than 4,300 Japanese dead were counted behind American lines.

The line of crosses tell a grim story at the 2nd Marine Division cemetery on Saipan in the summer of 1944. Marine Corps

Though the failed attack caused serious U.S. casualties — about 1,500 soldiers and Marines KIA and WIA — it also sapped the remaining Japanese forces. Saipan was secured July 9. Total U.S. losses in the four-week battle — the most of any campaign in the Pacific to date — were grievous. Marine units sustained 3,152 KIA and 7,285 WIA. The 27th Division counted 3,674 killed and wounded.

In contrast, the Japanese garrison was annihilated: only 1,810 prisoners were taken during the battle. In the months of "mopping-up" that followed, U.S. patrols killed or captured hundreds more of the diehards.

'Great Marianas Turkey Shoot'

While ground combat consumed Saipan, a huge battle force of the U.S. Fifth Fleet steamed west, screening the Marianas from expected Japanese naval and air attacks. When the enemy fleet was discovered in the Philippine Sea on June 18, 1944, the war's greatest battle between aircraft carriers commenced.

Task Force 58, under Adm. Marc Mitscher and comprising 15 carriers, seven battleships, 21 cruisers and 69 destroyers, rushed forward. The Japanese had nine carriers, five battleships and more cruisers than the U.S. fleet. In the air, in all categories except float planes, the Japanese were outnumbered 2:1.

On June 19, the Japanese struck, launching four air attacks with 417 planes. Their approach was detected by radar and 315 enemy planes were shot down by U.S. fighters and anti-air-craft fire. Two U.S. carriers, *Wasp* and *Bunker Hill*, were damaged. Meanwhile, U.S. submarines sank two enemy carriers — *Shokaku* and *Taiho*.

"As the Americans headed for advantageous attack positions, 75 Japanese planes met them in the air over the fleet. Simultaneously, the Japanese ships opened up with all the anti-aircraft fire they could muster. The darkening sky was filled with brilliant colors: green, yellow, blue, white, pink and purple, all from the thermite and phosphorous shells of the Japanese anti-aircraft fire," wrote John M. Lindley in *Carrier Victory*.

Next day, June 20, *TF 58* fliers pushed their planes beyond maximum range to strike back at the Japanese fleet. Heavy resistance was met, but another enemy flattop, *Hiyo*, was sunk and four more Japanese carriers damaged. Two-thirds of their remaining aircraft were shot down and a battleship and cruiser crippled.

With all but 35 of their 430 carrier planes and 3,500 seamen lost in the Battle of the Philippine Sea, the Japanese fleet withdrew. U.S. losses during the far-ranging action were 16 pilots, 33 air crewmen and about 100 planes. The one-sided engagement became popularly known as the "Great Marianas Turkey Shoot."

Despite the outcome, Capt. Arleigh Burke believed "we could have gotten the whole outfit! Nobody could have gotten away if we had done what we wanted to."

An F-6F Hellcat readies for takeoff into the Battle of the Philippine Sea — the "Great Marianas Turkey Shoot" — in June 1944. Admiral Nimitz Museum

Fighter ace Lt. (jg) Alex Vracin celebrates his score of six Japanese planes in the Battle of the Philippine Sea, known as the "Turkey Shoot" because of the volume of enemy planes downed in a short period of time during the Marianas invasion of June 1944. U.S. Navy

A Japanese dive bomber plunges seaward after taking a direct hit from anti-aircraft fire from the Navy carrier *USS Kitkun Bay*, in the Philippine Sea, June 1944. Japanese naval forces approaching the Marianas caused U.S. warships to withdraw eastward, though, leaving shore troops temporarily without naval gunfire and air support. National Archives

Guam Reconquered

Guam, more than 100 miles south of Saipan, was also to have been assaulted in mid-June, three days after Saipan was invaded. But when Saipan turned out to be tougher than expected, the attack on Guam was held up.

More than three times larger than Saipan, Guam measured 228 square miles and was defended by 18,500 Japanese. Because of the long delay prior to the actual attack, Guam was on the receiving end of the longest pre-invasion naval and air bombardment of any amphibious operation during the war.

Two separate landings were made on July 21. The 3rd Marine Division, which had been aboard transports for seven weeks, led the way north of Apra Harbor near Agana. The 1st Provisional Marine Brigade and one regiment of the 77th Infantry Division landed south of the harbor near Agat. Ultimately, 30,214 Marines and 17,958 soldiers would fight on the island.

"I landed on Guam with the third wave to find the beaches literally covered with dead Marines. Just about every palm tree had its top blown off. Blood and carnage was everywhere. Shells from the large ships at sea were exploding on the mountains and hills away in the distance. American planes were flying overhead and strafing an area ahead of the beach. Japanese mortar shells were dropping in their pattern of threes all over the place," said Louis Webb, 1st Marine Division.

Guam was island-fighting at its worst. For four dogged days, the bitter battle for the beachhead raged. Marines and soldiers fought their way

Helldivers and a lone ship return from a strike on Guam in July 1944. Guam, part of the island-hopping battleground of the U.S. war in the Pacific, was the first U.S. possession recaptured from the Japanese. U.S. Navy

Action in the landing on Guam intensifies, as a tank moves across to cover the Marines wading past a wrecked Japanese plane. Aerial and naval bombardment continued all around them during the landing on July 21, 1944. Defense Dept./Marine Corps

Soldiers of the 30th Infantry Regiment, 77th Infantry Division, assaulted Guam on July 21, 1944, coming ashore at Agat Beach on the Orote Peninsula. They soon occupied the high ground overlooking the beachhead. The rest of the division followed two days later. **U.S. Army**

1st Lt. Richard C. Bryson of the 3rd Marine Division marches up the Agana-Piti road under rifle cover, careful to avoid the mines planted to knock out tanks on Guam in June 1944.

Defense Dept./Marine Corps

forward inch by inch across successive ridges, suffering heavily from combat and exhaustion. Their first objective, Orote Peninsula, was cleared after five days by the 1st Marine Brigade.

When the agonizing fighting moved inland to higher jungle-covered ground, tactics became only more difficult. The Japanese holed up in dark ravines and higher ground beyond, and their tanks, mortars and artillery took a heavy toll of the American ranks.

On the night of July 25, the Japanese counterattacked en masse. Marine Sgt. Alvin M. Josephy, Jr., recalled that the enemy charged "throwing grenades and howling '*Banzai-ai!*' like a pack of wild animals. . . . All along the line shells lit up the night like the Fourth of July." Cooks and hospital patients had to take up weapons at deep points of enemy penetration. One portion of the line was hit seven times.

Approximately 5,000 Japanese — many drunk, some armed only with baseball bats or crude spears — made the suicide charge. While overrun in many places and sorely pressed, the U.S. line held. By daylight, 3,500 enemy troops had been killed, and it was clear that the *banzai* attack had failed. U.S. units suffered a thousand casualties in the attack.

Three days later, the Japanese again attempted to puncture the beachhead perimeter. It was a failed effort that cost the enemy commanding general his life. Retreating to the interior, they made their last defensive stands at Mt. Barrigada, Yigo and Mt. Santa Rosa.

Despite their terrible losses, organized Japanese resistance did not end

By Aug. 8, 1944, most of the fighting on Guam had ceased, except for clearing small pockets of enemy troops hiding in caves, dugouts and pillboxes. Though given the chance to surrender, many Japanese, who felt it was honorable to die "for their emperor," were killed by dynamite charges or hand grenades. **U.S. Navy**

until Aug. 11. Eventually, the entire enemy garrison was killed or captured. Small numbers of them held out in the hills — in some cases, for years after the war had ended. (The last *zanryusha*, or straggler, on Guam did not surrender until 1972.) Fighting on the island claimed the lives of 1,567 Marines and 213 soldiers of the 77th Infantry Division.

Tinian Tornado

Tinian, which lay only 3½ miles south of Saipan, is 12½ miles long and about five miles at its widest. It was defended by 8,000 enemy troops when the 4th Marine Division landed, along with two regiments of the 2nd Marine Division, on its high, rocky coastline shortly after sunrise on July 24, 1944.

Landing forces encountered Type 98 hemispherical anti-boat mines known as "steel basketballs with horns." Lt. Michael F. Keleher of the 25th Marines remembered the impact on an LVT. "That vehicle, weighing seven tons, was flipped into the air and folded up like a Parker House Roll."

During the landings, Japanese coastal artillery raked the naval gunfire support group. Battleship *Colorado* was hit 22 times and destroyer *Norman Scott* six times. Sixty-two sailors were killed and 245 wounded before the enemy guns were silenced.

Next day, the balance of the 2nd Division came ashore and together the two Marine divisions stormed over the island. Furious though the fighting on Tinian was, however, it was largely over within nine days. During the fighting, Pvt. Joseph W. Ozbourn, 4th Marine Division, and Pfc. Robert L. Wilson, 2nd Marine Division, both earned Medals of Honor. Each threw himself on a grenade to save the lives of fellow Marines.

The island saw the first operational use of napalm bombs. Army pilots dropped 150 jettisonable wing tanks filled with a mixture of gasoline and napalm jelly, which was originally dropped as a defoliant.

U.S. losses were 328 KIA and 1,571 WIA. In contrast, the Japanese garrison was wiped out; only a handful surrendered. In the three months after Tinian's fall, another 542 enemy troops were killed by U.S. patrols.

U.S. Fifth Fleet commander Adm. Raymond A. Spruance said, "Tinian was probably the most brilliantly conceived and executed amphibious operation of World War II." It soon became famous as the largest B-29 base in the world.

U.S. capture of the southern Marianas — particularly of Saipan — was a watershed in the Pacific war. After the decisive battle for Saipan, the Japanese leadership realized it had no chance of avoiding defeat. The shock waves reached all the way to Japan itself, toppling Prime Minister Hideki Tojo's military government from power.

Marines on Guam salute the Coast Guard for getting them ashore. Bearing the sign are Pfc. William A. McCoy and Pfc. Ralph L. Plunkett. U.S. Coast Guard

The assault on Tinian — just 3½ miles south of Saipan — began the morning of July 24, 1944, with both the 2nd and 4th Marine divisions landing along the northwest edge of the island. (A diversionary force bluffed an invasion from the south.)
Once in control of the northern half of the island three days later, artillery units, using 155mm howitzers and smaller 75mm guns, opened up on enemy forces to the south. By Aug. 1, the island was in American hands. Dept. of Defense

'Yankee Samurai'

Some 6,000 mostly Japanese-American, or *Nisei*, graduates of the Military Intelligence Service Language School (MISLS) of Fort Snelling, Minn., served from the icy tundra of Kiska and Attu in Alaska's Aleutians to the boiling jungles of Burma and India, and on still-classified missions with the OSS — Office of Strategic Services, the CIA forerunner.

Nisei agents also went on forays into the caves of Yenan to rendezvous with two then-obscure Chinese partisans named Mao Tse Tung and Chou En Lai. *Nisei* MISLS grads played a major, if unheralded, role in nearly every battle in the Pacific war.

Perhaps the Nisei's biggest intelligence coup was the capture and translation of the Z Plan, Imperial Japan's strategy for defending the Mariana Islands. "Never in military history did an

Sometimes called the "Yankee Samurai," the Japanese-American 306th Language Detachment helped turn the momentum of the Battle of Okinawa with their translation of a captured artillery chart. U.S. Army

army know so much about the enemy prior to an actual engagement," remarked Gen. Douglas MacArthur.

Immediately before the U.S. landings in the Philippines in October 1944, *Nisei* translators broke Tokyo's *Kata*

Kana code and learned of Japan's master plan for the defense of the islands.

Serving as an intelligence sleuth in the Philippines, Charles Tatsuda wrote in a letter home: "The fighting has been tough — close combat, picking off a great deal of the enemy with rifles and not with big guns."

Kiyoshi Ishibashi was a member of the MISLS team in Calcutta, India. His unit broke codes by listening for "one-word" signals carefully concealed in routine messages. Later, in Burma, Ishibashi's group "monitored and translated all Japanese aircraft broadcasts. We had to be careful in combat zones of our own soldiers mistaking us for the enemy," he said.

Such service allowed the Nisei to "get on with being Americans," said MISLS veteran Bud NaKasone. "Americans got a better view of us through this kind of bravery."

Guam, Saipan and Tinian all became critical forward bases for the burgeoning U.S. Pacific Fleet's naval and amphibious forces. But most important, the conquered islands in the Marianas became major air bases from which newly developed long-range strategic bombers, the B-29s, could reach the Japanese home islands.

Nonetheless, the price of victory in the Marianas was high. Total U.S. losses during the summer-long campaign amounted to about 24,000 dead and wounded, including 4,500 U.S. soldiers, 19,300 Marines and some 500 sailors and airmen.

Peleliu: 'The Devils Anvil'

"We managed to take the beach by having a bunch of us get killed — it was as simple as that. But, my God, what a price we paid." That's how veterans of the Pacific's "forgotten battle" described the deadly assault on Peleliu. A chronicler of this bitter battle aptly called the campaign "the devil's anvil."

After completing conquest of the Marianas, U.S. strategists turned southwest toward the Palau Islands in the western Carolines, stepping stones to the Philippines. Located about 1,000 miles west of the great Japanese naval stronghold at Truk and only 500 miles east of Mindanao, the Palaus formed a major crossroad in the western Pacific. Their loss would cut off large Japanese forces occupying the Netherlands East Indies and seal the fate of the enemy garrisons already isolated in western New Guinea.

Marine Pfc. Gerald Churchby and Pfc. Douglas Lightheart, cradling his .30-caliber machine gun in his lap, take a break during the fierce fighting on Peleliu on Sept. 14, 1944.
Cpl. H.H. Clements, Marine Corps

But more important, enemy airfields on Peleliu and Angaur islands, both of which lay within the southern tip of the Palaus, were needed to cover the U.S. invasion of the Philippines. Once secured, the Palaus would serve as staging points for the continuing U.S. movement around Truk.

Though the Palaus campaign — code-named *Operation Stalemate II* — began to take shape in late summer 1944, the region had been under constant air attack since June. U.S. Fifth and Thirteenth Air Force bombers kept the enemy off balance until the eve of the American invasion.

Beginning Sept. 6, Adm. William F. "Bull" Halsey's U.S. Third Fleet raided Yap, the Palaus and Mindanao islands to keep the Japanese guessing where the main blow would fall. In these softening-up attacks, Halsey's carrier aviators devastated enemy airfields and naval anchorages, meeting almost no opposition.

In fact, by D-Day, Sept. 15, 1944, Japanese air power had been written off as no threat to the amphibious forces advancing into the western Pacific. Though the Japanese in the Palaus expected to be attacked, the assault phase of the Peleliu invasion went through without interference from enemy planes.

In addition to 202,000 seamen aboard 800 ships, *Stalemate II* consisted of 49,650 troops of the III Amphibious Corps and 1,600 aircraft. Principal assault troops were the 16,000-man 1st Marine Division, which drew Peleliu as its assignment, and the Army's 81st Infantry Division, which had Angaur as its main target.

Volcanic in origin and enclosed by a coral reef, Peleliu rose 550 feet above sea level and was covered with thick jungle. The island's northern part was dominated by Umurbrogol Mountain — a natural labyrinth of steep, craggy ridges honeycombed with caves and covered by scrub brush.

After Third Fleet warships worked over the seven-square-mile island for three days with 2,200 tons of shells, the Marines landed three regiments abreast on a mile-long beach. They were opposed by more than 11,000 Japanese protected by a maze of heavy steel-and concrete-reinforced underground fortifications.

Furthermore, mixed coral and concrete casemates and pillboxes fronted all the beaches. Roads were covered by strongly entrenched anti-tank guns and automatic weapons. Inland traps were constructed to channel an invader's movement into lines of fire. Artillery and heavy mortars studded the high ground.

Despite the fierce pre-invasion naval and air bombardment, the Japanese unleashed a storm of coordinated fire upon the first waves of troop-carrying landing craft bearing down on the island. The stunning array of concealed Japanese mortars, artillery and machine guns created havoc on the beaches.

Maj. Frank Hough, author of *The Island War*, recalled that the "assault waves crossed the reef amid the debris of those which had preceded them: wreckage of gear and vehicles, [Marine and Navy dead] bobbing sluggishly in the shallow water or draped grotesquely across protruding coral heads."

66

The shore at Peleliu was a mass of flames and smoke. This landing was going to be heavily opposed and at a high cost of life. . . . The shore was a bloody mess, devastating and sickening.

At 1010 hours an amphib took the company of infantry into the beach. At 1035 hours it returned and took us to shore. The helmsman told us that he had lost seven men on that first trip. His advice was short: 'Hit the beach, find a hole and get inland as fast as possible' because the beach was an inferno of death.

We drove right onto the beach under heavy mortar fire and leaped ashore. We had made it without losing a man. We hit the nearest hole and dug in. Mortars were hitting on the beach. The heat was terrible. Booby traps and mines and boat obstacles were evident at the receding of the tide.

99

— ROBERT E. BLUTHARDT
1st Marine Division

Above: A battle-weary Marine is loaded for combat on Peleliu in September 1944. Progress was slow because of the island's rough terrain, but by Oct. 9, 1944, the enemy was backed into a small area in central Peleliu and it took several more weeks to ferret them out. Dept. of Defense

Top: Members of the 1st Marine Division ford a river on bloody Peleliu Island during the fall months of 1944. Marine Corps

In the south, dragon's teeth funneled the 7th Marine Regiment into a single-file, head-on approach, which made their ranks easy prey for Japanese gunners. In the north, the 1st Marine Regiment came under flanking fire from behind a protruding rock formation. Only in the center did the 5th Marine Regiment land in good shape.

Then, once ashore, the Marines found their way inland blocked by extensive minefields and pillboxes carved into the raw coral. In fact, the Japanese defenses blended in "so well with the natural terrain that a man had to walk practically up to the narrow firing apertures before recognizing them for what they were," according to one account.

1st Lt. William Sellers, 2nd Lt. Raymond Stramel and Pfcs. Joseph Hendley and William Getz, Marine Corps veterans of Peleliu, together recalled in Henry Berry's book *Semper Fi, Mac:* "We managed to take the beach by having a bunch of us get killed — it was as simple as that. But, my God, what a price we paid. Everywhere you looked you saw dead and wounded Marines . . . so many of them, some horribly mangled, others with a piercing hole."

Late in the afternoon, Japanese infantry with strong armor support counterattacked the shallow beachhead. The 5th Marines and 2nd Bn., 1st Marines, beat off the most threatening fanatical charges and inflicted severe losses on the enemy, including several hundred men killed and 13 tanks destroyed.

After they failed to unhinge the U.S. lodgement, the Japanese pulled back into the caves and pillboxes of Umurbrogol, determined to hold out as long as they could. On Sept. 17, the 1st Marines, who already had absorbed 1,000 of the division's 1,500 casualties since landing, ran up against the massif.

Within three days, the 1st Marines had suffered another 700 casualties

Anguish on Angaur

When it became clear that the Marines had won and ensured at least a foothold on Peleliu, the 81st Infantry Division and 710th Tank Battalion landed on the tiny island of Angaur on Sept. 17, 1944. Angaur, which lay only 10 miles south of Peleliu, was defended by about 2,600 Japanese troops.

The 321st and 322d Regimental Combat Teams — two-thirds of the 81st Division — went ashore simultaneously, though on separate beaches, and seized beachheads the first day. After linking up, they fought their way together across the island.

"On Angaur, because of the narrow beach areas and small island combat

A GI of the 81st Infantry Division who was wounded on Angaur in September 1944 is given plasma prior to evacuation. U.S. Army

area, we had to lay in foxholes made in the coral at night. There was always the danger of being run over by our own tanks," wrote Joseph Hetra of the 405th Ordnance Co., 81st Inf. Div.

The 81st Division's battle for Angaur — too often overlooked in Pacific war history — was fierce and costly. Nonetheless, the GIs overwhelmed the enemy's resistance within 72 hours and secured the island in four days. The 321st RCT went on to Peleliu while the 322nd RCT mopped up.

Organized fighting on Angaur, however, continued until Oct. 21 when the last pocket of Japanese soldiers was overrun in the northwest. By then, U.S. casualties numbered 264 KIA, 1,355 WIA and 940 non-battle losses. In contrast, at least 1,300 Japanese were killed. Only 45 surrendered.

---

on Peleliu. In the regiment's indomitable 1st Battalion alone three companies were reduced to 15 percent strength. Marines started referring to Umurbrogol Mountain as "Bloody Nose Ridge."

After six days of fighting and running into Umurbrogol, the bloodied 1st Marines were pulled off the embattled ridgeline. The 7th Marines, who had gone about securing the southern end of the island, were thrown against the mountain but soon suffered similar losses.

On Sept. 23, the 81st Division's 321st Regimental Combat Team (RCT) landed on Peleliu and joined the grinding action around Umurbrogol. The 5th Marines, meanwhile, in spite of severe casualties, captured the island's northern part and doubled back to invest the ridge from behind.

Soldiers and Marines pinched the enemy from his mountain stronghold. By mid-October, the 1st Marine Division had been reduced to less than half strength. About 700 Japanese remained alive, and responsibility for the battle was handed over entirely to the 81st Division.

The 323nd RCT, which in *Stalemate II*-related action had captured Ulithi, an undefended atoll to the north in the western Carolines chain, took over the brunt of the battle for Peleliu. GIs inched forward day by day, preceded by air, artillery, mortar and napalm attacks. With armored bulldozers, tanks and half-tracks in close support, they finished the grueling job Nov. 27, 1944.

The long, drawn-out Army-Marine Corps struggle for Peleliu ranked with Tarawa and Iwo Jima as one of the bloodiest battles of the Pacific war. Fighting was costly: Marines — 1,336 KIA and 6,032 WIA; Army — 110 KIA and 717 WIA; and Navy — 195 KIA and 505 WIA.

Though they held out a long time, the Japanese garrison of 11,000 or more troops was practically annihilated. In the end, U.S. forces took but

We are between Peleliu and Angaur. To our right, the battleship New Jersey. *To our left, the rocket ships. The cruiser* Honolulu *is toward shore from us. There are so many ships and planes I could never count them, and all guns are going. We are dropping anchor in the bowels of hell.*

— CURTIS F. ANDERSON
USS *Windsor*

Thousand Yard Stare by Tom Lea. "As we passed sick bay it was crowded with wounded, and somehow hushed in the evening light I noticed a tattered Marine standing quietly by a corpsman, staring stiffly at nothing. His mind had crumbled in battle, his jaw hung, and his eyes were like two black empty holes in his head. Down by the beach again, we walked silently as we passed the long line of dead Marines under the tarpaulins," remembered Lea at Peleliu. U.S. Navy Art Collection

❝

In one cave I recall seeing 8 or 10 Japs lined up against a wall with their rifle muzzles in their mouths, or what was left of them. They had obviously committed hari-kari *by putting their toes in the trigger guards and squeezing the triggers.*

❞

— SGT. GILBERT A. AMBROSE
Marine Air Group 11

300 or so prisoners. Most were captured near the end of the bloody campaign, when the Japanese defenders started running out of food and water.

Peleliu and Angaur were rapidly converted into advanced U.S. bases for bombing missions against the Philippines. Ulithi, with its large lagoon and numerous flat islets, promptly evolved into an immense U.S. Pacific Fleet supply and ship repair depot.

"Ulithi was Admiral Nimitz's secret weapon — the Navy's fabulous supply and repair base that kept our fleet at the Japs' front door," said Arthur Blott, who served there with Service Squadron Ten.

Some 43,000 Japanese troops in the northern Palaus were effectively isolated by U.S. victories. Encircled enemy forces, without supplies or hope of escape, surrendered at the end of the war. Others hid in caves and swamps for years afterward: the last contingent held out until April 1947.

Iwo Jima: 'Nightmare in Hell'

"Each man had his own thoughts, many later confessing to having uttered silent prayers. There were those who believed that God would keep them safe, however high the casualties. On the other hand, some had premonitions of death. The young recruits were not sure what to make of the situation. Many had joined the Marines 'to see action' but now a dawning had come that action was likely to be a terrible thing.

"A very few, among both recruits and veterans, felt truly aggressive, eager to land and begin fighting, believing themselves to be alert enough and clever enough to survive. Bravado was commonplace. One man tilted back his head, cast his eye across the sunny sky, and announced, 'What a perfect day to die!' " recorded Richard Wheeler in his book *Iwo.*

Back on course and headed north again after the Peleliu diversion, the Marines opened one of the war's most dramatic chapters in February 1945 with the invasion of Iwo Jima, a combined land, sea and air operation of historic scope. It was then, and remains today, an epic in the annals of amphibious warfare. But the most costly per capita combat of the Pacific war on land lay ahead.

Eight hundred miles south of Tokyo and only 675 miles north of Saipan, Iwo Jima ("Sulphur Island") was the principal island of the Volcano chain. These volcanic islands lay within the route of U.S. forces destined to attack Okinawa and, more important, directly in the path of Japan-bound B-29 Superfortress bombers flying from the Marianas.

Radar and radio-listening posts on Iwo Jima gave the Japanese essential advance notice of impending B-29 raids. Such warning allowed fighter aircraft to be scrambled and civil defense to be organized more effectively. In addition, the island's airfields permitted enemy fighters to pick off crippled B-29s returning to the Marianas.

With Iwo Jima in U.S. hands, the situation could be reversed. The island was within P-51 Mustang fighter aircraft range of Japan, and in U.S. control would give the B-29 crews fighter escort to their targets and back, as well as emergency landing sites.

Iwo Jima was considered crucial to Tokyo and no one doubted the Japanese would fight hard to hold the island. Because its loss would be a severe psychological blow, fortifications had been perfected over eight months. The island's eight square miles were honeycombed with caves, bunkers and pillboxes, which harbored 24,000 troops.

Iwo Jima was subjected to an unprecedented softening-up campaign. For six months, beginning in autumn 1944, the island was kept under nonstop air assault by U.S. Seventh Air Force bombers and Fifth Fleet carrier planes.

"Ships of the Seventh Fleet also were bombarding Iwo at that time," recalled Bernard O'Leary, who served aboard the *USS Case*. "That bombardment was at night and we fired starshells. Mt. Suribachi showed up like a big haystack."

Beginning Feb. 16, 1945, Iwo Jima shook under a pre-invasion naval bombardment lasting three days. Meanwhile, *Task Force 58*, the most powerful carrier force ever to put to sea, struck the Japanese mainland to pin down enemy air support. More than 500 of Tokyo's planes were destroyed.

In addition to 1,800 carrier-based and Seventh Fighter Command planes and tens of thousands of seamen on nearly 800 ships, the Iwo Jima operation — code-named *Detachment* — included about 75,000 troops of the V Amphibious Corps. Main assault units included:

• *Marines* — 3rd, 4th and 5th divisions; 2nd and 4th 155mm Howitzer battalions; 2nd Armored Amphibian Tractor Battalion; 3rd, 5th, 10th and 11th Amphibian Tractor battalions; Company B, Amphibious Reconnaissance Battalion, V Amphibious Corps; 8th Ammo and 36th Depot companies, as well as the 2nd Bomb Disposal Company.

• *Army* — 471st, 473rd and 476th DUKW battalions; 147th Infantry Regiment (attached to the 3rd Marine Division); 506th Anti-Aircraft Artillery Battalion; and the 483rd Anti-Aircraft Automatic Weapons Battalion.

Pfc. Ira Hayes, Pfc. Franklin Sousley, Sgt. Mike Strank, Pharmacist's Mate Second Class John H. Bradley, Pfc. Rene Gagnon and Cpl. Harlon Block — all of 2nd Plt., Co. E, 28th Marines — plant the larger American flag on Mt. Suribachi at 3 p.m. on Feb. 23, 1945.

Joe Rosenthal, Associated Press

• *Navy* — 31st, 62nd, 70th and 133rd Naval Construction battalions and the 8th and 41st Naval Construction regiments. Coast Guardsmen manned 18 LSTs and two transports along with seven Navy ships.

Casualties were sustained even before the actual assault. During the preliminary naval gunfire phase, Japanese coastal artillery hit the cruiser *Pensacola* six times. It lost 17 KIA and 120 WIA. Destroyer *Leutze* counted seven KIA and 33 WIA.

In addition, Navy underwater demolition teams (UDTs) or frogmen — charged with scouting the beaches for offshore mines and obstacles — and a dozen gunboats supporting them, were badly shot up. Their losses, including bombing of the *APD Blessman* and LCI gunboats one thousand yards off shore, were 43 KIA, 153 WIA and one MIA. Of that number, 18 frogmen were killed and 23 wounded — some when the gunboats were hit.

In the south, Mount Suribachi, a dormant cone-shaped volcano, towered menacingly over the island, dominating the invasion beaches. Along with the rock-strewn northern part of the island, Suribachi was one of the island's few natural strong positions and the Japanese had made it even stronger.

Mining engineers had hollowed out the rugged 556-foot massif and reconstructed it from within until it bristled with over 200 gun emplacements and 21 blockhouses. Elsewhere on the island, artillery, mortars, anti-tank guns and machine guns were sited in positions reinforced with concrete walls four to eight feet thick.

At 9 a.m., Feb. 19, the 4th and 5th Marine divisions began landing on the loose volcanic ash beaches. The landing was picture perfect, and at first enemy resistance was sporadic and ineffective. But within 20 minutes after landing, when the Marines had driven 250 yards inland, the Japanese opened up.

Maj. Frank Hough, author of *The Island War*, recalled that "artillery and mortars of all shapes and sizes commenced pounding the beach...harmless-appearing sand hummocks spat automatic weapons fire from narrow apertures only a few inches above ground level...land mines were everywhere."

The battle to secure the beachhead was ferocious, but by late afternoon of the first day the Navy had moved more than 30,000 troops ashore. Within another 48 hours after landing, however, 1,500 sailors and Marines lay dead ashore and afloat; another 3,000 were WIA. "A nightmare in hell," *Time and Life* correspondent Robert Sherrod called it.

"Whenever you're in the assault you feel that every shot is aimed at you, and you alone. Machine gun tracers arch like Roman candles fired straight ahead instead of skyward. Near an enemy mortar pit you can hear 'thunks' as shells are dropped into firing tubes, and sometimes you can see their up-and-down trajectories and hear their in-flight whirring sound before the deadly 'whomps' of explosion," said one Marine with the 2nd Bn., 25th Regt., 4th Div. on Green Beach one day after the invasion.

"Artillery and rocket fire are worse, but somehow less personal. You can hear the incoming whine of shells, but you can't hear the lanyard pulled or see the missiles coming. Seldom on Iwo, from D-Day until the battle was over, did you see the enemy — just the sights and sounds of deadly fire from his weapons. You could see comrades moving and hear the shouted commands of officers and non-coms. And, once the attack began, you soon would hear those terrible cries of 'Corpsman! Corpsman.'"

Offshore, *kamikazes* — Japanese suicide planes — crashed into numerous U.S. ships with brutal effect on Feb. 21. Escort carrier *Bismarck Sea* was sunk and 326 seamen were killed. Another carrier, *Saratoga*, was hit by five *kamikazes*, which caused severe damage and killed 123 men and wounded 192. Net tender *Keokuk* was set afire and lost 17 KIA and 44 WIA.

Suribachi, after the Japanese troops and guns defending it had been largely silenced, fell on the fifth day, Feb. 23. A 40-man patrol of the 5th Division's 2nd Battalion, 28th Marines, cleared the summit. Despite enemy fire, patrol members raised the Stars and Stripes, signalling the capture of the key position.

Marine Staff Sgt. Louis R. Lowery, a *Leatherneck* magazine combat photographer, took pictures of the event. A few hours later, the flag-raising (with a larger flag) was shot by Associated Press photographer Joe Rosenthal, who snapped the famous photo that thrilled the world. (On Jan. 11, 1994, the last surviving member — John H. Bradley — of the six who planted the flag, died.)

"Six men from Co. E, 28th Marines, had replaced the small American flag with a larger one," said Dave Severance, Company E commander. "The first flag was to be saved as a memento for the 2nd Battalion. Also, a larger flag could be seen clearly by Marines advancing."

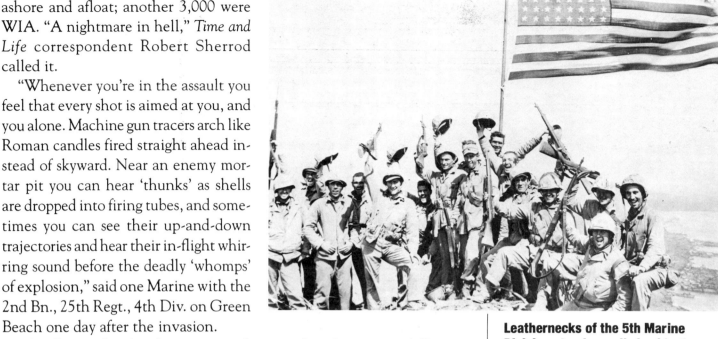

Leathernecks of the 5th Marine Division stand proudly beside the American flag planted atop Mt. Suribachi on Iwo Jima in February 1945. Marine Corps

A chaplain celebrates mass with Marines on Iwo Jima, February 1945. U.S. Navy

Marines hit the Japanese on Iwo Jima with all they had, including these 4.5-inch automatic, gravity-fed rocket launchers mounted on three-quarter ton trucks. Marine Corps

66

The forward observer teams would spend about three days up on the front lines and then return back to the artillery battery for a couple of days before returning to the front. On one of these occasions we were issued a fresh egg!

I never saw anything that took the minds off the danger each of us was experiencing. It took a couple of days to figure out just what to do with a raw egg when we were getting shot at! I ended up making a tiny fire in the corner of my fox hole, cooked the egg in my mess kit. I think it was the best egg I ever ate!

99

— MANSEL DEWAYNE MARTIN
A Battery, 1st Battalion
13th Marines, 5th Marine Division

The fall of Suribachi ended the battle for the beachhead. Though artillery and mortar fire continued to make matters in the rear unsafe, men and machines began pouring across the beaches in unending streams. Soon 60,000 GIs were fighting ashore.

By Feb. 24, the 3rd Marine Division had landed in strength and was positioned in the center between the 5th and 4th divisions. For the next five weeks, the Marine divisions ground forward line abreast up the island's ever-rising and broadening central tableland.

At every point, the heavily dug-in Japanese met the U.S. advance with fearsome resistance. For the Marines, the battle's lexicon came to be dominated by strange-sounding place names like Bloody Gorge, Hill 382, the Meatgrinder, Charlie-Dog Ridge, The Amphitheater, Turkey Knob, The Quarry and Cushman's Pocket.

Japanese redoubts were embedded so ingeniously into ridges and ravines, and hidden in caves connected by subterranean passages, that it proved impossible to wipe them all out. Many strongpoints were simply covered up by bulldozers with rubble and sand, entombing the fanatical enemy troops.

That fanaticism was shown near Tachiiwa Point during a *banzai* charge on March 8. Combat was fierce; a single Marine company expended 20 cases of grenades. The carnage was clear: 784 Japanese bodies were counted versus 90 U.S. KIA and 257 WIA.

Final breakup of the enemy's main line of resistance did not occur until March 9, D day plus 18. It happened when the 3rd Division finally succeeded in cutting through to Iwo Jima's northern shore and splitting the Japanese defenders into two isolated groups.

The few Japanese still organized were hemmed in. But it was not until March 26 that Marines overran the last part of Iwo Jima and the island was declared secured. A final, futile attack on that day accounted for 262 more Japanese dead, with the loss of 53 Americans.

Testifying to the strength of the fortifications, some 2,400 additional Japanese were killed or captured as fighting flickered on into June.

By the time it was all over in mid-summer 1945, 22 Marines and five Navy men had earned the Medal of Honor. This was the greatest number of MOH recipients for any single engagement of WWII. One, for example, was earned by Pfc. Douglas T. Jacobson who personally dispatched 75 Japanese on Hill 382.

Capt. Irving Schechter, in Henry Berry's book *Semper Fi, Mac,* called Iwo Jima "as horrible as any action in Marine Corps history . . . if you were going to survive, you just had to be lucky, that's all."

The grueling five-week battle for "that stinking island," as the men who were there called it, was a campaign unparalleled in WWII for its intensity and possibly the sheer scale of its ferocity. It cost the U.S. armed forces a total of 28,686 casualties: 6,821 KIA and 19,217 WIA.

The Marines lost 30 percent of their assault force. Moreover, 2,648 Marines were disabled by combat fatigue. Some 633 Navy aviators and seamen were dead and 1,158 WIA; ashore, another 248 Navy corpsmen, Seabees and other specialists were killed and 759 WIA. The Army had nine KIA and 28 WIA.

The Japanese sacrificed 23,300 lives. Even though Lt. Gen. Tadamichi Kuribayashi, the garrison commander on Iwo Jima, had ordered that "every man will resist until the end, making his position his tomb," 1,083 Japanese ultimately surrendered.

Iwo Jima was rapidly turned into a base for the U.S. bombing campaign over Japan. As early as March 4, 1945, long before the island-fighting was finished, the first shot-up B-29 crash-landed there. On March 11, P-51

Ground crewmen prep the P-51 Mustang — *Is This Trip Necessary?* — with auxiliary fuel tanks for its next assignment out of Iwo Jima in April 1945. U.S. Air Force

'The Ship That Wouldn't Die'

On March 19, 1945, as the aircraft carrier USS *Franklin* was launching a fighter sweep against naval bases on the island of Kyushu, a Japanese attack bomber appeared out of the low, thin clouds and dropped two 500-pound, armor-piercing bombs along the length of the carrier.

At 7:07 a.m. the first bomb ripped through the flight deck and exploded on the hangar deck. The second bomb penetrated further into the *Franklin*, igniting ammunition, bombs and high-octane fuel drums. Resulting explosions knocked out the combat information center and all radio communication. The large ship, which now lay dead in the water less than 60 miles off Japan, was soon a raging inferno.

Most of the ship's 100 planes, loaded with "Tiny Tim" rockets and fuel, were prepared for takeoff when the bombs hit. Those not blown overboard or still located on the hangar deck exploded as the flames engulfed them. "The explosions were really out of this world," said Capt. Stephen Jurika, Jr., the *Franklin's* navigator. "One followed the other interminably."

Surviving crew members battled valiantly to bring the fires under control and were helped by the crew of the USS *Santa Fe.* Two of the *Franklin's* survivors received the Medal of Honor for their heroic efforts — Lt. Cmdr. Joseph T. O'Callaghan, the ship's chaplain, and Lt. Donald Gary. O'Callaghan, "the bravest man I've ever seen," according to the ship's captain, Leslie E. Gehres,

became the first chaplain ever to receive this honor.

Unbelievably, the *Franklin* was able to regain power as it was towed to Ulithi in the Caroline Islands by the cruiser USS *Pittsburgh*. After stopping briefly at Pearl Harbor for more repairs, the battered and burned-out flagship of *Task Force 58* limped home to the Brooklyn Navy Yard. Remarkably, the *Franklin* had covered nearly the entire 12,000 miles under its own power.

Of the 3,500 men aboard the *Franklin*, 832 died and 300 were wounded. Their ship, however, survived. After three *kamikaze* attacks during the Battle of Leyte Gulf and two direct bomb hits that should have sunk her, the USS *Franklin* richly deserved her nickname, "The Ship that Wouldn't Die."

The crew of the cruiser *Santa Fe* observes the smoking carrier *Franklin*, which, on March 19, 1945, incurred the loss of 832 men and another 300 injured when two Japanese bombs exploded on its deck, igniting fires and explosions of armed, fueled aircraft that continued for five hours. The *Franklin* was saved just 55 miles off the coast of Japan, and, after returning to Pearl Harbor and the mainland U.S., was rebuilt, but never returned to combat. U.S. Navy

The Fifth Fleet provided pre-invasion shelling of Okinawa, including this LSM(R) — Landing Ship, Medium; Rocket — firing volleys at enemy fortifications along the shores of Tokishiki Shima in March 1945. **U.S. Navy**

"

March 27, 1945 . . . We're at sea again. The jumping, rolling, tossing sea again. My belly isn't the only thing with the jitters . . . they affect my whole body. Okinawa. Just looking at it on the map breaks us out in a cold sweat. Okinawa spells Kamikaze Corps to us. Somebody's gonna get it and we may be lucky or unlucky. You see, the Navy loses a lot of men but you don't particularly hear about it. . . .

"

— ORVILLE RAINES
Yeoman 3rd Class
USS Howorth

Mustangs began operating from Iwo Jima and flying fighter escort for the B-29s. P-47s also performed as fighters.

By the end of the war, 2,251 B-29 Superfortresses would land there. More than 800 of them — returning to the Marianas hampered by engine problems or damage from enemy fire — made emergency landings. Without Iwo Jima in U.S. hands, many of their 9,000 crew members most likely would have been lost.

Okinawa: 'Ultimate Battle'

Before combat had even fully subsided on Iwo Jima, the largest invasion of the Pacific was under way; it proved to be the most costly. This was the last stepping stone to the home islands.

To the enemy it was *Tennozan* — "the ultimate battle." The Japanese general on Okinawa gave explicit orders: "Each soldier will kill at least one American devil." And "the present position will be defended to the death, even to the last man." Three months later, in July 1945, the Ryukyus were in American hands.

As the largest and principal island of the Ryukyus chain, Okinawa's value lay in its location northeast of Formosa and the Philippines, and west of the Bonins. Only 350 miles from Kyushu, Japanese-occupied Okinawa (it was conquered by Tokyo in 1875) had the only two naval anchorages between Formosa and Kyushu from which an invasion of Japan could be launched.

Sixty miles long, 2 to 18 miles wide and covering 485 square miles, the island was large enough to base and train troops for the forthcoming invasion of Japan. Finally, in U.S. hands Okinawa would make a superb air base to strike at the heart of Japan.

Sensing Japan would soon be invaded, the Japanese fortified Okinawa to delay the U.S. drive. By the time U.S. forces appeared in the Ryukyus, the Japanese 32nd Army had a force of 120,000 troops defending the island. (This was about double the 65,000 troops that American intelligence believed the Japanese had.) That total included a 20,000-member Okinawan home guard called the *Boeitai*. Japanese troops were told, "The victory of the century lies in this battle."

The island was extremely rugged and mountainous, with elevations of 1,000 feet or more. In addition, about 80 percent of the land was covered by pine forests interspersed with dense undergrowth. The Japanese took good advantage of the terrain.

Since their intention was to hold out as long as possible, the Japanese concentrated their strength in a massive underground defensive network in the south. Their battle cry: "One plane for one warship. One boat for one ship. One man for 10 enemy. One man for one tank."

The amphibious assault of Okinawa, code-named *Operation Iceberg*, reflected the greatest concentration of land, sea and air power ever used in the Pacific.

The supporting armada of U.S. Fifth Fleet ships totaled 1,457 vessels

of all types, including the British Pacific Fleet, and 548,000 men. The invasion was also supported by the bomber and fighter-bomber aircraft of the U.S. Seventh Air Force and B-29 Superfortresses of XXI Bomber Command.

The 183,000 troops landing on Okinawa composed the most experienced amphibious army in history. The principal combat units of the assault force, which fought under Lt. Gen. Simon Bolivar Buckner as the U.S. Tenth Army, were primarily battle-tested veterans of Pacific island-fighting and included:

• *XXIV (Army) Corps* — 7th and 96th Infantry divisions; 419th Field Artillery (FA) and 1176th Engineer groups; and 866th Anti-Aircraft Artillery (AAA), 88th Chemical Mortar, 71st Medical, 780th Amphibian Tank and 534th Amphibious Tractor battalions.

• *III (Marine) Amphibious Corps* — 1st and 6th Marine divisions; 2nd, 5th, 8th and 16th AAA; 1st and 3rd Armored Amphibian Tractor; 1st, 4th, 8th and 9th Amphibian Tractor; 1st, 3rd, 6th, 7th, 8th and 9th Field Artillery; and 1st Separate Engineer, 802nd (Army) Engineer, 71st and 130th Naval Construction battalions (eventually, the 8th, 10th, 11th and 12th Seabee brigades served on Okinawa).

> *I saw a fast new fighter, a 'Tony,' heading straight for USS Sigsbee's bridge. I braced myself against the bulkhead. I felt a hard push on my back and heard a loud roar. My helmet flew into the air, and I went sprawling onto the deck. Dust, smoke, clattering steel chunks and fragments were everywhere. The captain, Cmdr. Gordon P. Chung Hoon [Annapolis '34], had not ducked at all.*
>
> *He stood straight up on the wing of the bridge, glaring at the onrushing plane. He was in command of his ship, and in command of himself, completely. I heard him say, 'Steady, gang.' The plane hit our depth charges. Later, the captain went below aft and worked in waist-deep oil and water and darkness, directing the repair crews. He kept the ship from sinking. Next day, we held a burial at sea for the four [of 23] that could be buried.*

— JOHN R. WILLIAMS
Signalman 1st Class
USS Sigsbee
April 14, 1945

- *Western Islands Landing Force* — 77th Infantry Division.
- *Tenth Army Troops/Reserve* — 2nd Marine and 27th Infantry divisions; 20th Armor Group, 80th Medical and 144th Coast Artillery groups; 53rd AAA Brigade; and 713th Armored Flame Thrower Battalion.

Beginning in February 1945, U.S. ships and planes pummeled Okinawa with an intense, methodical naval and air bombardment. In response, Japanese suicide planes unleashed *Ten Go* — "heavenly operation" — against the fleet, consisting of *kikusai* — "floating chrysanthemums" or mass formation attacks.

Between March 26–31, *kamikazes* knocked 16 ships out of action or severely damaged them. Carrier *Franklin*, hit by two bombs, suffered close to 1,000 casualties, but she got home under her own power — the most heavily damaged carrier ever to be saved.

The invasion began March 26 when 77th Division battalions landed in the Kerama Retto group in the western Ryukyus to obtain a protected anchorage for refueling and resupply ships. The 77th secured the main objective in four days at a cost of 31 U.S. KIA and 81 WIA. In the Keramas, the troops made an interesting find: 350 *renraku tei* — explosives-laden suicide boats.

Nearly 1,000 Navy frogmen cleared Okinawa's shore in preparation for L-Day, April 1. Consequently, 28 American lives were lost during the landing instead of expected far greater casualties.

III Amphibious and XXIV corps landed against light opposition on the beaches north and south of Hagushi and seized Yontan and Kadena airfields. By April 6, Tenth Army held the center of the island.

Seven hundred Japanese planes, however, ravaged *Task Force 58* on April 6–7, sinking a destroyer, an escort carrier, two LSTs and an LCT, and damaging two troop transports and six other vessels. *TF 58* claimed 249 kills. In addition, remnants of the Japanese navy sortied from the Inland Sea to attack ships off Okinawa.

A U.S. submarine west of Kyushu, on April 7, sighted the Japanese naval task force, which consisted of the superbattleship *Yamato*, a cruiser and eight destroyers. Three hundred U.S. carrier planes attacked and sank all the enemy vessels except four destroyers, which fled back to Japan. *Yamato* — the biggest and most powerful battleship in the world — went down with 3,063 men.

By April 8, the Marines had secured all of the northern part of Okinawa except Motobu Peninsula, where the Japanese dug into the 1,500-foot Yae Tae hills. The peninsula fell on April 19 after fierce fighting.

During this period, *kamikazes* continued to mount devastating raids. On April 12–13, a second mass air attack by 400 planes caused great damage to Allied shipping. Attacks on April 15–16 and April 27–28 were less successful, but still caused grievous casualties aboard the ships.

One ship, the destroyer *Laffey*, withstood 12 hits in 80 minutes while fighting through 20 *kamikaze* and bombing attacks and downing nine planes. Some 32 sailors were KIA and 71 WIA. Tragedy struck the hospital ship

USS Comfort, off Leyte, April 28 when a *kamikaze* hit the operating room killing six nurses, five doctors, eight enlisted men and seven patients.

Meanwhile, the 27th Division seized Tsugen Shima, southeast of Okinawa, on April 10–11. The 77th Division landed 6,100 men on 11-square-mile Ie Shima, an island northwest of Okinawa, on April 16. U.S. casualties totaled 239 KIA, 879 WIA and 19 MIA versus 4,700 enemy soldiers killed and 149 captured in six days of brutal fighting. America's most beloved war correspondent — Ernie Pyle — also was killed on Ie Shima by a Japanese sniper.

Beginning April 9, XXIV Corps ran up against the formidable Shuri Line, the main line of Japanese resistance on Okinawa. Their fortifications were anchored on an ancient castle from which the defensive network took its name.

The line was softened up for 10 days by artillery, aircraft and naval gunfire. This was the most massive and concentrated artillery pounding of the Pacific war. Yet the Japanese dug in so firmly that U.S. troops made little progress when they attacked April 19. The assault on Kakazu Ridge alone cost 22 U.S. tanks.

GIs renewed the attack five days later but found the Japanese had secretly withdrawn behind an even stronger line. So III Amphibious Corps joined XXIV Corps in the south to prepare to throw the entire Tenth Army against the entrenched enemy.

On May 5, however, the enemy, with tanks and artillery support, surged forward from their fortifications, striking the U.S. front in an enormous counterattack centered around Kochi Ridge. The offensive was well-planned and skillfully-coordinated with *kamikazes*.

Though it was stopped by U.S. infantry, artillery and naval gunfire and

Pfc. Paul E. Ison of the 1st Marine Division charges across Death Valley on Okinawa, May 10, 1945. Marine Corps

"

One afternoon there was close to a hundred Japanese kamikaze *planes that flew over us. About six broke formation to come after us. We knocked down four, and another destroyer got one but missed the last one. The* kamikaze *pilot crashed into that destroyer and left a hole big enough to drive two trucks through.*

It killed about 40 men.

Another time we shot one kamikaze *out of the air. He came spiraling down at us but luckily hit our guy wire, rolled off the side of the ship and exploded in the water about 20 feet from us.*

"

— EDGAR EICHLER
Machinist Mate 3rd Class
USS Bennion, April 1945

cost the Japanese about 5,500 casualties, the counterattack inflicted 700 U.S. losses and helped upset American plans for resuming the offensive, which got under way again May 11.

That day GIs drove against the Japanese line, stretching from the Asa River estuary to Yonbaru. Through May 20, Marines and soldiers suffered terribly in continuous fighting for Wana Ridge, Sugar Loaf Hill, Hills 55 and 110 and other godforsaken terrain features.

"One of the most horrendous bloodlettings in the history of American combat" is how Henry Berry, author of *Semper Fi, Mac,* described the fighting. "In actuality, the entire fighting south of the Asa River on Okinawa was a bloody nightmare."

At Wana, according to Lt. Col. Arthur J. Stuart of the 1st Marine Division's 1st Tank Battalion, the tank-infantry teams, stuck with each other ". . . alive, wounded, dead, maimed, crying in anguish, limping, bleeding — no matter how, they came out together."

A Peleliu veteran, E.B. Sledge, later recalled of Sugar Loaf: "When enemy artillery shells exploded, the eruptions of soil and mud uncovered previously buried Japanese and scattered chunks of corpses. The ridge was a stinking compost pile. If a Marine slid down the muddy ridge, he was apt to reach the bottom vomiting. Fat maggots tumbled out of his muddy pockets, cartridge belt, leggings. . . . The conditions taxed the toughest almost to the point of screaming. . . . The war was insanity."

U.S. attacks bogged down repeatedly in nonstop rain that turned the roads and battlefield into a sea of mud and hindered battlefield maneuvering. By May 28, after the heaviest of the rains stopped, the advance resumed again.

Next day, the 1st Division's 1st Battalion, 5th Marines, succeeded at last in overwhelming the Japanese defending Shuri Castle. As a result, the Japanese were compelled to abandon the main Shuri Line. Nonetheless, the feat was bittersweet since the Tenth Army had already suffered grievous losses.

"I was a Navy pharmacist's mate (corpsman) attached to the III Corps Medical Battalion, III Amphibious Corps, and we were very much along the Shuri Line," wrote John E. Buckingham. "During these battles, we were the receiving unit for thousands of wounded and battle-fatigued Marines, mainly from the Sixth Division. They received medical and surgical treatment necessary to either get them back into the lines, or evacuated to the hospital ships offshore.

"In many respects, we resembled the MASH unit of the Korean War. Our battalion consisted of about 100 Marines — drivers, cooks, etc., and 250 dedicated Navy doctors, dentists and corpsmen from all walks of life."

At this stage, the Japanese were retreating in the face of overwhelming firepower. "Yard by yard they slowly advanced, moving from rock to rock, shooting at the visible Nips in front of them. The entire escarpment was giving off funeral pyres of skyward-curling smoke as caves full of screaming Nips were closed with satchel charges, creating the stink of mangled flesh,"

Kamikaze attacks peaked during the battle for Okinawa. Two struck within seconds of each other on May 11, 1945, and set off an explosion on the USS Bunker Hill just off Kyushu, killing 396 and injuring 264 sailors. National Archives

Navy Corpsmen: Respected and Revered

Unarmed Navy corpsmen were often the first link in a chain that carried wounded Marines to safety.

"We were the receiving unit for thousands of wounded and battle-fatigued Marines," said John E. Buckingham, then a pharmacist mate with III Corps Medical Battalion attached to the III (Marine) Amphibious Corps during the Battle of Okinawa. "We gave medical and surgical treatment necessary to either get them back into the lines or evacuated to the hospital ships offshore."

Sometimes corpsmen were called upon to join the fight. On Guam in 1944, a medical officer and a corpsman died defending their hospital from an attack.

On Iwo Jima, the exploits of corpsmen are legendary. Despite being wounded three times in one week, George Wahlen, 2nd Bn., 26th Marines, 5th Div., stayed on the battlefield retrieving casualties amid murderous concentrations of fire. John Willis, 3rd Bn., 27th Marines, 5th Div., also disregarding his injuries, helped repel a Japanese attack by hurling back eight grenades the enemy had thrown at him. A ninth grenade exploded in his hand, killing him instantly. Both men received the Medal of Honor.

Another corpsman on Iwo Jima, John Bradley, became part of history when he and a group of Marines raised the Stars and Stripes over Mt. Suribachi.

On Peleliu, the corpsman's task was especially daunting.

"One corpsman asked a wounded Marine if many corpsmen were being wounded, and he immediately responded, 'No,'" recalls James Quin, a corpsman attached to the 1st Marine Division on the island. "There was a general sigh of relief until he added, 'Most of them are getting hit between the eyes.'"

A total of 677 Navy medical personnel attached to Marine units died in the Pacific and 2,218 were wounded, according to a 1950 report entitled *The History of the Medical Department of the U.S. Navy in World War II*. The most corpsmen casualties during one operation occurred on Iwo Jima, where 209 were killed and 641 were wounded. On Okinawa, 118 died and 442 were wounded. On Saipan, 77 corpsmen died in battle and 337 were wounded.

wrote Mason Pawlak, *Yank* correspondent with M Co., 381st Inf. Regt., 96th Division on Okinawa's Hill 99 on June 14.

As the Japanese were driven in upon themselves, fresh elements of the reserve units, including the 8th Marines, moved ashore to bolster the tired Tenth Army. Japanese defenses weakened steadily.

On June 22, organized enemy resistance ceased after two remaining pockets — Hill 85 and the Ara-saki area — fell to the 77th Infantry and 6th Marine divisions.

Still, that was followed by 10 days of heavy mopping-up, including the 381st Infantry eliminating the last elements of the 24th Japanese Division in the south. The Tenth Army also launched a four-division clean-up drive in the north, which didn't end until Aug. 4 when the 27th Division reached Hedo Misake.

Okinawa ranks as the costliest single battle of the Pacific war for both sides, second only to the Battle of the Bulge in terms of U.S. casualties. Between them, the Army's 96th, 7th, 77th and 27th Infantry divisions sustained 4,436 KIA and 17,343 WIA. Combined, the 6th and 1st Marine divisions suffered 2,793 KIA and 13,434 KIA.

The Japanese counted 107,539 dead and 10,755 captured. Another 23,764 enemy dead were estimated to have been sealed in caves or otherwise buried. Tragically, some 42,000 Okinawan civilians also were killed. In addition, they lost 7,800 planes (at least 1,465 of them *kamikaze*), 16 ships sunk and four ships damaged.

American losses in ships between April 1 and July 1, also the highest in U.S. history, were 36 sunk and 368 damaged. Some 20 percent of Navy KIA (4,907) in the entire war was sustained off Okinawa. Also, 763 aircraft were shot down. *Kamikazes* were the culprits in most cases.

Among the U.S. dead was Gen. Buckner, the highest-ranking American officer killed in the Pacific war. He died June 18 in a Japanese artillery barrage while visiting the front on Mezado Ridge. Buckner's favorite toast, incidentally, was, "May you walk in the ashes of Tokyo."

Okinawa also demonstrated the lethal ingenuity of man. To clear caves and tunnels, the U.S. used the recoilles rifle for the first time, along with flame-throwers. "Blowtorch and corkscrew" tactics, as Buckner called them, sealed caves. Flame-throwing tanks provided the blowtorch, while dynamite charges and grenades served as corkscrews. In fact, flame-throwers accounted for 25 percent of Japanese dead on Okinawa.

The Japanese were ingenious, too. Besides the *kamikaze* and *renraku tei*, the Japanese developed the *kaiten* — "turning of the heavens" — two torpedoes lashed together with a seat for a driver. Some 106 of the drivers died. Then there were the *ohkas* — "cherry blossoms" — rocket-propelled cylinders or piloted buzz bombs.

These and more traditional weapons, such as giant mortars and artillery, took a heavy psychological toll among GIs — producing the most and worst cases of combat fatigue in the Pacific war. The Tenth Army even opened a special field hospital to treat its victims.

One example shows why the psychiatric casualty rate was so high. On Ishiromi Ridge, GIs were raked by deadly 50mm knee mortars and "riflemen were blown to bits," remembered 2nd Lt. Robert F. Meiser. Of the 204 men of E Co., 307th Regt., 77th Inf. Div., only 48 came out unscathed after three days of such punishment.

Despite the terrible price, America's overwhelming victory carried the war to Japan's doorstep. Still, as Cmdr. Louis A. Gilles, Fifth Fleet intelligence officer, cautioned: "The Japanese are defeated, but we have not yet won the victory." The writing, however, was on the wall even in Tokyo. Reported veteran Japanese diplomat Mamoru Shigemitsu: "Okinawa left little room for doubt as to the outcome of the war."

British observers may have best characterized the battle for Okinawa as "... the most audacious and complex enterprise ... yet undertaken by the American amphibious forces ... more ships were used, more troops put ashore, more supplies transported, more bombs dropped, more naval guns fired against shore targets" than in any other Pacific operation.

★ ★ ★

Okinawa Death Factory

Branch	KIA	WIA	Other Casualties*
Navy	4,907	4,824	—
Army	4,675	18,099	15,613
Marines	2,938	13,708	10,598
Total	**12,520**	**36,631**	**26,211**

*Mostly combat fatigue.

Casualties by Division

Division	KIA	WIA
96th	1,518	5,912
7th	1,125	4,943
77th	1,058	3,968
27th	735	2,520
6th Marine	1,637	6,689
1st Marine	1,156	6,745

RETURN TO THE PHILIPPINES

Follow Me! U.S. Army in Action series. When the 3rd Battalion, 34th Infantry Regiment, 24th Division, landed on Red Beach on Leyte, Philippines, on Oct. 20, 1944, regimental commander, Col. Aubrey S. Newman, shouted to his men: "Get up and get moving! Follow me!" The infantrymen quickly broke through the line of well-camouflaged pillboxes.

Liberating Leyte, Luzon and the South

Liberating Leyte

"

Recapture of the Philippines would be a profoundly important step toward the defeat of Japan, for from those islands the Allies could cut Japanese lines of communication to the rich, conquered territory of the Netherlands East Indies, Indochina, Thailand, Burma, and Malaya. In the Philippines the Allies could establish bases from which to support subsequent advances against Formosa, the China Coast, or Japan itself.

"

— ROBERT ROSS SMITH
The Approach to the Philippines

THOUGH THE HORRIFIC STRUGGLE for Okinawa is generally considered the last battle in the Pacific, the war, in fact, in the Philippines continued right up to the armistice date.

In many respects — in terms of numbers of men engaged, the extent of casualties and the military objectives — liberation of the Philippines qualified as a full-fledged war. Consequently, its latter campaigns — Leyte, Luzon and the Southern Philippines — are covered distinctly.

Sunrise on Oct. 20, 1944, off the central Philippines, signaled the dramatic return of U.S. forces to the islands. An armada of nearly 750 ships — the greatest invasion fleet yet assembled in the Pacific war — covered Leyte Gulf.

Leyte — 115 miles long and 15 to 45 miles wide — covering 2,785 square miles, was blanketed by jungle interspersed with rice paddies. And it was extremely rugged and mountainous, with elevations of up to 4,000 feet. But its eastern landing beaches were the best in the Pacific.

Those beaches became the target of a massive invasion force. U.S. Far East Air Forces (FEAF) counted 2,500 planes. U.S. Seventh Fleet — often called "MacArthur's Navy" — had more than 100 warships, 500 planes, 107 transports and cargo ships, 223 oceangoing landing vessels and 400 other assorted craft.

The U.S. Sixth Army comprised 193,841 troops:
- X Corps — 1st Cavalry and 24th Infantry divisions.
- XXIV Corps — 7th and 96th Infantry divisions.
- In reserve — 32nd and 77th Infantry divisions.

Starting Oct. 12, China-based B-29 Superfortresses and U.S. Third Fleet carriers began reducing Japanese air strength in the Philippines. In only one week of air action, more than 600 enemy planes and 40 ships were destroyed at a cost of 100 U.S. planes.

The first landings, made principally by the 6th Ranger Battalion, occurred Oct. 17, A-Day (Assault) minus three. Seven companies landed on several different islands on the eastern approaches to the gulf; all fell with little opposition. The Rangers destroyed enemy installations and set up navigation lights to guide the invasion fleet into the gulf. Finally relieved on Nov. 14, the Rangers moved to Leyte to patrol for the Sixth Army.

Meanwhile, the Seventh Fleet bombarded the landing beaches with drum-like fire, and carrier planes bombed and strafed airfields and defenses. Navy underwater demolition teams (UDTs) cleared and charted obstacles offshore.

"In the pre-dawn hours of the invasion, lookouts on the destroyer *USS Hale* spotted blinker signals from the beach, asking to evacuate some very important personnel," recalled Mike Renault Rolley, who was aboard that ship. "Me and three other crewmen boarded a whaleboat and headed for the beach.

"A small group of men ran toward the beach, followed by a hail of machine-gun fire. Our coxswain brought the boat in and we managed to haul in our guests and miraculously no one was injured even though our whaleboat was riddled with bullets."

Filipino Col. Keaglioni, head of intelligence and resistance forces, boarded the *USS Hale* and reported exact enemy positions of artillery and airfields.

> **"**
>
> *We found White Beach in shambles. The airfield wasn't much to look at, just smooth sand and no facilities. Planes came in, out of fuel or shot up, some landed, some crashed, some slid along with sand spraying, others cartwheeled.*
>
> *We manned dozers to lay an airstrip and shoved planes into the ocean as fast as we could. The ocean edge of the strip looked like junkyard row.*
>
> *Planes on end, smashed, water washing over them. This lasted into the night, and we lined up jeeps with engines running and headlights on to guide more planes in . . .*
>
> **"**
>
> — WILLIAM S. LEWIS
> Boatswain's Mate 1st Class
> 75th Naval Construction Battalion

Above: Curious Filipino civilians came out of hiding once U.S. ground forces secured the beachhead on Leyte, Oct. 20, 1944. A pre-dawn aerial and naval bombardment pummeled the landing sites at Tacloban and Dulag, leaving some trees and buildings still smoldering in the background. U.S. Coast Guard

Top: GIs on White Beach during D-day, Oct. 20, 1944, on Leyte tug at a jeep that's stuck in the water. U.S. Army

The Japanese 35th Army, 21,500 men, offered only minor resistance on Oct. 20. But on one section of the Leyte coast, a different story unfolded. "This is the thickest mess of lead I have ever had to take a boat ride through," said artillery Maj. Harold Liebe of the 24th Infantry Division. By midnight, the following day, the U.S. had 132,000 men and 200,000 tons of equipment ashore. Several coastal airfields, as well as the port facilities at Tacloban, were in U.S. hands.

Japanese soldiers quickly opted to fight in the mountains and rice paddies. Ormoc, a post on the west coast, became their principal stronghold. Yet by the end of October, the Leyte Valley and all of the airfields in the east-central part of the island were occupied by Americans.

Already bitter fighting, however, was suddenly made more difficult by typhoons, which signaled the start of the rainy season. Violent tropical rainstorms and deep mud soon overtaxed the supply lines. Forward units became dependent upon hand-carried supplies, and medical evacuation of casualties resorted to native bearers.

With the weather as their ally, the Japanese shifted reinforcements from neighboring islands: 45,000 troops reached the embattled 35th Army.

In early November, the 24th Infantry Division, working to overcome a Japanese delaying action, attacked a rugged hill complex soon dubbed "Breakneck Ridge," near the fishing port of Carigara. The enemy was dug into foxholes known as *takotoubo* — "octopus traps."

GIs had run into the Imperial Japanese army's finest division, the crack 1st, recently removed from the Kwantung Army in Manchuria and secretly rushed to the Philippines. The struggle for Breakneck Ridge accounted for the bloodiest combat of the entire Leyte campaign.

Fighting lasted until mid-December when the Japanese committed the unthinkable — *tenchin* — "turn around and advance." The 24th and 32nd Infantry (which had relieved the 24th on Nov. 16) divisions sustained 1,498 casualties, compared to about 5,252 Japanese dead. But GIs advanced only two miles.

Japanese air strength in the Philippines also increased. Planes bombed U.S. airfields, struck at supplies on the beachhead, and launched deadly *kamikaze* suicide attacks in growing numbers on Allied shipping.

Japanese troops blocked entry into the Ormoc Valley, delaying the U.S. advance, and keeping GIs from closing in on Limon until Nov. 30. But the southern part of the island was vacant, and 7th Infantry Division elements pushed across the mountain spine of central Leyte via an unguarded trail that crossed the island's narrow middle.

Squeezed in a tightening vice, the 35th Army engineered a major effort to regain the initiative in late November, supported by a series of heavy air attacks. The Japanese Kaoru Airborne Raiding Detachment tried unsuccessfully to crash-land transport planes onto U.S. airfields.

An airdrop, *Operation Wa,* on Dec. 5, achieved more success when 350 paratroopers seized a U.S. airfield at Buri, destroying supplies and installations before they were wiped out after a few days. Pvt. Ova A. Kelley killed eight Japanese soldiers in a one-man charge, earning the Medal of Honor, posthumously.

A supporting ground offensive was disrupted by swift U.S. reaction. Only two Japanese battalions advanced far enough to get off a counterattack. Like the paratroopers, they caused little damage.

The final U.S. push on Leyte began Dec. 5 with simultaneous drives into the northern Ormoc Valley and the central highlands and southwest.

"The U.S. 11th Airborne Division was attacked by Japanese paratroopers on Dec. 8 — the only time in the Pacific war when paratroopers were attacked by other paratroopers," wrote George MacNeilage, a veteran of "The Angels." "They came in over the coconut trees just before sunset and dropped onto our airstrip, destroying all our liaison planes used to direct artillery fire. It took several days to clear the enemy from the area. Use of 75mm cannons from a mountain top completed the cleanup."

To hasten the fall of Ormoc and with it the island, the 77th Infantry Division landed south of the city. By Dec. 11, despite furious resistance, the 77th captured Ormoc and great quantities of Japanese supplies.

When the battle ended, according to the 77th Division's operations report, Ormoc had become ... "a blazing inferno of bursting white phosphorus shells, burning houses and exploding ammunition dumps, and over it all hung a pall of heavy smoke from burning dumps mixed with the gray dust of destroyed concrete buildings blasted by artillery, mortar and rocket fire."

Then FEAF and carriers finally succeeded in cutting off the stream of Japanese reinforcements. Marine Aircraft Group 12 and Night Fighting Squadron 541 also made "a major contribution," according to the Sixth Army, to this effort. (Some 1,500 Marines of V Amphibious Corps Artillery also fought on Leyte.) Total enemy troop strength had reached 65,000. But by this time, that figure had been reduced to 15,000.

GIs compressed the remainder of organized Japanese resistance on the island into a labyrinth of spiny ridgelines along the narrow corridor of the Ormoc Valley. From there the enemy had no hope of escaping.

Their last stand, in effect, took place at Kilometer 79 on the Ormoc highway. About 500 Japanese troops held out against U.S. attacks from Dec. 19–21 before fleeing into the mountains.

Organized resistance on Leyte *officially* ended Christmas Day. On Dec. 26, 1944, the U.S. Eighth Army began costly mopping-up operations which

As the Weapons Troop of the 12th Cavalry moves from the beach at Leyte, they pass splintered trees and fires caused by the heavy bombardment that preceded the invasion force on Oct. 21, 1944.
MacArthur Memorial Museum

Despite fierce opposition from the Japanese, U.S. ground troops surged into the Ormoc Valley, relying on howitzers and 60mm mortars to pound enemy fortifications. By the end of November 1944, the 32nd Infantry Division had captured Limon.
U.S. Army

On Dec. 25, 1944, we flew to Tacloban, Leyte. We jokingly asked where we could seek shelter in the event of an air raid. The gun crew said we could share their emplacement, if it was necessary.

Shortly after turning in we were startled by the sound of Red Alert [three shots from a 90mm gun]. We heard aircraft approaching from the north. With all haste we were in the gun emplacement!

We had to squat down to remain below sand bag level. Suddenly, there was a long and violent string of explosions. The gun crew screamed for us to keep our heads down. Daisy Cutters! We compacted into the smallest possible objects pressed against the wall of the emplacement.

As the anti-personnel bombs exploded about 20 yards offshore, they generated an ugly sand storm. As the aircraft departed we staggered out spitting, sputtering and wiping copious quantities of sand from our hair, eyes, nose, ears, mouth, pockets and shoes.

— SGT. WILLIAM A. ELLIS
65th Troop Carrier Squadron
433rd Troop Carrier Group
54th Wing, Fifth Air Force

An American 15mm howitzer crew shells enemy fortifications on Leyte Island during the fall of 1944. America returned to the Philippines when the Southern Attack Force (U.S. XXIV Corps) landed at Dulag on Oct. 20, 1944, while the Northern Attack Force (X Corps) pushed ashore at Tacloban the same day. U.S. Army

lasted well into mid-1945. "Mopping up, hell," said Eighth Army commander Gen. Robert Eichelberger. "We have killed 27,000." Indeed, when the war ended in the summer of 1945, thousands of Japanese soldiers still roamed Leyte.

At its zenith, U.S. strength on Leyte numbered 254,000 troops. Units which fought there, in addition to the original assault divisions, included the Americal, 38th Infantry and 11th Airborne divisions, and 164th, 108th and 112th regimental combat teams.

Gen. Douglas MacArthur called the six-month battle for Leyte "perhaps the greatest defeat in the military annals of the Japanese Army." At least 59,400 Japanese soldiers lost their lives on land or in the surrounding waters when their transports were sunk. Another 10,500 enemy airmen and sailors died.

Leyte Island cost the U.S. Army 3,593 soldiers killed and 11,991 WIA in ground combat through May 1945.

A U.S. battle report best summed up the GIs' experience on Leyte: "These bearded, mud-caked soldiers came out of the mountains exhausted and hungry . . . feet heavy, cheeks hollow, bodies emaciated, eyes glazed. They had seen comrades...mortally wounded [and] . . . others lie suffering in muddy foxholes.

"Yet their morale had not changed . . . they were proud that they had outfought the Emperor's toughest troops. . . . And they were proud that they had been able to accomplish all this despite conditions of extreme hardship."

Their victory in this historic campaign cut off Japan from its resources in Southeast Asia and the Netherlands East Indies. "Our defeat at Leyte," said Adm. Mitsumasa Yonai, Japan's navy minister, "was tantamount to the loss of the Philippines. When you took the Philippines, that was the end of our resources."

Leyte Gulf: History's Greatest Naval Battle

As Leyte Island was being invaded, in October 1944, off the Philippine Islands, the U.S. Third and Seventh fleets annihilated the Japanese navy in a series of four clashes unprecedented in scope and decisiveness.

Leyte Gulf was history's largest engagement of naval forces in terms of the number of ships involved. It also was the last major naval battle of WWII and marked the end of Tokyo's navy as an effective fighting force.

Sho ("victory")-1, the code name for the Japanese plan to defend the archipelago, was triggered when U.S. ships were detected approaching the Philippines.

A Northern Force of four decoy carriers hoped to lure the U.S. Third Fleet away from the real Japanese objective. Then a Center Force, including super battleships *Yamato* and *Musashi*, would slip secretly into Leyte Gulf through San Bernardino Strait. At the same time, Southern Force would enter the gulf through Surigao Strait.

On Oct. 17, the Japanese Combined Fleet activated *Sho-1* and within days its warships began converging on the Philippines. It consisted of four carriers with 116 planes — about all that was left of the Japanese naval air arm by this time — nine battleships, 19 cruisers and 33 destroyers. Another 200 supporting land-based aircraft stood ready on airfields in the Philippines.

In contrast, the U.S. Third Fleet alone had 17 carriers with 1,100 aircraft, six battleships, 17 cruisers and 64 destroyers — the most powerful armada ever assembled. U.S. Seventh Fleet, which would land and support the assault forces, had another 157 combat vessels.

Nothing was known of the Japanese movements until submarines *Darter* and *Dace* sighted Center Force in the Sibuyan Sea and sank two enemy cruisers and damaged a third on Oct. 23. "It looks like the Fourth of July out there!" said Cmdr. Bladen D. Claggett, observing the aftermath through *Dace's* periscope. "One is burning. The Japs are milling and firing all over the place. What a show! What a show!"

Next, three waves of 50 to 60 Japanese planes from Luzon swept in on the Third Fleet. A lone dive-bomber hit the light carrier *Princeton*. Damaged beyond repair by fire, it had to be sunk by other U.S. ships. Light cruiser *Birmingham*, which had come alongside *Princeton* to fight fires, was damaged severely when the carrier exploded; *Birmingham* lost 237 killed and 300 wounded.

"The explosion was as surprising as it was terrifying," a survivor recalled.

A dive bomber attack sets fires aboard the *USS Princeton*, causing extensive damage during the Battle of Leyte Gulf in October 1944. U.S. Navy

> 66
>
> *It looks like the Fourth of July out there! What a show! What a show!*
>
> 99
>
> — CMDR. BLADEN D. CLAGGETT
> USS *Dace*

The Battle of Surigao Strait marked the last time in naval history a battle line was employed in action. U.S. Navy

66

The explosion was as surprising as it was terrifying. I think it can be compared to a small volcano.

99

— Survivor *USS Birmingham*

"I think it can be compared to a small volcano...Flying fragments, some huge, some small, burst outwards and upwards, showing the deck of the [carrier]...from stem to stern."

U.S. planes retaliated, damaging three Japanese battleships and putting 19 torpedoes and 17 bombs into *Musashi*, which sank with most of her 2,000-man crew.

Southern Force entered Surigao Strait under cover of darkness. Blacked out and waiting at the strait's mouth were six U.S. battleships, eight cruisers, 28 destroyers and 39 PT boats from the Seventh Fleet. The PT boats attacked, sowing confusion and uncertainty among the Japanese.

"I was the bow gunner on PT 151 when we snuck in between two Japanese destroyers and fired a 'fish' at the light cruiser in the Japanese battle line," remembered Franklin Mellion. "The two destroyers put their blueish-green lights on us and I opened up with my 37mm gun. They were firing five-inch shells at us that sounded like freight trains going by, and star shells to light up the sky, but we got away."

On Oct. 25, U.S. and Australian destroyers attacked with torpedoes. An enemy battleship took the first hit and exploded; a second battleship was hit twice and crippled. In addition, a PT boat knocked out a light cruiser, and all four Japanese destroyers were sunk or dropped out of line with severe damage.

As remnants of the Japanese force continued steaming ahead, U.S. ships guarding the mouth of the strait crossed the "Japanese T." Battleships *Maryland, Pennsylvania, California, West Virginia* and *Tennessee* opened fire with deadly effect.

Gunfire quickly left a Japanese cruiser and battleship adrift and burning. (The battleship later sank when destroyer *Newcombe* hit it with two torpedoes.) A second echelon of two enemy cruisers and four destroyers appeared on the scene and were similarly mauled.

A firsthand observer remembered: "The devastating accuracy of this gunfire was the most beautiful sight I have ever witnessed. The arched line of tracers in the darkness looked like a continual stream of lighted railroad cars going over a hill. No target could be observed at first; then shortly there would be fires and explosions, and another ship would be accounted for."

As dawn arrived, U.S. cruisers and destroyers chased the Japanese survivors back down the strait, sinking a cruiser and two destroyers. Just two Japanese cruisers and three destroyers escaped the ambush. The Battle of Surigao Strait marked the last time in naval history a battle line was employed in action.

The main body of U.S. naval forces had been lured north by the decoy carriers, leaving the San Bernardino Strait unguarded. This enabled Center Force to work its way toward Leyte Gulf, undetected, during the night.

At sunrise Oct. 25, while the Surigao Strait fight still raged, Japanese ships discovered U.S. escort carriers near the entrance to the gulf and opened fire on the unsuspecting group of "baby flattops," code-named *Taffy 3*.

Destroyers screening the carriers engaged the much stronger enemy force. *Johnston* forced a cruiser out of the battle before losing a duel with a battleship and three cruisers; only 141 of the 327 men aboard her survived. *Hoel*, which took 40 hits, and destroyer escort *Samuel B. Roberts* also sank.

Taffy 1 and *Taffy 2*, 130 miles away, launched their planes in support, knocking out an enemy cruiser and sinking two more. The planes and destroyers fought until exhausting their ammunition, and then faked attacks to divert Japanese fire from the escort carriers. *Gambier Bay*, however, sank while *Fanshaw Bay* and *Kalinin Bay* were damaged.

But the Japanese unexpectedly broke off contact and fled. The chief quartermaster, ironically, exclaimed, "My God, Admiral [Sprague], they're getting away."

Later the same day, U.S. ships off Samar became the first to endure crash-dive attacks by the infamous Japanese *kamikaze* suicide planes. Escort carrier *St. Lo* was sunk and four other carriers damaged. "I was aboard the escort carrier *Kitkun Bay* when it was hit by a *kamikaze* off Samar," recalled John Bartley. "The Japanese plane hung on the side and the dud bomb landed in the engine room."

U.S. casualties in the costly Samar engagement were 1,130 sailors and aviators dead and 913 WIA.

Approximately 300 miles away, planes from the Japanese decoy carriers had staged diversionary attacks against Third Fleet carriers on Oct. 24, luring the fleet from Leyte Gulf as planned.

The opposing carrier forces clashed the next day northeast of Luzon's Cape Engano. Some 787 aircraft got off four strikes in rapid sequence. Despite the enemy's evasive tactics and heavily concentrated anti-aircraft fire — perhaps the most violent barrage put up by carriers on either side during the war — all four Japanese carriers and a destroyer were sunk.

Third Fleet later overtook the enemy. Of 17 ships, only one cruiser, two battleships and five destroyers escaped. But the fleet arrived too late to help *Taffy 3*, which was barely spared off Samar.

In the combined battles of the Sibuyan Sea, Surigao Strait, Samar and Cape Engano during Oct. 22–27, 1944, the Americans lost one light carrier, two escort carriers, two destroyers, one destroyer escort, one submarine and 3,000 men.

Yet U.S. accomplishments in this epic sea engagement were decisive. The Navy's overwhelming victory at Leyte Gulf was nothing short of a disaster for Japan. Besides ensuring the seaward flank of the U.S. amphibious forces invading the Philippines, the bulk of the Imperial Combined Fleet was destroyed.

"After this battle," stated Adm. Jisaburo Ozawa, "the surface forces became strictly auxiliary, so that we relied on land forces, special [kamikaze] attack and air power. There was no further use assigned to surface vessels, with the exception of some special ships."

The Japanese lost four carriers, three battleships, 10 cruisers, 11 destroyers, some 300 planes and 10,500 sailors and aviators. With their navy ren-

Operating in the waters off Samar Island on Oct. 25, 1944, the ships of *Taffy 3* — including the escort carriers *Fanshaw Bay*, *St. Lo*, *Kitkun Bay*, *White Plains*, *Kalinin Bay* and *Gambier Bay*, plus three destroyers and four destroyer-escorts — withstood a new and terrifying weapon: the *kamikaze*, meaning "divine wind."

From the flight deck of *Kitkun Bay*, pilots and crewmen watch as two *kamikazes* descend on the *USS Fanshaw Bay* in the distance. Both planes were hit and plunged harmlessly into the water. U.S. Navy

Operation Sho got off to a discouraging start. On Oct. 23, 1944, Vice Adm. Takeo Kurita's force was ambushed by American submarines *Darter* and *Dace*, as shown in John Hamilton's painting. Kurita's flagship, *Atago*, was sunk, along with heavy cruiser *Maya*, in the Battle of Leyte Gulf.
Navy Office of Information

Planes of the Seventh Fleet Air-Sea Rescue Squadron watch over U.S. ships at Lingayen Gulf, which formed a formidable task force to invade Luzon in January 1945. **Signal Corps**

Anti-aircraft gun crewmen from a U.S. Navy cruiser scan the skies for menacing *kamikazes* during the amphibious landing at Mindoro in the Philippines on Dec. 15, 1944. **U.S. Navy**

dered ineffective, hundreds of thousands of Japanese troops on islands scattered throughout the Pacific were left without hope of support.

Historian Samuel Eliot Morison summed it up best: The climactic battle of Leyte Gulf, he wrote, determined that the U.S. "would rule the Pacific until the end of the war, and by so doing hasten the war's end."

Lingayen Gulf: Gateway to Luzon

Despite great successes in the decisive naval Battle of Leyte Gulf and the fierce fighting for Leyte Island, the struggle for Luzon in early 1945 became the U.S. forces' most difficult and closely run contest in the sprawling Philippines campaign.

Luzon — 40,420 square miles in area — is the largest and most important of all the hundreds of islands making up the Philippines. Manila Bay was the best of Luzon's several excellent harbors.

Generally mountainous, Luzon's peaks rise steeply from the sea. Nonetheless, the large central lowlands plain on which Manila sits was valuable to Japan for its abundant resources — fertile farm land, rich mineral wealth and great forests.

Luzon's defense was entrusted to Japan's most famous general, Gen. Tomoyuki Yamashita. In 1942, he had sacked Singapore and then Luzon's Bataan Peninsula, becoming known as the "Tiger of Malaya" to the Japanese and the "Butcher of Bataan" to Americans.

Now Yamashita led the XIV Area Army. Of the 350,000 Japanese troops remaining in the Philippines, 275,000 were on Luzon. About 150,000 were in the rugged northern part of the island, 105,000 in the south and about 20,000 based around Manila.

The U.S. committed two armies totaling more than 280,000 GIs — more troops than had been deployed by the U.S. in North Africa, Sicily, Italy or southern France — making Luzon the largest land campaign of the Pacific war.

In addition, Lt. Gen. George C. Kenney's combined U.S. Far East Air Forces (FEAF) had over 2,000 Army Air Forces, Navy and Marine Corps planes. Vice Adm. Thomas C. Kinkaid's U.S. Seventh Fleet — "MacArthur's Navy" — had over 850 ships, including several Australian and Dutch vessels, and 3,000 landing craft.

To assist the assault forces and protect the ships supplying the Luzon operation, constant air support was needed. Thus the Allies first had to take Mindoro, in the Visayan Islands, and secure sites for airfields there.

En route to Mindoro, the Visayan Attack Force came under nonstop attack by *kamikazes*. On Dec. 13, heavy cruiser *Nashville* was hit off Negros Island and lost 133 KIA and 190 WIA. Several other ships were disabled or sunk.

To cover the landings and suppress the *kamikazes*, air attacks were made all over Luzon by carrier planes of Adm. John McCain's *Task Force 38.* Between Dec. 14-16, the Japanese lost 179 planes and the U.S. 65.

On Dec. 15, the 24th Infantry Division's 19th Regimental Combat Team

(RCT) landed on Mindoro, backed by the 13th and 148th Field Artillery battalions, 179th Coastal Artillery Battalion and 94th Anti-Aircraft Artillery (AAA) Group. The 503rd Parachute Regimental Combat Team put two battalions ashore on Green and Blue beaches. They moved quickly inland and by late afternoon had secured airstrips and the town of San Jose.

Eleven days later, a Japanese naval force of two cruisers and six destroyers bombarded the U.S. beachhead on Mindoro. A U.S. PT boat sank one of the destroyers. This large sortie was the last by the Japanese navy in the Philippines. Together with *kamikaze* attacks against U.S. ships, the naval raid claimed a total of 475 men KIA and 385 WIA. Meantime, the 866th and 1874th Engineer Aviation battalions had completed airfields on the island. The 866th received the Meritorious Unit Citation for its work at San Jose, a strip later attacked by Japanese planes.

The initial U.S. objective on Luzon was Lingayen Gulf — Luzon's point of greatest vulnerability — about halfway up the island's west coast. It had good landing beaches and was within easy striking distance of Manila. The invasion fleet left Leyte on Jan. 2, 1945. By knocking out rail lines, roads, bridges and tunnels on Luzon, FEAF planes and U.S.-Filipino guerillas prevented Yamashita from moving troops to the landing area.

Japanese naval and air forces launched furious attacks on the approaching fleet. Midget submarines, *kamikazes* and small explosive-packed surface craft and suicide motor boats made the seas around Luzon harrowing for the Navy.

On Jan. 6 alone, 11 warships were damaged, a minesweeper sunk, a cruiser crippled and hundreds of sailors killed. All told, the Luzon ordeal cost the U.S. Navy 24 ships sunk — including the escort carrier *Ommaney Bay* — and 67 damaged.

The actual invasion of Luzon, code-named *Operation Mike I*, commenced Jan. 9. Lt. Gen. Walter Krueger's U.S. Sixth Army swarmed across Lingayen Gulf's beaches. The principal units of this large assault-landing force included:

• XIV Corps — 37th and 40th Infantry divisions; 251st Anti-Aircraft Artillery (AAA) Group; and 1129th Engineer Group.

• I Corps — 6th and 43rd Infantry divisions; 197th AAA; and 1136th Engineer Group.

• Other troops — 4th Engineer Special, 68th AAA, 5202nd Engineer brigades; 14th AAA, 931st Engineer, 135th Medical, and 168th and 191st Field Artillery groups.

• Reserve — 25th Infantry Division; 158th Regimental Combat Team; 13th Armored Group; and 6th Ranger Battalion.

"The 25th Division was actually 'in reserve' only two days," recalled

On Dec. 15, 1944, the 19th Regimental Combat Team from the 24th Infantry Division and the 503rd Parachute Infantry Regiment Combat Team landed on Mindoro unopposed. They quickly pushed inland to seize airfield sites. Mindoro, located in the Visayan Islands, had to be taken in preparation for the invasion of Luzon.
U.S. Army

John Bellerose of Cannon Company, 161st Regiment. "It was ambushed, then a week later engaged the Japanese 2nd Armored Division, well entrenched, in the battle of San Manuel."

Eighth Army's X and XI Corps formed an additional reserve, fielding the 24th, 32nd, 33rd and 38th Infantry, 1st Cavalry and 11th Airborne divisions as well as the 112th Regimental Combat Team.

The landings caught almost every major Japanese combat unit in motion, which forced the enemy into a piecemeal commitment of troops. By nightfall, 68,000 GIs controlled a 15-mile beachhead 6,000 yards deep. Within two days, 175,000 troops were ashore. "The 534th Amphibious Engineer Regiment joined the infantry in the initial waves onto the beach," said Joseph Samaritano, an engineer with that unit. "After the beachhead was secured we began off-loading the ships."

MacArthur believed the invasion was "a situation unique in modern war. Never had such large numbers of [enemy] troops been so outmaneuvered." The Sixth Army immediately launched its advance south toward Manila.

As the GIs approached Clark Field, the Japanese were strongly entrenched in hill positions, and I Corps encountered heavy fighting. Once it was captured, the engineers went to work. "The 1913th Engineers rebuilt Clark Field and repaired bridges and roads that were damaged," remembered Bill McConnell, of the 1913th. "This work was being done when the Japs still had a few big guns in the hills around Clark Field firing down on us."

'Crippling Blow' to Third Fleet

As the U.S. Third Fleet prepared for the invasion of Luzon, Philippines, on Dec. 17, an approaching storm hindered refueling efforts. The U.S. ships moved northwest to evade the tropical disturbance, which was only 300 miles to the east, then changed course again to the southwest. But the storm — now reaching typhoon strength and only 150 miles away — seemed to be stalking them.

With winds topping 110 knots and monstrous waves pitching them back and forth, the ships were helpless. Planes and vehicles broke free of lashings, tossed into piles like discarded toys. "Seas looked like rolling mountains," remembered Motor Machinist Mate Denver P. Roush.

Three destroyers were especially vulnerable. With fuel bays nearly empty, their massive guns and ammunition

The *USS New Jersey* absorbs the force of waves created by the notorious typhoon of Dec. 17, 1944, that bashed the Third Fleet as it prepared for the invasion of Luzon. The fleet suffered 790 men lost at sea and 21 ships damaged, nine of which were put out of action. National Archives

made them dangerously top heavy. With every broadside, the *Hull*, *Spence* and *Monaghan* were thrown on their sides.

Seawater rushed in, shorting out electricity and flooding engine rooms. Tragically, all three destroyers sank, trapping most of their crews. Of 250 crewmen aboard the *Monaghan*, only six survived; only 24 of 325 from the *Spence* lived; and 62 of 250 on the *Hull*.

Mother Nature had unleashed her full might on the U.S. Third Fleet, claiming 790 lives, damaging 21 ships (nine put out of action) and destroying 150 planes.

"There were also 36 LCTs caught in the storm," recalled Charles Heffernan. "I was in *LCT 1077* and we were scattered over the South Pacific for about three days."

Fleet Adm. Chester W. Nimitz said the typhoon "represented a more crippling blow to the Third Fleet than it might be expected to suffer in anything less than a major action."

XIV and XI Corps moved next to liberate Manila and southern Luzon, cutting the Japanese forces on the island in half. Simultaneously, I Corps focused on taking the mountain strongholds in the north.

Manila: 'Charnel House of the Dead'

Almost four weeks after landing on Luzon in January 1945, Lt. Gen. Walter Krueger's U.S. Sixth Army found itself locked in desperate battle on the wrecked and rubbled streets of Manila, once the beautiful capital city of the Philippines.

Gen. Tomoyuki Yamashita, one of Japan's best-known generals and greatest military leaders, had been placed in command of the XIV Area Army's 275,000 troops on Luzon in autumn 1944.

Yamashita entrusted Rear Adm. Sanji Iwabuchi with the defense of the Philippine capital. Iwabuchi commanded Japan's 16,000 naval troops based in the Manila area and he was personally determined to fight to the finish.

With 1.1 million residents occupying 250 square miles, metropolitan Manila was one of the largest cities in Southeast Asia. Many of its buildings were made to survive earthquakes. Consequently, the Japanese were presented with numerous defensible positions.

Fortifications were erected in late 1944. By January, the defenders were braced for attack. Most of all, the Japanese wanted to keep control of Manila Bay, so they greatly fortified the port area and Corregidor, an island 25 miles southwest of Manila guarding the bay's mouth.

Iwabuchi had the equivalent of some two divisions totalling about 20,500 men. They were arrayed in battalions of army, naval and Imperial marine infantry and assorted support troops.

They were armed with ample stocks of field, anti-tank and dual-purpose anti-aircraft artillery, automatic weapons, mortars and naval guns dismounted from stranded ships. It was a formidable enemy force, and wresting Manila from it proved a long and bloody ordeal.

Gen. MacArthur knew the battle to liberate Manila would be rough, and he prepared accordingly. The main body of U.S. forces employed, two-thirds of XIV Corps, totaled about 35,000 troops.

The battle started Jan. 28–29. U.S. XI Corps — the 38th Infantry Division, 34th Regimental Combat Team and supporting units totalling 40,000 men — landed north of the Bataan Peninsula, the defenders of which the U.S. forces hoped to seal off from the fight for Manila.

"Troops from L Company, 34th Infantry, loaded up some native canoes and with Browning automatic rifles in the bow of each canoe filled with riflemen, paddled across the bay to reconnoiter around a water tower on the other side," recalled Nicholas Marasco. "There were no enemy soldiers, but that action put us as the first troops back to Bataan."

GIs captured Olongapo and pushed inland to the Zambales foothills.

Three GIs search the streets and buildings of Fort Stotsenburg on the southwestern edge of Clark Field, Luzon, during the recapture of the airfield in late January 1945.
Smithsonian Institution

A soldier on Luzon watches through binoculars as Manila burns on the horizon during February 1945. U.S. Army

Men of Co. F, 145th Infantry Regiment, 37th Infantry Division, move past the rubble of what once was the majestic Manila Post Office that crumbled in the shelling by heavy guns and tanks.
Smithsonian Institution

On Feb. 23, 1945, the 129th Infantry Regiment, 37th Infantry Division, crossed the Pasig River in assault boats and stormed the Mint Building as part of the assault on Intramuros — the Walled City. U.S. Army

Their drive stalled, however, when they ran into a complex of heavy fortifications concealed along a narrow jungle road dubbed "Zig Zag Pass." It took two weeks of combat to clear the pass. But XI Corps finally established a line reaching from Subic Bay to Manila Bay and sealed off Bataan Peninsula. The Japanese paid dearly; the Americans suffered 1,400 casualties, including 250 KIA.

On Jan. 30, the 1st Cavalry and 37th Infantry divisions poured through holes in the enemy lines north of the city. Leaving behind supporting units to follow later and mop up, their tank and truck "flying columns" — watched over by dive bombers of Marine Air Group 24 and 32 — covered up to 30 miles per hour as they raced toward Manila. The 112th Cavalry Regiment kept the supply lines open to Manila, operating in the Santa Inez Valley. "Marine Lt. Gordon Lewis and Cpl. Samuel Melish flying in an SBD-5 Douglas Dauntless had been shot down on Jan. 28, the first Marines casualties on Luzon," pointed out W. M. Phillips of FM B-244 — the *Bombing Banshees*.

Next day, 11th Airborne Division elements landed from the sea in the Nasugbu Bay area 50 miles southwest of Manila. Assault units included the 187th and 188th Glider Infantry regiments, and 674th and 675th Airborne Field Artillery and 152nd Anti-Aircraft Artillery battalions.

These forces were soon joined by the airborne's 511th Parachute Infantry Regiment and 457th Airborne Field Artillery Battalion, which dropped on Tagaytay Ridge. As they rushed northwest to enter Manila through the back door, the 11th Airborne was cheered by Filipinos waving the Stars and Stripes.

Paratroopers were stopped Feb. 4 when they ran into the main line of Japanese fortifications making up the southern side of the Manila defense zone. By then, however, the U.S. formations descending upon the Japanese from the north had already won the race to Manila.

The 8th Cavalry and 44th Tank Battalion had rumbled into Manila on Feb. 3. Taking the Japanese by surprise, the GIs had little trouble liberating 4,000 Allied civilian prisoners of war from Santo Tomas University, where they had been interned. Next day, the 37th Division released 530 civilians and 810 POWs from Old Bilibid Prison.

As U.S. forces began to invest Manila on Feb. 4, the defending Japanese withdrew across the Pasig River, which runs through the city. In their wake, they demolished bridges and torched government buildings, military facilities and supplies.

An inferno ensued as fires engulfed large parts of Manila's highly flammable residential areas. The conflagration was so threatening that U.S. troops, when they were not under enemy sniper and artillery attack, spent much of the following two days fighting the blazes.

Elsewhere the going was also difficult. Though the paratroopers moving up from the south overcame parts of the city's outer defensive perimeter, they could not break through. Nor could XIV Corps in the north get through to link-up with them.

Moreover, Bataan's 4,000 defenders kept XI Corps from sealing off the peninsula until Feb. 7. Eight days later the 151st Infantry Regiment and 139th Field Artillery landed at Mariveles, on the peninsula's southwest tip. By month's end, Bataan was entirely in U.S. hands. Some 3,510 Japanese had been KIA and 340 taken prisoner. Another 150 gave themselves up seven months later, when Japan surrendered. U.S. losses on Bataan were 315 KIA and 1,285 WIA.

When the 1st Cavalry and 37th divisions finally pushed deeper into Manila and then south across the Pasig River, combat erupted in the heart of the city. Then street-fighting raged for almost a month. The Japanese were desperately determined to postpone the impending catastrophe — even if only for a few days — by using all their resources. Their strongpoints were mutually supporting and made maximum use of all kinds of obstructions.

Not only collapsed buildings, but entire neighborhoods destroyed by bombing and shelling were used. All approaches to the city's interior were barricaded, with reinforced positions built to give full fields of fire.

Fighting "was block-by-block, building-by-building," wrote Ronald Spector, author of *Eagle Against the Sun*. "Small assault squads worked their way from roof to roof, then chopped their way into the top floor and fought their way down, making liberal use of grenades, flamethrowers and demolitions."

Indifferent to the effect of the battle on the residents, the Japanese ravaged the city. About 100,000 Filipino civilians died in the carnage. Of all Allied cities during the war, only Warsaw, Poland, suffered more devastation than Manila.

In Manila, the Japanese made their last stand in Intramuros, a 150-acre section of the city built by the colonial Spanish in the 16th century. It was enclosed by ancient stone walls 40 feet thick and 16 feet high.

On Feb. 23, after six days of massive artillery bombardment, the 37th Division attacked. The 3rd Bn., 129th Inf., crossed the Pasig River in assault boats and infiltrated Intramuros from the north. In the east, the 145th Infantry rushed through a breach and gate in the wall.

(That same day, the 1st Bn., 511th Parachute Inf. Regt., and other elements of the 11th Airborne Division, jumped 25 miles behind enemy lines to rescue 2,122 POWs at Los Banos.)

Japanese defenders made extensive use of underground hideouts, such as sewers, tunnels, basements and dungeons of old Spanish buildings, in particular, that were considerably improved and extended, as fortified positions during the period of preparation.

During house-to-house combat in Manila, soldiers from the 37th Infantry and 1st Cavalry divisions routed out the enemy. The maze of tunnels and archways of the Intramuros district — Manila's Walled City — was extremely hazardous, but by March 3, 1945, had been cleared of Japanese troops.
National Archives

66

Dead and more dead lay sprawled and scattered on both sides of the thoroughfares, and the atmosphere was filled with such nauseating odor as to cause people to vomit what little they had in their stomachs.

99

— Eyewitness to the
Rape of Manila

'Brilliant Operation': Corregidor Conquered

In addition to a last-ditch defense of Manila, Adm. Iwabuchi had deployed 6,000 Japanese troops to Corregidor. They would fight to the death to hold the 2.75 square-mile island, which controlled access to Manila Bay and was called "The Rock."

On Feb. 16, troops of the 503rd Parachute Infantry Regiment and 462nd Airborne Field Artillery Battalion parachuted on to Corregidor, suffering numerous jump casualties. Many missed their landing zones, but enough arrived as planned to seize positions from which they could cover the follow-up amphibious landing.

The land assault was made by the 24th Division's 3rd Battalion, 34th Infantry, which seized a 200-yard-deep beachhead. For nearly a week thereafter, however, the infantrymen engaged in fierce fighting.

Japanese held out in prewar American-made tunnels carved into a rocky mass called Malinta Hill. U.S. engineers sealed off exits daily, but the Japanese dug their way out every night and counter-attacked the American lines.

Yet each of these suicidal attacks were futile. "It was like a massacre in a lunatic asylum," wrote one veteran. Still, it

On Feb. 16, 1945, the 503rd Parachute Infantry Regiment readies for a jump onto Corregidor at 500 feet from a C-47. They had two small drop zones on the cliff plateaus. Many missed and crashed into buildings and trees, or floated out to sea. Others set up machine gun and 75mm howitzer positions to cover the seaborne landing. U.S. Army

A flag-raising ceremony attended by Gen. Douglas MacArthur marks the occupation and control of Corregidor after the fighting ended there March 2, 1945. U.S. Army

was not all one-sided. Company K, 34th Infantry, started with 161 men and ended with 33 fit for duty.

On several occasions, the Japanese blew up underground ammunition stockpiles beneath the Americans on Malinta Hill. In one blast, fire shot out of tunnel mouths and scores of GIs and as many as 1,400 Japanese died.

Another blast, even greater than the first on Malinta, showered ships offshore with debris. "I have never seen such a

sight in my life," said a U.S. officer. "Utter carnage, bodies laying everywhere, everywhere."

Organized fighting ended March 2, with the U.S. flag being raised over shell-and bomb-scarred Corregidor. Japanese losses were 5,635 KIA and 35 captured. U.S. Army casualties were 240 KIA and 675 WIA, plus 285 Navy losses — a total of 1,200 or 25 percent of the 4,560-man assault force.

It was a severe price for the rocky real estate, but with one consolation. MacArthur called the capture of Corregidor "one of the most brilliant operations in military history."

66

All in all, our aim is extermination.

99

— Japanese soldier in Manila

Using grenades and bazookas, the 145th Infantry knocked out the last large pocket of resistance on Feb. 24 and split the Japanese, who had not evacuated the city, into small groups. The last of these groups held out in the Finance Building until March 3 — one month after the battle for Manila had begun.

Japanese behavior was atrocious: Of 100,000 Filipino civilian deaths, at least half were killed in atrocities. Wrote a Japanese soldier in his diary, "All in all, our aim is extermination." When the 1st Cavalry Division entered the city it found mounds of Filipino dead and bodies stacked in dungeons. It was, as one observer put it, a "charnel house of the dead."

As an eyewitness recounted, "Dead and more dead lay sprawled and scattered on both sides of the thoroughfares, and the atmosphere was filled with such nauseating odor as to cause people to vomit what little they had in their stomachs." GIs donned gas masks to mitigate the obnoxious smell of decaying flesh.

U.S. units sustained 1,010 KIA and 5,565 WIA in taking Manila. Some 12,500 Japanese died; only 915 surrendered. Urban warfare in its most brutal form had come to the Pacific for GIs to witness firsthand.

From Manila, mobile elements cleared the area south of Laguna de Bay and advanced rapidly toward the Bicol Peninsula. On April 1, the 158th Infantry and 147th Field Artillery Battalion landed at Legaspi on the Albay Gulf and cleared southeastern Luzon.

GIs destroyed strong enemy forces totalling 41,000 troops — killing 21,000, taking 1,550 prisoners and capturing over 1,800 guns, mortars and machine guns — during the southern Luzon campaign. They also displayed exceptional courage — seven GIs were awarded the Medal of Honor.

This dramatic triumph clearly illustrated how wrong Japan's leaders were in judging their ability to delay defeat. But such important victories are rarely, if ever, cheaply won. The fighting to clear southern Luzon cost the U.S. approximately 2,325 dead and 9,935 WIA.

Northern Luzon would be a tough nut to crack, too. But first to the southern Philippines, a bewildering array of islands ideal for concealment and defense.

Sweeping the Southern Philippines

Web-footed warriors of five U.S. Army divisions seized the southern Philippines in an amphibious blitzkrieg termed "a strategic masterwork." Code-named *Operation Victor*, the campaign involved 1,000 Army and Marine planes, a large part of the Seventh Fleet and the Americal, 31st, 24th, 40th and 41st Infantry divisions. All told, more than 85,000 ground troops were deployed against 110,000 Japanese.

Landing craft played a vital role in moving soldiers from one island to another. "We were always in the first three waves and stayed with the troops until a strong beachhead was established," recalled Elmer Hallen, a veteran of the 658th Amphibious Tractor Battalion.

Because of the amphibious nature of the warfare in the region, another unique unit was employed: the 295th Joint Assault Signal Company (JASCO) — a combined Army artillery, signal corps, infantry and Navy outfit. JASCOs performed essential combat support services.

Victor III, on Palawan Island, launched the operation. It was the site of a POW camp where the Japanese had recently carried out a mass execution of 140 U.S. POWs. Bombers and naval gunfire softened up the beaches for the 41st Division's 186th RCT landing Feb. 28, 1945, at Puerto Princesa, which was captured with its two airfields. Occupation of the island was completed March 8 after sharp fighting. Four days before, 1st Bn., 21st Inf. Regt., began the four-day fight for Lubang Island. Loss of Palawan and Lubang isolated significant parts of the Japanese 35th Army.

Starting March 9, U.S. warships and Thirteenth Air Force bombers pounded the coast of Zamboanga Peninsula, on the tip of Mindanao's southwest corner, preparing it and the Sulu Archipelago for *Operation Victor IV*. Invading units included the 162nd and 163rd Infantry, 41st Division; 146th,

> *JASCOs contained 500 or 600 Army, AAF and Navy communications specialists trained in joint procedures. They provided the essential links between the land, sea and air elements in operations against the enemy.*
>
> *On Mindanao, between April 17 and July 1, 1945, the Shore Fire Control Section of the 295th Joint Assault Signal Company was converted into field artillery forward observer parties. Air liaison parties landed with assault infantry units and directed air bombardments. They remained continuously with front-line infantry battalions. Finally, the Communications Section assisted forward combat elements, helping to earn the 295th a unit citation for its actions in the campaign.*
>
> — GEORGE L. KEDENBURG
> 295th JASCO veteran

Infantry and armored troops from the U.S. Americal Division move through crowded streets of Cebu City in the southern Philippines March 26–27, 1945. Fighting raged for nearly three months before the island was fully secured. U.S. Army

205th and 218th Field Artillery battalions; and the 166th and 202nd Anti-Aircraft Artillery battalions.

By the following evening, U.S. forces had advanced inland toward the Mindanao mountains and were closing in on Zamboanga City, which was secured March 11. First serious enemy opposition developed northeast of San Roque in a bitter contest for a fortified village. After several days, the Japanese survivors fled into the interior.

Assault parties also hit nearby Romblon and Simara islands, unopposed. Japanese resolve stiffened on Zamboanga, however, and fighting soon became fierce, especially in the Masilay and Pasananca areas.

Combat — some of the worst of the entire southern Philippines campaign — see-sawed back and forth on the peninsula until organized Japanese resistance crumbled March 29. The Army received able assistance from Marine pilots who could allegedly "drive tacks with their bombs."

Zamboanga cost the 41st Division 220 KIA and 665 WIA.

Beginning March 18, in *Victor I* and *II*, the Eighth Army assaulted the Visayan Islands: Bohol (164th Regimental Combat Team), Panay (213th Field Artillery Battalion), Negros (185th Regimental Combat Team; 213th Field Artillery Battalion) and Caballo (151st Regimental Combat Team).

Within a week, Cebu was invaded by the 132nd and 182nd Infantry, Americal Division; 221st, 246th and 247th Field Artillery battalions; and 478th Anti-Aircraft Artillery Battalion. From the Talisay area, GIs advanced to the Mananga River line before the end of D-day. Next day, they broke through Japanese defenses and took Cebu City.

But the Japanese dug in for a prolonged fight on the surrounding hills. Hard, close-in fighting developed March 29. GIs suffered heavy losses when enemy engineers mined and tunneled into a spur of a contested mountain beneath them and blew it up. By the time Cebu was declared secure June 21, 420 GIs had been killed and 1,730 WIA.

GIs were now poised for the biggest and bloodiest battle in the south. But they were well-established on the Zamboanga Peninsula, and guerrillas possessed most of northern Mindanao. To speed up the island's capture, an amphibious end run to Mindanao's west coast was made in an effort to dislodge the main line of Japanese resistance.

The 19th and 21st Infantry, 24th Division; 11th, 13th and 52nd Field Artillery battalions; and 116th Anti-Aircraft Artillery Group seized a beachhead in central Mindanao, north of Cotabatu, April 17. After discovering that U.S.-led guerrillas had already captured Malabang, the principal target, GIs landed at Parang and quickly seized the high ground overlooking Polloc Harbor. The 24th Division extended its beachhead up to 20 miles from Cotabato.

Farther southwest in the Sulu Archipelago, recon elements of the 163rd Regimental Combat Team seized Sanga Sanga and Jolo islands.

While landings usually encountered minimal resistance, stubborn and prolonged fighting almost always followed in the foothills. Negros Island (in the Visayan's), for example, cost 1,610 U.S. casualties. The 503rd Parachute RCT, which arrived by small craft on Negros April 6 and stayed until early November 1945, sustained many of these casualties.

When the 31st and 24th divisions landed on Mindanao, Eighth Army's U.S. X Corps was at full strength.

The 24th Division headed for Davao Bay, cutting the main body of Japanese forces on Mindanao in two. Theirs was the longest sustained overland march by any U.S. unit in the entire Pacific war. Soldiers traversed 100 miles of wilderness that harbored swarms of locusts and fearsome *Moros* (native Moslems).

Excursions on the Mindanao River also made military history. X Corp's *V-5 Operation* sent six Navy gunboats with 100 GIs aboard, behind enemy lines, to capture Ft. Pikit. The Boat Battalion of the 533rd Engineer Boat and Shore Regiment, Third Engineer Special Brigade, carried men of the 24th Division 83 miles on the river in four days.

Retreating Japanese resorted to deadly booby-traps. While attempting to disarm a rigged bomb, one mine-disposal crew was obliterated. "Nothing was left of the squad except a blackish smear on the tree trunks," recalled Pvt. Joseph Turner.

Driving east, 24th Division elements took desolate Davao City on May 4, and then pursued Japanese remnants into the surrounding hills. A column of the 31st Division drove north up the Pulangi River Valley along the Sayre Highway.

On May 10, the 108th RCT and 164th Field Artillery Battalion landed along the coast of northern Mindanao's Macajalar Bay. It took the 108th Regimental Combat Team two weeks to advance 40 miles to Impalutao and link up with the 155th Inf., 31st Inf. Div., on May 24.

"The 108th RCT had already been in 51 straight days of combat on Luzon when we were given the mission to land on Mindanao," wrote Dick Ruppert, a veteran of Able Company, 108th. "In a series of difficult engagements, we routed the enemy through rugged terrain. We lost 41 killed and 148 wounded, as well as hundreds who fell to disease and fatigue."

Fighting for control of the island continued until July 25 when organized resistance in the Saranganai Bay area ended. Mindanao was secured at the cost of 820 Americans KIA and 2,880 WIA. Mopping-up lasted through Aug. 11, only a few days before the cease-fire.

Rooting the Japanese diehards out of the primeval rain forests and abandoned abaca fields where visibility was rarely more than 10 feet was lethal work. Eliminating pillboxes under these circumstances tested the mettle of even the bravest. One example was Pfc. James H. Diamond of Co. D, 21st Inf. Regt., 24th Inf. Div., who saved the lives of numerous patrol members by sacrificing his own, earning the Medal of Honor.

Web-footed GIs of the Eighth Army had conducted 14 major and 24 minor amphibious landings in just 44 days in the southern Philippines.

An M-8 armored car navigates a river bank on Mindanao in April 1945.
U.S. Army

Prior to an attack on enemy locations in April 1945 on Mindanao, an 81mm mortar crew unloads and inspects each round. U.S. Army

A 60mm mortar crew fires on Japanese positions during an action on Mindanao, where combat lasted into August 1945. U.S. Army

Medics treat one of the many casualties at the front line near Damortis on Luzon in January 1945. The Japanese were firmly entrenched in the mountains, with pillboxes and dugouts along the Rosario-Pozorrubio-Binalonan line which, along with the rough terrain, rendered much of the U.S. artillery and armor attacks ineffective. Dept. of Defense

Supported by U.S. and Filipino guerrillas, the U.S. forces seized all the airfields, principal towns and roads necessary for reestablishing civil government.

Historian William Manchester, in his book *American Caesar*, called the Army's campaign — one of history's and the entire war's most complex and audacious — "a strategic masterwork, magnificently executed, with a minimal loss of life." U.S. troops suffered 2,070 dead and 6,990 WIA in all the *Victor* operations.

Extraordinary triumphs of combined arms dealt a crushing blow to enemy morale. The Japanese had an entire field army practically annihilated. Another 53,000 troops who were isolated and effectively removed from the war surrendered after Aug. 15.

The southern Philippines campaign remains a classic example of how a numerically inferior field force, backed by sea and air power, used speed and mobility to outmaneuver a stronger but immobilized enemy. Operation *Victor* marked the capstone of the U.S. victory in the Philippines.

Northern Luzon: Last Leg to Victory

As GIs cleared the southern portion of the archipelago, the northern half of Luzon preoccupied another American force. Fighting was fierce and casualties high right up until the armistice. And the Japanese defenders had plenty of fight left in them even when the war ended. Fighting spirit combined with difficult terrain presented an awesome task to Army units.

Mountain strongholds in the north harbored two Japanese armies: *Shobu* Group (152,000 men) and *Shimbu* Group (60,000 men). They were commanded by Gen. Tomoyuki Yamashita, soon tagged the "Gopher of Luzon" by troops in the field. In earlier days he was known as the "Tiger of Malaya."

Two dams — Wawa on the Marikina River and Ipo on the Angat River — that controlled the water supply to Manila were the primary American targets as 1945 dawned. To reach them, GIs had to cross open rice fields and then penetrate the Sierra Madre Mountains that provided sanctuary to the *Shimbu* Group.

"The mountains looked ominous," according to a campaign history. "You knew the Japanese were in them, but you couldn't see them; you knew on the other hand that they'd be able to see you all too well as you started across the valley. The prospects were thoroughly unpleasant."

Natural caves connected to horizontal tunnels honeycombed the hillsides. Enemy 75mm and 105mm artillery pieces were concealed along with naval guns and rockets in the deadly openings on the slopes.

The 1st Cav's 2nd Brigade attacked toward the Wawa Dam in late February 1945. Closing off the cave complexes proved a formidable ordeal. Before the hills around the dam were finally cleared on May 27, the 6th and 38th Infantry divisions joined the action. (During the fighting, helicopters were used for the first time to evacuate wounded.)

Meanwhile, Ipo Dam was deemed the more important objective. "The entire region bore an oppressive, weird aspect," said the official history.

"Wildly tossed rock outcroppings were pervading the features. Some stretching horizontally across the land, some pyramiding dizzily to sudden, jumbled heights, these sharp grayish outcroppings and sharp pinnacles looked like the product of a fantastic nightmare."

Nightmare aptly described what the men of the 43rd Division, along with the Filipino Marking Regiment, went through in taking the dam between May 6–17. Japanese lines overlooking Highway 52 were finally obliterated by artillery and the Fifth Air Force using napalm.

Farther north, beginning in late February, I Corps launched a three-pronged attack against the *Shobu* Group with 70,000 men of the 25th, 32nd and 33rd Infantry divisions.

Heading for Baguio, headquarters of the *Shobu*, they had to pass through the Cagayan Valley, 40 miles wide and 150 miles long. Towered over by the Central Cordillera and Caraballo ranges, its passes were well-defended.

The 33rd Division went up Highway 11. But climbing the mountains completely drained the men. I Co., 130th Inf. Regt., for instance, went 24 hours without water. When finally relieved, the outfit was "a pitiful sight."

On April 16, one 33rd Division regiment endured a ferocious assault. "For sheer desperation," the battle report said, "this counterattack was unmatched in the fighting. Machine gunners and automatic riflemen cut down the swarms of frenzied enemy as they heedlessly rushed into final protective lines. The shrill battle cries of the Nips and the moans of their wounded could be heard above the roar of battle."

At the same time, April 17–20, along Highway 9, the 37th Division engaged the Japanese in four days of carnage at Irisan Gorge. This prompted a Japanese withdrawal from Baguio. Before the delayed U.S. entry into the town six days later, 10,000 enemy troops escaped.

By March 1945, the Japanese were retreating and U.S. forces on northern Luzon, including this 105mm howitzer motor carriage M-7, advanced up the roads to Bauang and Baguio. Going was slow given the terrain and stubborn enemy defenses. U.S. Army

Left: An 8-inch howitzer in action in the Ipo Dam area on northern Luzon in May 1945. The dam was taken by the 103rd Infantry Regiment, 43rd Division, on the 17th. U.S. Army

U.S. troops took two other routes into the Cagayan Valley. On the Villa Verde Trail, the 32nd Division hit a stone wall at the Salacsac passes near Santa Fe. It took nearly three months, between March 5 and May 28, to break through five miles of the heavily forested passes.

"This was," as the official report stated, "combined mountain and tropical warfare at its worst." Combat fatigue claimed an increasing toll among the troops, over and above the 825 men KIA and 2,100 WIA sustained by the 32nd Division in traversing the treacherous trail.

Route 5 was equally brutal. The 25th Division required two months to go the five miles to Balete Pass, the main gateway to the Cagayan Valley. Col. Harold Riegelman wondered how "life could survive the rain of steel and fire" after observing I Corps mortars in action in the area.

Between March 10 and May 13, "Tropic Lightning" troopers captured places like Myoko Ridge and Lone Tree Hill. But it still took two more weeks to reach Santa Fe, where the 25th Division made contact with the 32nd. Combined, the two divisions lost 1,510 KIA and 4,250 WIA in opening the gateway to the Cagayan Valley.

Within two weeks, the 37th Division reached the valley's flatlands, linking up with the Filipino 11th Infantry. Next target: the Japanese base at Aparri on Luzon's northern coast. The 511th PIR, 11th Airborne Division, dropped near the town June 23, only to find the enemy garrison already wiped out by a Ranger task force and Filipino guerrillas.

Though this marked the strategic end of the campaign, MacArthur's formal announcement ending the fighting was premature.

Remnants of the *Shobu* Group — 65,000 strong — retreated into the Central Cordillera. Some 80 percent formed a pocket in the Asin Valley, the so-called "last-stand area." Rooting them out would take three U.S. divisions — 6th, 32nd and 37th — and Filipino guerrillas six weeks.

"Instead of mopping up," wrote Robert R. Smith in *Triumph in the Philippines,* "the division [6th] soon found itself involved in mountain fighting as rough as that experienced at any time or at any place throughout the Luzon Campaign."

The main effort concentrated along Route 4 toward Kiangan. It was taken in mid-July, and by July 29 the Japanese were completely encircled. That day, Cpl. Melvin Mayfield of Co. D, 20th Inf., 6th Div., earned WWII's

Above: Enemy artillery positions in Balete Pass on Luzon proved very troublesome until C Battery, 90th Field Artillery, neutralized them during the night of April 19, 1945.
National Archives

Top: GIs fire a .30-caliber machine gun at the enemy on northern Luzon in early 1945. U.S. Army

A Japanese POW taken near Baguio during the northern Luzon campaign in April 1945. Maj. Gaetano Faillace, U.S. Army Reserve

Left: Paratroopers of the 511th PIR, 11th Airborne Division, drop near Aparri, Luzon, on June 23, 1945. Smithsonian Institution

last Medal of Honor. During a gallant, one-man assault, he single-handedly cleared enemy caves, inspiring Filipinos to fight on.

Fighting continued to the very end. Pfc. Edward Mullins of A Co., 1st Bn., 128th Inf. Regt., 32nd Div., was killed in action near Bagabag on Aug. 15 just 45 minutes before the war ended. Battery C, 1st Field Artillery Bn., 6th Div., fired the last shot of WWII on land in the Mt. Puloy Antipolo area, according to A.R. Larason, who was then battalion commander.

During those last six weeks, U.S. units sustained 155 KIA and 495 WIA. *Shobu* lost 13,500 men killed, starved or died of disease. Yet they were ready to fight for at least another month, according to plans.

A major breakout was scheduled, complete with *banzai* attacks on all fronts to cover the effectives' escape. "Thus, the war ended with about one-third of the *Shobu* Group's peak strength still alive and still capable of conducting organized, stubborn delaying actions," wrote Smith.

Not until Sept. 5, 1945, three weeks after the armistice, did the last major Japanese unit on Luzon officially surrender to the 37th Division at Tuguegarao. Still later, Japanese diehards filtered out of the mountains.

Finally, the Philippines were free from Japanese militarism. Liberating the islands was a massive and costly undertaking. From the time of the October 1944 Leyte landing, 16,233 American soldiers died in action. When those who were killed in 1942 are added to the tally (13,847), the price tag jumps to 30,080 Americans killed in action — 54.5 percent of all Army combat deaths in the Pacific.

The prospect of even more massive casualties was foremost on the minds of U.S. strategists when they launched the bombing campaign against Japan — the concluding chapter in the Pacific war.

Men from Co. C, 1st Bn., 123rd Infantry, 33rd Division, use a make-shift ladder to descend a steep cliff at Cervantes, Luzon, on June 15, 1945. U.S. Army

★ ★ ★

STRATEGIC AIR OFFENSIVE AGAINST JAPAN

...nd I was there

"... and I was there!" by Phil Oliver. America's famed U.S. Twentieth Air Force carried out the B-29 bomber offensive against mainland Japan in 1945. These images depict the airmen who made that victory possible.

Phil Oliver

Reaping the Whirlwind

**Torching Tokyo:
Firebombing of Japan**

66

*No part of the Japanese
Empire is now out of range.
Japan has sowed the wind;
now let it reap the whirlwind.*

99

— GEN. HAP ARNOLD
Army Air Forces Chief of Staff

ON NOV. 1, 1944, *Tokyo Rose* — a B-29 reconnaissance plane flown by Capt. Ralph Steakley — flew over Tokyo at 32,000 feet and shot more than 7,000 photos. The plane's primary mission was to locate and photograph the vital Nakajima engine works factory just north of the city.

Tokyo's anti-aircraft guns opened up but could not reach the intruder, nor could Japanese fighter pilots wary of being blasted out of the sky by the heavily armed Superfortress.

Months before, the new B-29 long-range bomber was deployed to Calcutta, India. Once the Marianas were secured and bases were established on Guam, Saipan and Tinian, the Superfortresses of the new XXI Bomber Command, Twentieth Air Force, were ready to use the photos taken by the *Tokyo Rose.*

At dawn, on Nov. 24, 110 Superfortresses roared toward Tokyo, led by the *Dauntless Dotty* of the 73rd Wing. But cloud cover made it difficult for bombardiers to locate their targets. Though 1,000 bombs were dropped, only 48 hit anywhere close to the target area.

Despite the dismal results, Gen. Hap Arnold, Army Air Forces chief of staff, was confident: "No part of the Japanese Empire is now out of range. Japan has sowed the wind; now let it reap the whirlwind."

Though the B-29s had dropped 1,550 tons of bombs in November and December of 1944, the assessment was bleak: only one bomb in 50 hit within 1,000 feet of the aiming point, causing only minor damage. Worse yet, 188 airmen had been killed or lost at sea when forced to ditch.

While the high-altitude capability of B-29s afforded safety from anti-

aircraft guns and defending aircraft, far too many missions were compromised by either cloud cover obscuring the targets, or bombs drifting off course because of the newly encountered jet stream.

The Japanese were concerned about this new threat, however, and sent their own bombers from Iwo Jima to hit the B-29 bases. On Nov. 27, four Superforts were destroyed on the ground and 13 were damaged, while 10 of the enemy fighters were shot down. Through early January 1945, losses from enemy attacks totalled 11 B-29s destroyed and 43 damaged on the ground alone.

Iwo Jima and the enemy planes based on that five-mile long volcanic island were a constant problem for U.S. bomber crews. An enemy radar site there also alerted the home islands of approaching bombers.

During the first months of 1945, brutal combat took place on Iwo Jima. One pilot, Chester Marshall of the 878th Bomb Squadron, remembered, "Our flight to Tokyo carried us close to Iwo Jima and the fighting taking place down below telegraphed a message to us that the struggle for the island was not yet over, and people were still dying down there."

But once Iwo Jima was secured, the Superfortresses could fly straight to Japan unmolested.

Disappointed with the results of the high altitude-missions relying on massed formations of bombers, Maj. Gen. Curtis E. LeMay, commander of XXI Bomber Command, ordered the firebombing of Japanese cities. LeMay's strategy often called for gunners on the sides to act as "scanners" (lookouts) for possible mid-air collisions and taxi operations. So their presence was essential even if they didn't have ammunition. And instead of flying in formation, LeMay wanted his bombers to approach their targets in single file and at low altitude.

Naturally, many pilots weren't too keen on flying in enemy airspace

66

Although we had been trained at 25,000 feet altitude, we were astonished to learn that our missions would be flown at 16,000 feet on daylight missions, and at 9,000 feet for incendiary night missions!

99

— MASTER SGT. MERLE E. BOUGES
B-29 crew member
73rd Wing, Saipan

An echelon of the 869th Squadron, 497th Bombardment Group, heads for an industrial target during the fire-bombing missions over Japan in the spring and summer of 1945.
U.S. Army Air Forces

On May 26, 1945, 500 B-29 Superfortresses went cloud-hopping on the way to devastating Tokyo with high incendiary bombs. Japanese radio said Tokyo was "literally scorched to the ground." Nineteen of the Superforts from the Twentieth Air Force were lost during the mission. Army Air Force

❝

As long as our bombers stayed at 25,000 feet they could fly over the Jap anti-aircraft fire. Then suddenly, they started coming in at 5,000 or 6,000 feet. Right off the deck. It was like you could reach up and touch them. The Japs had a field day. Right in our area alone we counted 14 B-29s that went down in one night. They really got creamed!

Before the men bailed out, they'd put their planes on automatic pilot. These planes would then fly around. Finally, they'd go splat out in the bay.

❞

— STAFF SGT. JAMES CAVANAUGH
POW at Subcamp No. 2
Kawasaki, Japan

without the firepower to ward off swarms of pesky interceptors. Nor were they pleased about flying on the deck instead of in the upper stratosphere where enemy planes couldn't reach them. But LeMay felt the extra space could be better used to cram each B-29 with napalm and thermite bombs. The lower altitude bombing runs would improve accuracy, too.

"Everybody was panic-stricken when they said they were going to remove the guns from our B-29s," recalled Ray Brashear, pilot with the 878th Bomb Squadron. "Later, we learned that the Japanese had no night fighters able to intercept us and that the fuses for their anti-aircraft guns were not set for low altitudes."

A trial run was conducted on Feb. 24, as 100 B-29s hit Singapore, with 40 percent of the warehouse district totally destroyed by the incendiaries or the resulting fires.

"We believed, and meant to prove, that by destroying Japan's materials — burning down her cities — and then by tremendously heavy attacks against transport we could paralyze the country and make defense against invasion impossible," stated Brig. Gen. John Samford, chief target planner, XXI Bomber Command.

During a XXI Bomber Command staff briefing, the merits of striking key cities was discussed: "These operations are not conducted as terror raids against the civilian population. The Japanese economy depends heavily on home industries carried on in its cities close to major factory areas.

"By destroying these feeder industries, the flow of vital parts could be curtailed and war production disorganized. A general conflagration in a city like Tokyo or Nagoya might have the further advantage of spreading to some of the priority targets located in the urban areas."

The success of the Singapore mission validated LeMay's revolutionary strategy. Still, there were a few skeptics among those crewmen who flew the first firebombing mission over Tokyo, just after midnight on March 9, 1945.

As B-29 Superfortresses from the 73rd, 313th and 314th Bomber Groups approached Tokyo they passed by majestic Mt. Fuji. Flying at low altitude, they could hear air raid sirens blaring throughout the capital city only a few thousand feet below. And as they dropped their payloads, the flight crews could feel the intense heat of a metropolis engulfed in flames. They choked on the dense smoke clouds that blocked out the moon.

"I remember the tremendous fires of hundreds of city blocks just going up in smoke," said Brashear of the 878th Bomb Squadron. "If you flew into a smoke column, you would think your aircraft was coming apart. It was so turbulent, you couldn't read your cockpit instruments."

Though enemy fighter pilots took off to meet the approaching bombers, they kept their distance, unaware the B-29s were often lightly armed. "We lived with the anxious thought that sooner or later the Japanese would discover our secret and we knew it would be like shooting ducks in a barrel when they discovered we weren't equipped with the gun turrets."

Tokyo began to glow bright red as incendiaries were dropped and high winds fanned the flames, engulfing entire sections of the city. Houses made of wood and paper were reduced to ashes. Reconnaissance photos revealed that more than 15 square miles of Tokyo was reduced to rubble, and 23 military targets destroyed. Some 83,793 people were dead; one million left homeless. Fourteen B-29s were lost and 42 damaged.

On March 11, 307 B-29s struck Nagoya followed two days later by a raid on Osaka involving 279 bombers. Kobe was devastated on March 16 by 331 Superfortresses.

Firebombings had the desired effect: civilian morale plummeted. Absenteeism at factories rose to 40 percent as families looked for housing or simply moved to safer locations away from the bombed cities.

One by one, Japan's industrial centers were checked off a list of vital targets, and entire cities were turned into wastelands. (The only deterrent was the slow resupply of incendiaries to the bomber groups.)

LeMay felt strongly that his bombers, if allowed to continue to strike hard at the enemy, could eventually break down the Japanese will and force them to surrender.

But momentous events intervened and changed the course of history.

'A Rain of Ruin': Hiroshima and Nagasaki in Ashes

Col. Paul Tibbets, commander of the 509th Composite Group, needed seven B-29 crews for his secret mission. One would remain in reserve on Iwo Jima, one would fly over the primary target early and report on weather conditions, two more would scout out the secondary targets, one would serve as an escort carrying monitoring equipment, another escort would be loaded with cameras, and of course the primary plane, the *Enola Gay* — named for Tibbets' mother — would deliver the atomic bomb.

During raids on Yokohama, Japan, in 1945, B-29s of the XXI Bomber Command destroyed 44 percent of the city. Much of the damage was due to incendiaries and high winds, which quickly engulfed the city in flames. XXI Bomber Command

"

We gained some emotional strength from the great Tokyo fire raid. It was a hell of a big fire. And it was very beautiful. The raid began in the middle of the night. The sky turned reddish orange and was bright enough to read by. The burning was right across the canal from us at Omori prison camp. The flames shot as high as some of the planes. The planes came in low and you could see them drop those big bundles of incendiaries.

The feeling in the camp was of pure jubilation, knowing Tokyo was being burned and that our forces were close enough so they could put on that kind of show.

"

— PFC. JACK BRADY
Prisoner, Omori Camp, Japan

Terror From the Deep: Tragedy of the *USS Indianapolis*

After receiving heavy damage from a *kamikaze* attack near Okinawa on March 31, 1945, the heavy cruiser *USS Indianapolis* limped back to Mare Island at San Francisco for repairs. In July, and while still under repairs, the *Indianapolis* was assigned the mission of transporting vital parts for a secret weapon to the remote island of Tinian in the Marianas Islands.

Capt. Charles Butler McVay, skipper of the *Indianapolis*, was simply told for every day he could shave off the delivery time, the war would end that much sooner.

He didn't know what was in the 15-foot-long wooden crate or the unwieldy heavy bucket brought on board his ship. Or why two "artillery officers" who couldn't even wear their uniforms properly had accompanied and maintained a constant watch on these materials. But McVay understood the importance of his cargo when he received a radio message: "*Indianapolis* under orders of Commander-in-Chief must not be diverted from its mission for any reason."

At dawn on July 16, the *Indianapolis* cast off without escort for Tinian. After refueling at Pearl Harbor, the ship steamed off again, arriving at Tinian 10 days later, where members of the Army Air Forces' 509th Composite Group waited. The two "artillery officers" — members of the top-secret Manhattan Project — supervised unloading of the crate and bucket, then disappeared into a heavily guarded Quonset hut to assemble the new super weapon.

On July 29, midway between Guam and the Philippines, the Japanese submarine *I-58* spotted the shadowy silhouette of the *Indianapolis* and fired two torpedoes into her starboard side.

"I waited until it got close enough to see what it was," wrote *I-58* commander Capt. Mochitasura Hashimoto. "When I saw what a big ship it was, I aimed my torpedoes, and fired."

On July 29, 1945, the *USS Indianapolis* was struck by two torpedoes fired from the Japanese submarine I-58. After 82 hours in the water, only 316 of the original crew of 1,199 were finally rescued after being spotted by a patrol plane. U.S. Navy

Of the 1,198 men on board, 800 survived the blasts, only to cling to lifeboats and debris in shark-infested waters. The ship continued on course before sinking, scattering the survivors over several miles.

On Guam, the combat intelligence office intercepted a message from the Japanese submarine boasting that it had sunk a U.S. warship during the night. But there were no distress calls from any U.S. ships, so the message was deemed bogus.

For three days, *Indianapolis* survivors drifted helplessly, warding off sharks. "A nasty looking fin was cruising up and down only a few yards from us. That scared me about as badly as anything ever has," wrote Radioman 2nd Class Herb Minor after his rescue. "I'd read so many stories about huge schools of sharks gobbling men up and leaving nothing but the bloodied waters."

Many of the men, too weak to endure, were preyed on by the sharks or simply disappeared into the depths of the Pacific.

On Aug. 2, while on a routine patrol, Lt. Wilbur Gwinn of VPB-152 Squadron spotted an oil slick from his Ventura and swooped down for a closer look. Initially stunned by what he saw, Gwinn ordered his crew to drop survival gear to the stranded crewmen. Then he radioed back: "Sighted 30 survivors 011-30 North 133-30 East. Dropped transmitter and lifeboat emergency IFF on 133-30."

By the next day, all the survivors from the *Indianapolis* — only 316 of the original 1,198-man crew — including Capt. McVay, were rescued. Some 882, or nearly 75 percent of the crew perished. The search was called off Aug. 8.

Two days before, on Aug. 6, the secret weapon that the *Indianapolis* had delivered to Tinian — an atomic bomb nicknamed *Little Boy* — was dropped on Hiroshima. Ironically, among the dead was the entire family of Capt. Hashimoto, commander of the sub that sank the mighty *Indianapolis*.

After three days at sea, enduring sweltering heat and swarms of sharks, survivors of the July 29, 1945, sinking of the *USS Indianapolis* returned to the U.S. aboard the *Hollandia*. Courtesy of the *USS Indianapolis* Association

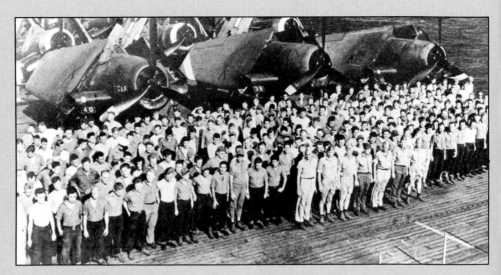

LeMay, as head of the XXI Bomber Command, chose Hiroshima on the southwestern coast of Honshu as the primary target. In addition to its numerous war factories, it also served as headquarters for the Japanese 2nd Army. Kokura and Nagasaki would be the alternates if Hiroshima was obscured by clouds.

At 1:37 a.m. on Aug. 6, 1945, the three scout planes took off for Hiroshima and the alternate sites to relay weather conditions back to Tibbets while the *Enola Gay* was en route.

An hour later, with military photographers crowding around, the *Enola Gay* — with 12 crewmen and a 4.5-ton bomb on board — rolled down the runway on Tinian and lifted off into history.

While in flight, Tibbets turned over the controls to his co-pilot and visited with his crew, which had been restricted from talking to anyone and were unaware of just how powerful this new bomb was.

"Have you figured out what we're doing this morning?" Tibbets asked his tail gunner, Tech. Sgt. Robert Caron. "Are we carrying a chemist's nightmare?" Caron asked. "No, not exactly," the colonel responded. "How about a physicist's nightmare?" Caron continued. Tibbets simply nodded.

Caron asked one more question: "Are we splitting atoms?" Tibbets didn't indicate whether Caron was right or not.

As the *Enola Gay* and her two escorts passed over Iwo Jima and swung

The crew of the B-29 Enola Gay that made history with the A-bomb drop on Hiroshima, Aug. 6, 1945.

Standing: Lt. Col. John Porter, ground maintenance officer; Maj. Theodore J. "Dutch" Van Kirk, navigator; Maj. Thomas W. Ferebee, bombardier; Col. Paul W. Tibbets, pilot and commanding officer of the 509th Group; Capt. Robert A. Lewis, co-pilot; and Lt. Jacob Beser, radar counter-measure officer.

Kneeling: Sgt. Joseph S. Stiborik, radar operator; Staff Sgt. George R. Caron, tail gunner; Pfc. Richard H. Nelson, radio operator; Sgt. Robert H. Shumard, assistant engineer; and Staff Sgt. Wyatt E. Duzenbury, flight engineer. U.S. Air Force

northwest, Tibbets used the intercom to finally explain to his crew what their important mission was. "We are carrying the world's first atomic bomb . . . and Bob, you are right. We are splitting atoms."

At dawn, the scout plane *Straight Flush* streaked across Hiroshima. Capt. Claude Eatherly reported clear skies: "Advice: bomb primary." Surprisingly, no enemy fighters or anti-aircraft guns challenged the *Straight Flush*.

An hour later, the *Enola Gay* and its two monitors were on the outskirts of Hiroshima. Though Japanese radar and spotters were alerted to their approach, they were unmolested by any defenders.

As the aiming point — Hiroshima's Aioi Bridge — appeared in the bomb sight, Maj. Thomas Ferebee, the bombardier, released *Little Boy* at 08:15. Tibbets pounced on the throttle, and swung his Superfortress into a hard right bank to put some distance between his crew and what they had just unleashed.

Surprisingly, the detonation was muffled. The sky, though, seemed to glow as if all three planes were flying at the sun. From his tail gunner's turret, Caron saw the billowing gray cloud tumbling toward him, but was too stunned to speak. The concussion from the shock wave blindsided the *Enola Gay* and its two shadows, and everyone thought they'd been hit by flak.

Caron caught his breath and shouted "there's another one coming!" just as a second jolt rocked the plane. As the *Enola Gay* continued on, Caron watched the sky over Hiroshima turn from a red core to purple.

"A column of smoke rising fast. It has a fiery red core. A bubbling mass, purple-gray in color, with that red core. It's all turbulent. Fires are springing up everywhere, like flames shooting out of a huge bed of coals.... Here it comes, the mushroom shape. It's like a bubbling molasses," remembered Caron. Beneath that beautiful changing set of colors, though, the entire city was in flames. With communication lines severed in the blast, Hiroshima was literally cut off from the rest of Japan. By 3 p.m. the *Enola Gay* had returned to Tinian.

President Harry Truman, on board the cruiser *Augusta* and returning from the historic meeting at Potsdam, received the news via radio. In a radio address to the American public, Truman announced: "The force from which the sun draws its power has been loosed upon those who brought war to the Far East.... If [the leaders of Japan] do not now accept our terms they may expect a rain of ruin from the air, the like of which has never been seen on this earth."

In Tokyo, the cabinet was divided. Some sought peace immediately, but others demanded a suicidal last stand, calling all citizens to defend their homeland. Still not believing the reports trickling in about Hiroshima, War Minister Korechika Anami dispatched a nuclear physicist and a military officer to survey the damage and report back. Yet despite confirmation that an atomic blast had occurred, the cabinet refused to give into Truman's surrender demands.

The Japanese government was perilously close to collapsing from within, unable to decide the best course of action. By not deciding, it forced President Truman to order another atomic bomb. Others would follow as quickly as they could be assembled on Tinian. Unlike *Little Boy*, which relied on uranium 235, this next bomb would use plutonium.

Christened *Fat Man*, after the first blast at Alamogordo in New Mexico, this third device was loaded onto the B-29 *Bock's Car*, named for Capt. Frederick Bock. But it would be flown instead by Maj. Charles Sweeney, pilot of the monitor plane during the atomic blast at Hiroshima.

At 3:49 a.m. on Aug. 9, *Bock's Car* took off for the primary target — Kokura, Japan — located on the island of Kyushu. Six hours later, after its scout plane had said visibility was good, Capt. Sweeney started his bombing run.

"Smoke from fire bombings the night before had drifted over and blocked our view of the aiming point," Sweeney recalled. "We could see bodies of water right next to the aiming point and we could have bombed by off-set, or we could have bombed by radar, but we were told to bomb visually."

Twice the plane swung around for another try, but the smoke prevented an accurate drop. Flak from anti-aircraft guns was rocking the plane and fuel was getting low, so Kokura was scratched.

The secondary target was Nagasaki, which was surrounded by mountains. But on approach, it too was obscured by cloud cover. Sweeney told

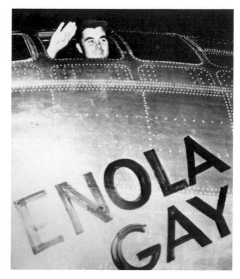

Col. Paul W. Tibbets, Jr., waves from the cockpit of the *Enola Gay*, the plane — named after his mother — that dropped the first atomic bomb, Aug. 6, 1945, on Hiroshima.
National Archives

66

I believed then and continue to believe today that President Truman made the right decision to drop the bomb. As the father of 10 children and the grandfather of 21, I am certainly grateful that the war ended when it did. And it is my fervent hope that there will never be another atomic mission. Ever.

99

— Charles W. Sweeney
Squadron Commander and Pilot of the *Bock's Car* in the mission over Nagasaki. Writing in the *Wall Street Journal*, July 19, 1995

Borneo: The Last Invasion

Operation Oboe had three targets on Borneo: Tarakan, Brunei Bay and Balikpapan. The U.S. Seventh Fleet and Thirteenth Air Force supported the Australian assault forces at all three invasion points.

At Tarakan Island in May 1945, a Navy shore party and about 500 Army troops also participated. While most resistance was light at Tarakan, three minesweepers were hit by 75mm guns from a concealed enemy battery. Two sweepers survived, but the YMS-481 was sunk with the loss of six men.

At Brunei Bay, 17 minesweepers moved in to clear the harbor. On June 8, four men were killed and 12 wounded when their minesweeper, *Salute*, hit a contact mine. Underwater demolition teams (UDTs) reconnoitered the beaches without incident, and PT Squadrons 13 and 16 destroyed a schooner and five barges. MacArthur called the operation "flawless."

Balikpapan, the oil center of Borneo, hosted the Navy's last major amphibious operation in WWII, conducted by VII Amphibious Force. A 16-day bombardment preceded the landing. Two weeks before the July 1 landing date (F-day), minesweepers protected the Cruiser and Destroyer Covering Group, which suffered seven men killed and 43 wounded.

UDTs 11 and 18 sustained no casualties, benefiting from the support of seven LCS(L) gunboats. However, *LCS(L)-28* was hit by three 75mm shells, wounding five men. "This job at Balikpapan was one of the bravest and best by the 'frogmen' during the entire war," wrote naval historian Samuel E. Morison.

"The 727th Amphibian Tractor Battalion — operators of the 'water buffaloes' — carried the Australian assault forces ashore for the initial landings and for subsequent 'leap frog' operations to isolate and neutralize Japanese positions," wrote veteran James E. Ball.

Firepower supplied by *Task Group 78.2* and Marine Air Group 2 accounted for 460 enemy dead at Balikpapan. Some 800 Seabees went on to build a base there. The last invasion of the Pacific war was complete.

A U.S. Coast Guard landing craft unloads Australian troops at Balikpapan, Borneo, in July 1945. U.S. Coast Guard

the crew they could only take one run at the aiming point — the Mitsubishi arms complex. Traces of the city peeked through the clouds, not enough, however, for such a critical mission. But then, at the last moment, the clouds opened up and the target came into view.

Fat Man was delivered at 11:01 a.m. *Bock's Car* and its monitor plane swung around high to escape the aftershocks, but two minutes later both planes were buffeted by five jolts as the shock waves bounced off the surrounding mountains.

As the only pilot from the 509th Composite Group to fly both atomic bomb missions, Sweeney noted, "The second bomb seemed to be more powerful than the one over Hiroshima. The flash seemed to be brighter, and the concussion was slightly greater."

Several hours later and with its engines sputtering, *Bock's Car* landed on Okinawa, its fuel tanks nearly empty.

Later that night the Japanese cabinet met, and again debated making a last stand against the inevitable invasion to come. The two sides argued into the early hours of the next morning.

Finally, Emperor Hirohito, who normally acted only after the cabinet had come to a unanimous decision, one way or the other, spoke: "I cannot bear to see my innocent people suffer any longer. It pains me to think of those who served me so faithfully, the soldiers and sailors who have been killed or wounded in far-off battles, the families who have lost all their worldly goods — and often their lives as well.

"The time has come when we must bear the unbearable. I swallow my tears and give my sanction to the proposal to accept the Allied proclamation. . . ."

Without further dissent, the cabinet agreed to the terms spelled out in the Potsdam Proclamation, with the stipulation that "the supreme power of the Emperor" not be compromised.

Rebel factions vowed to continue the fight, but their efforts were put

Unlike its counterpart, the *Bock's Car* has never achieved national notoriety for its mission over Nagasaki in that fateful August of 1945.
Courtesy of Friends Museum

The nose of the plane that dropped the atom bomb on Nagasaki, Aug. 9, 1945, displays its name, origination and destination. In an odd twist of fate, Capt. Fred Bock of Salt Lake City, usually the skipper of *Bock's Car*, flew alongside in *The Great Artiste* while Maj. Charles Sweeney piloted the carrier of the bomb.

Benzedrine and coffee became the best friends of crews such as this one aboard a B-29 Superfortress during the air raids over Japanese cities late in the war. Flights would last 15–16 hours, and shifts often ran 24 hours or more. One pilot said the colors of sunrise and sunset often ". . . softened our strain and anxieties." U.S. Air Force

Junk Battle Off China: A First and Last

Soon after Japan's surrender, the Sino-American Cooperative Organization (SACO) — a secret behind-the-lines unit — ordered its field units in China to shut down and return to one of the regional offices at Hankow, Shanghai or Chungking.

Unit 8 at Tsingtien, led by Lt. Livingston "Swede" Swentzel, commandeered two sailing junks at Hainan for the eight American servicemen and shoved off for Shanghai. Besides machine guns and Tommy guns, the GIs also lugged a bazooka on board.

Five days after the cease-fire, on Aug. 19, the motley group encountered a much larger black junk armed with a 75mm howitzer and Japanese on board. Japanese fired on the junks, killing two of the Chinese crewmen and wounding two others.

The Americans returned fire, peppering the enemy junk with bullets and firing three rockets into her, killing 48 Japanese. Waving a dirty shirt from a bayonet, the 39 survivors surrendered. All but four were wounded in the attack. The enemy vessel was seized and escorted to Shanghai.

Ironically, this final naval battle of WWII was not waged by aircraft carriers, battleships or submarines, but by simple wooden sailing junks. It also was the first U.S. naval battle under sail since the American Civil War.

down once the emperor's wishes were broadcast to the Japanese people. Though thousands perished at Hiroshima and Nagasaki, the atomic bombs and the threat of further destruction forced the Japanese to surrender, sparing the lives of many thousands more Japanese and Americans.

The Final Raids

Still, the conventional air war against Japan continued unabated until Aug. 14. That day and night, 809 B-29s of the Strategic Air Forces based in the Marianas and escorted by 173 fighters, hit eight primary targets in the Tokyo area. One pilot of the Seventh Fighter Command, based on Iwo Jima, was downed by flak.

Before the cease-fire took effect at 7 a.m. on Aug. 15, 143 unprotected B-29s of the 315th Bomb Wing attacked the Nippon Oil refineries at Akita, some 270 miles northwest of Tokyo.

"Our last mission destroyed 67 percent of the Japanese refining capability," noted Jim Smith, a B-29 crewman with the 315th. "There was not enough oil left in Japan to cremate the dead, and the military diehards sorely needed the Akita petrol if they were to resume the war."

Because of engine trouble, which delayed take-off from Northwest Field on Guam, the B-29 *The Uninvited,* piloted by Capt. Dan Trask, was 30 minutes late over the refinery and thus became the last plane to drop a bomb on Japan in WWII, at 0339 hours on Aug. 15. "We were still in the air returning to Guam when President Truman announced the Japanese surrender," recalled Smith.

Meanwhile, at sea, Adm. William Halsey sent a message to his Third Fleet after learning of Japan's surrender: "Cease firing, but if any enemy planes appear, shoot them down in a friendly fashion."

A mission that morning involving Hellcats of the carrier *Yorktown's* VF-88 was already airborne and over Tokyo's Tokurozama airfield when the pilots were told to abort because of the surrender announcement. But at the same time, the six Hellcats were attacked by 15-20 enemy fighters. Nine Japanese planes were shot down, but so were four of the Navy planes. Later in the day, Japanese aircraft approached the ships of *Task Force 38* and also were shot down.

In what is considered the last dogfight in Japanese airspace, two B-32 reconnaissance planes flying over Tokyo were attacked by 14 enemy fighters on Aug. 18 — three days after the cease-fire. Though three of the Japanese planes were shot down, one of the B-32s was strafed, killing Sgt. Anthony Marchione and wounding Staff Sgt. Joseph Lacherite of the 20th Combat Mapping Squadron, 6th Photo Group.

The Twentieth Air Forces' strategic air offensive against the home islands, initiated June 5, 1944 and ending Aug. 15, 1945, was an unqualified success. But it came with a price: 512 B-29s were lost overseas — 494 in combat. Among the crews, 576 were KIA and 2,406 MIA (presumed dead), bringing the total killed to 2,982 airmen.

★ ★ ★

On Aug. 10, 1945, during a series of U.S. bombing raids after the dropping of the atomic bombs, Japanese Lt. Minoru Wada becomes the first captured enemy officer to brief U.S. pilots for a strike against his own command.

From the belly of a U.S. Marine Billy Mitchell bomber, Wada transmits information to the air strike coordinator for the group as it heads for the long-sought headquarters of the 100th Japanese Army Division on Mindanao in the Philippines, where Wada had been captured in the jungle. U.S. Marine Corps

Penetrating the 'Great Northern Shield'

The rocky and barren Kurile Islands (even today a bone of contention between Japan and Russia) extend northeast of Japan's main islands, and in WWII, provided the empire's "Great Northern Shield."

After a disastrous start on Sept. 11, 1943 — a loss of seven B-25s and two B-24s, the worst in the history of the 11th Air Force), the Army suspended air operations against the Kuriles until Nov. 9, 1943. The Navy flew its first bombing mission in the Kuriles on Dec. 20, 1943.

Surface bombardment of the Japanese homeland commenced Feb. 4, 1944, when the Navy shelled Paramushiro, the "Gibraltar of the North." By the end of the war, *Task Force* 94 and 92 had bombarded the Kuriles 12 times and conducted six sweeps in the Sea of Okhotsk.

Beginning in 1944, the Army moved its air base from Adak to Shemya, a tiny atoll 25 miles east of Attu in the Aleutians. The 28th Composite Group (the 404th Heavy Bomb and 77th Medium Bomb squadrons plus seven other units) flew the perilous air route from the base.

"Initially, living conditions were terrible," said Alfred B. Kinney, a veteran of the 11th Air Force. "Until the middle of 1944, we lived in winterized tents heated by coal stoves. Spring would bring a flooded Squadron area, and upon waking we would frequently find our personal belongings floating around the tent."

Meanwhile, the Navy established an airfield on Kiska and facilities for submarines and aircraft on Attu.

On April 15, 1944, *Operation Wedlock* began. A fictitious plan, it was designed to divert troops and attention away from a real attack in the Mariana Islands. It included imaginary sailors comprising a phantom Ninth Fleet. Communications and practice maneuvers were real, though, and the deception was successful.

An integral part of *Wedlock's* effectiveness was the continuous American air missions over the Kuriles. By the time Japan surrendered, the 404th Bombardment Squadron flew 699 sorties, dropped 1,262,100 pounds of bombs and lost 32 men. The 77th Bombardment Squadron flew 33 bombing missions and conducted 39 shipping sweeps, while losing 42 men.

The Navy's Fleet Air Wing Four lost 49 men while flying 113 attack missions, primarily against enemy ships and land targets on Paramushiro and Shimushu. The PV-1 Ventura, the Navy's versatile medium bomber that regularly out ran enemy fighters, was used extensively in the Kuriles. Renowned for its ability to absorb punishment and continue to fly, it gained the lasting respect of its crewmembers, who flew the "Empire Night Express."

"On one trip to Paramushiro, we took the airfield on the southeastern tip of the island, dropped our payload and started for home," recalls Lt. J. E. McLennan, VB-136, Fleet Air Wing Four, "The Ack Ack [anti-aircraft fire] was on true altitude, but they misjudged our speed.

"Our left engine began to run rough and cough a bit. We stripped the plane of everything that was moveable and dropped it out. After considerable flying, we picked up a LORAN [long-range radio navigation] bearing and split the runway dead center. Our good Pratt & Whitney 2800s [engines] brought us home."

Some airmen never did make it back. Faced with an emergency situation, a pilot had three options: crash on an enemy-held island, down the plane somewhere in the 650 miles of ice water between the Kuriles and Aleutians, or land on Russia's Kamchatka Peninsula. While the latter meant internment for a total of 242 U.S. airmen during WWII, it was their only chance of survival.

"In case of aircraft damage, the pre-planned escape route was to Petro-pavlovsk, Kamchatka," states John S. Smith, a former internee and member of the 11th Air Force. "Petro was a holding point until a group became large enough to move across Siberia to Tashkent, Russia. The trip was accomplished by various methods, from the Siberian railroad to flying in old C-47s with Russian crews. In all, five separate groups were held and released."

Submarine crews, however, never had such options, and they suffered the brunt of the casualties in the Kuriles. Of the 745 men killed in the campaign, 615 (83 percent) served aboard eight submarines. The subs conducted a total of 72 missions, sank 245,000 tons of shipping and tallied 88 victories, according to Kevin Hutchinson in *WWII in the North Pacific*.

The last U.S. shots fired in WWII occurred at the end of the Kurile campaign. The Navy credited the *USS Concord* with this distinction after the light cruiser shelled Shasukotan on Aug. 14, 1945. On Aug. 24, the 11th Air Force flew its last mission of the war when B-24s attempted to photograph the Soviet occupation of the Kuriles, but couldn't due to cloud cover.

Brian Garfield, author of *The Thousand-Mile War*, concluded: "The Kurile campaign was of far greater value than the bored Aleutian servicemen imagined."

B-25 bombers of the 11th Air Force, based in Alaska and the Aleutians, waged a little-known air war against the Kurile Islands. Courtesy Gerald Flynn

'Windship Weapon' Deals Death to the Home Front

For *Project FUGO* — "windship weapon" — paper balloons were glued together with paper paste and sent aloft to 38,000 feet with a five-bomb payload as they drifted across the Pacific. Of some 6,000 launched starting in late 1944, 361 definitely reached North America. Three touched down in Mexico and 36 landed in Alaska. British Columbia, Washington and Oregon were hardest hit. The first confirmations came when a fighter pilot shot one down over Alturas, Calif., in January 1945.

Igniting forest fires in the Pacific Northwest was the grand scheme behind the Japanese fire-balloon campaign, which was a dismal failure.

"I was stationed at Klamath Falls, Ore., and we were sent out on patrols through the mountains looking for strange objects which turned out to be 'windship weapons,'" recalled Byran English, a veteran of Co. K, 3rd Regt., 3rd Marine Div., who was recuperating at the R&R Center there for Marines with tropical diseases.

Some 5,000 feet up Gearhart Mountain near Bly, Ore., on May 5, 1945, a balloon-borne bomb exploded, killing Elsie Mitchell and five school children when they touched the strange-looking object. Navy Lt. H. P. Scott, a bomb disposal expert from the nearest naval air station, filed this report:

"Upon arrival at the scene [I found] a Japanese balloon together with various pieces of its equipment scattered around a nearby area. An explosion, evidently of a bomb carried by this balloon, had occurred and a woman and five children had been killed. It is surmised that one of the party either dropped or kicked the bomb, causing it to explode.

"It was necessary for me to render safe four incendiary bombs, a demolition charge, a flash bomb and various blow-out plugs from the balloon undercarriage before all the bodies could be removed.

"The examination of the fragments from the explosion proved that the bomb was a Japanese Army 15-kg. [33-pound] antipersonnel high-explosive. The balloon had evidently been on the ground for some time, as several of the parts were rusted, the paper [forming the balloon bag] was mildewed, and there were from six to eight inches of snow beneath the paper while the surrounding area was entirely free of snow."

A monument built of stone gathered from the mountain commemorates the site. Its inscription reads: "The only place on the American continent where death resulted from enemy action during World War II." (More properly, it should have read killed in the 48 states. Hundreds of Americans were killed fighting in Alaska's Aleutian Islands.)

29907 A.C.

One of the many Japanese balloons with fire bombs attached that came down in Oregon. This one was found on Feb. 23, 1945. Six picnickers in Oregon were killed by a fire balloon bomb in May 1945, causing the only U.S. casualties due to enemy action in the "Lower 48." U.S. Air Force

OCCUPATION OF JAPAN

God Shed His Grace on Thee by John D. Shaw. A Navy F-6F Hellcat, an Army P-38 Lightning and a Marine F-4U Corsair overfly the Statue of Liberty, commemorating the return of American troops from overseas after V-J Day. Many GIs, however, would remain in Japan to extend the blessings of democracy — symbolized by Lady Liberty — to the people of that defeated nation.

Counting Blessings and Extending Democracy

Sigh of Relief

> *It is hard to imagine a conquering army that could have undertaken the physical and spiritual rehabilitation of the erstwhile enemy with greater good will and deeper sincerity.*

— EDWIN O. REISCHAUER
Former Ambassador to Japan

THE WAR was over! Finally.

In the Pacific war, 108,656 Americans had been killed in action. Japan lost 485,717 men killed in battle against U.S. forces alone.

Now, half a million American servicemen no longer had to fear what everyone knew would be a savage fight to the death. Among those GIs were men of the 86th and 97th Infantry divisions, redeployed from the European Theater to link up with combat units already in the Pacific for the final assault on Japan.

"We knew that anytime you invade somebody's homeland they're going to be fortified," recalled Gottlieb Schock, a veteran of Service Co., 343rd Inf. Regt., 86th Inf. Div. "We had read about Tarawa and Iwo Jima and we knew we were in store for a pretty bitter fight, and so the news about the A-bomb was a wonderful relief." Instead of invading Japan, Schock ended up serving with the "Blackhawk" Division in the Philippines.

Calvin Hanawalt was a machine-gun crewman with H Co., 387th Inf., Regt., 97th Inf. Div. — which was in Czechoslovakia when Germany surrendered. "When we heard that we would be redeploying to the Pacific it was almost a mutiny!" After a 30-day furlough stateside, the 97th assembled on the West Coast for movement to the Pacific.

"We were scheduled to serve as a floating reserve, not in the initial invasion of Japan, but in the second wave," noted Hanawalt. "We were just getting ready to board the transports when we heard Japan had surrendered. It was like an enormous weight had been lifted. We still went over to Japan, but as occupation forces instead."

'Bring Daddy Home'

The Navy and Coast Guard launched *Operation Magic Carpet*, but there simply weren't enough vessels afloat to "bring the boys back home" as quickly as they and their loved ones wanted. "Bring Back Daddy Clubs" were organized by wives and parents of GIs, and elected officials were deluged with letters and calls asking for their help, especially as the holidays approached in late 1945.

Just as in Europe, each of the armed forces established a points system to determine who should return home first. Those who had been overseas the longest, fought in combat and earned battle ribbons racked up enough points to "get their ticket punched." Three months after V-J Day, though, 60 percent of all Army personnel were still overseas, in both Europe and Pacific; the figure was 75 percent for the Navy.

As the year dragged on, the slogan "Home alive in '45" was facetiously replaced with "Back to heaven in '47" and "Golden Gate in '48." The *Wall Street Journal* asked, "We wonder if anyone in Washington has any adequate idea of the resentment that is being built up in this country." *The Daily Oklahoman* went even further, cautioning politicians, "When given the next shot at the ballot box, we will demobilize you." Washington got the message.

GIs stationed on Guam delight in the news of the A-bomb falling on Hiroshima, Aug. 6, 1945. Two days later the Soviet Union declared war on Japan, and the U.S. dropped another A-bomb on Aug. 9 at Nagasaki. Within a week, Japan gave up. U.S. Army

---

Last American Killed In Action?

"The last days some of the best ones die."
— ROBERT CAPA, combat photographer

Who died last in WWII depends upon how you classify the combat death — on land, at sea or in the air. And whether he was killed before the armistice on Aug. 15 or between the cease-fire and the signing of the treaty on Sept. 2, 1945, or after the treaty.

On land, it was Pfc. Edward O'Dell Mullins of A Co., 1st Bn., 128th Inf. Regt., 32nd Inf. Div., near Bagabag in the Cagayan Valley of northern Luzon, Philippines. Just 45 minutes — at 6:15 a.m. — before the cease-fire was to take effect at 7 a.m. on Aug. 15, Mullins was killed by a Japanese sniper as his unit was disengaging from a firefight.

At sea, the distinction cannot be made because many men were killed at once. The transport *Lagrange*, while anchored in Buckner Bay, Okinawa, on Aug. 13, took a direct hit by a *kamikaze* carrying a 500-pound bomb, killing 21 men and wounding 89. The last U.S. Navy warship to sustain casualties — battleship *Pennsylvania* — also anchored in Buckner Bay, was torpedoed by a Japanese plane the day before: 20 sailors died and 10 were wounded.

Three days after the cease-fire, on Aug. 18, Sgt. Anthony J. Marchione, an aerial photographer aboard a B-32 of the 20th Combat Mapping Squadron, 6th Photo Group, was killed over Tokyo. His reconnaissance flight was attacked by 14 Japanese fighters. During the 25-minute dogfight two, and probably three, enemy planes were shot down.

Dec. 8, 1945 — more than three months after peace was officially concluded — U.S. Marines fought a lethal firefight with Japanese at Asan Point, Guam. A four-man patrol of the 4th Military Police Battalion was ambushed by snipers, killing three men: Lt. Ray W. Atchinson, Cpl. Howard W. Price and Pvt. Herbert E. Ward. Pvt. Ross, the sole survivor, was wounded.

During the sweep for the culprits, Co. K, 3rd Bn., 3rd Marines, lost one KIA — Pfc. W. C. P. Bates — on Dec. 14.

> *"*
>
> *We knew we would die in Japan. We had heard that a million men would be killed in the invasion. We were all scared to death. We were lucky that we didn't have to go.*
>
> *We had mixed feelings about going to fight the Japanese. We figured that our number shouldn't come up more than once, but we were soldiers and we did what we were told. We were grateful that we didn't have to die in Japan.*
>
> *We had been training for combat in the Pacific before the Battle of the Bulge. But the Battle of the Bulge was so savage that we were sent to Europe instead. We had had training in Japanese language, weapons, and warfare.*
>
> *We had even had glider training at Fort Bragg and amphibious training with the 4th Marine Division near Coronado, Calif., in preparation for combat in the Pacific. We had also heard that our division and the 86th Division would spearhead the invasion.*
>
> *Our division landed in France and made its way through Germany to Pilsen, Czechoslovakia, when the war in Europe ended. We were sent home in June, given a furlough, then put aboard a train for Seattle.*
>
> *Once we got there, the Army confined us and kept us in the dark about what was going on. After the bomb was dropped, we boarded transports and went to Japan for occupation duty.*
>
> *"*
>
> — PFC. ALBERT MIGLIO
> F Co., 386th Inf. Regt.
> 97th Infantry Division

Pvt. Beatrice Howard of the Transient Service checks in a group of Merrill's Marauders returning from Burma after the war ends in Japan, September 1945. Filing off a transport in Miami (front to back): Sgt. George E. Courtright, S/Sgt. Harold A. Phillips, T/4 Lawrence E. Doheny, T/4 Elva L. Tedford, Cpl. Herbert L. Henderson, Pfc. Robert R. Hickey (l.) and Sgt. John Lawryk (r.), T/5 David M. Waterhouse (l.) and Sgt. Lawrence O. Griffiths (r.), Sgt. Glen F. Richardson (l.) and S/Sgt. Ray C. Braden (r.), Pfc. Leo J. Desharnais (l.) and Pfc. Walter F. Deeback (r.).
U.S. Army Air Forces

A Nation Reborn From Ashes

Ernest Hoberecht, then with United Press, rode in the back seat of a Navy carrier plane that landed at Atsugi Airbase, well before GIs began arriving in late August 1945, to get a first look at a ruined Japan.

He told of jumping out of the plane as it sat a few minutes on the runway, with Japanese troops standing a quarter-mile away, and grabbing a few handsful of green grass, getting back in and flying off to land again on the carrier. "Those Navy guys were amazed to see green grass to prove we'd been there," he said.

A few days later, Hoberecht was back in Japan, this time with another American correspondent and one from England, all of whom got onto a Japanese train and rode right into Tokyo. After finding no stories, they returned to a carrier. "No one even bothered us that day," Hoberecht said, "even though it was a few days before the occupation began."

Others arrived early, too. One former POW imprisoned in Japan, Elroy Thomas, recalled seeing Army Air Forces Col. Johnson, "whose first name I don't recall, but he was an ace." A corporal also came to the POW camp. "He told us all to leave the camp and take the rickety narrow-gauged railway down to Osaka and wait there for others to help us," Thomas said.

After being a POW for 42 months, Thomas and his pals joyfully saw two

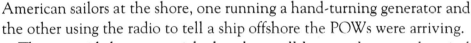

American sailors at the shore, one running a hand-turning generator and the other using the radio to tell a ship offshore the POWs were arriving.

Thomas said they were picked up by small boats, taken to a hospital ship, and after some shifting from ship to ship, later flown to the Philippines for further medical care.

That type of POW-collecting was going on all around Japan and Korea, since Priority No. 1 of the official occupation policy (code-named *Blacklist*), was to rescue Allied POWs as fast as possible. Roughly 17,000 (11,400 Americans) Allied POWs were held in 176 POW camps and sub-camps on the home islands.

Priority No. 2 dealt with actually landing forces on the enemy's homeland. On Aug. 27, 1945, victorious ships of the U.S. Third Fleet steamed into Tokyo's Sugami Bay at the head of what may have been history's greatest display of naval might. A vast fleet consisting of 23 aircraft carriers, 12 battleships, 26 cruisers, 116 destroyers and escorts, 12 submarines and 185 other smaller ships lay offshore.

Next day, Aug. 28, members of Underwater Demolition Team (UDT) 18 were the first to actually enter Tokyo Bay. "When the UDT team

Veterans of the China-Burma-India Theater arrive in New York on Sept. 27, 1945, aboard the transport *General A.W. Greely*. Office of War Information

Above: On Aug. 8, 1945, members of Underwater Demolition Team (UDT) 18 were the first Americans to actually enter Tokyo Bay. They had the honor of accepting the surrender of some of the first Japanese forces in Japan.
Courtesy of Kermit E. Hill

Right: The official surrender ceremony took place aboard the *USS Missouri* in Tokyo Bay on Sept. 2, 1945. The fall of the "Rising Sun" was now complete.

On Aug. 27, 1945, Allied ships anchor in Tokyo Bay, nearly a week before Japan signed the surrender document on board the *USS Missouri*. Majestic Mt. Fuji looms in the background. U.S. Navy photo

finished its primary mission, the signal was given by the Allied Command, and the occupation of Japan began," wrote Kermit E. Hill, then a 21-year-old ensign with UDT 18.

"Members spent September 1945, roaming some 300 miles up the Japanese coast, searching out Japanese weapons and gun emplacements, sinking suicide subs, destroying the speedy and treacherous suicide boats, making sure American occupation forces would not be ambushed.

"No medals were awarded to the men of UDT 18. The mission's success was their only reward. They silently accepted their assignment to swim into Tokyo Bay, walk up to the enemy and quietly, confidently and firmly announce their presence. 'We're here.' "

Two days later, Aug. 30, the first phase of Japan's occupation began, called L-Day, when the fleet's *Task Force 31*, spearheaded by the 2nd Bn., 4th Regt., 6th Marine Div., landed at Yokosuka Naval Base on the island of Honshu. The 4th's 1st and 3rd battalions were close behind.

Almost at the same moment, 3,518 paratroopers of the 188th, 187th and 511th Parachute Infantry regiments of the 11th Airborne Division swooped in aboard 123 C-54 transports to land at Atsugi Airbase, about 25 miles north of the naval base. An advance party of 154 Signal Corps men also flew into Atsugi. From Aug. 30 onward — day and night — warplanes of all kinds flew overhead, many using Atsugi to land or refuel.

Every branch of the service had a role in the early occupation. "Units of the Fifth Air Force, including my outfit — Headquarters Squadron, 63rd Air Service Group, arrived in August and assisted in the operation of Atsugi Airbase in Tokyo," said "Flying Buccaneer" veteran Norman Pruitt.

Expectations on both sides were askew. Allied forces expected some fights, at least from diehards. Homeland defense forces in Japan expected the invaders to loot, pillage and rape their women. None of that occurred,

Tokyo's Final Downfall

"To quell the Japanese resistance man by man and conquer the country yard by yard might well require the loss of a million American lives, and half that number of British." — WINSTON CHURCHILL, British Prime Minister

Operation Downfall — the scheduled invasion of Japan — was divided into two phases: *Operation Olympic* (later renamed Majestic) and *Operation Coronet*. *Olympic* called for 600,000 men hitting the beaches of Kyushu on Nov. 1, 1945. Next target would be Tokyo's Kanto Plain in March 1946 if the first invasion was not sufficient. A total of five million men — all U.S. except for three British Commonwealth divisions and the British Pacific Fleet — would be employed in both phases.

Backing up the assault troops were the Third and Fifth Fleets, Far East Air Force and Fifth, Seventh and Thirteenth Air Forces. An additional 250,000 ground troops were designated as reinforcements.

"All I could see was disaster!" said Col. Robert S. Sumner, then a first lieutenant with the Alamo Scouts, the Sixth Army's elite reconnaissance unit tentatively assigned to reconnoiter the beaches prior to the invasion. "I saw the whole operation laid out on rubber map and there were the cliffs, narrow beaches, and the estimates of the Jap garrisons . . . the possibility of success would have been practically nil!"

Japanese leaders knew the war was lost, yet under *Ketsu-Go*, or *Operation Decision*, they planned to kill as many Americans and other Allied soldiers as possible, even if it meant sacrificing a greater number of their own people.

Japanese women and teenagers trained to use simple hand tools and bamboo knives against the invaders. Children were asked to strap explosives around their waists then scurry under passing tanks to blow them up. Some 25 million of these civilians were organized into the National Volunteer Force.

More than 5,000 *kamikaze* pilots, plus manned torpedoes and suicide boats, would greet the invasion fleet. Japanese leaders felt they could even the score, if not swing the balance of power back in Japan's favor. More than 2½ million regular Army soldiers made up Japan's two general armies.

Preliminary estimates placed U.S. casualties at a horrendous 35 percent of the initial invasion force. One popular slogan in Japan, chanted by the masses during early 1945, reveals what that force would encounter: "One hundred million die proudly," according to Thomas Havens in his book *Valley of Darkness*. In fact, the general populace had been taught to think as a collective suicide unit — *Ichioku Tokko* — "the hundred million as a Special Attack Force."

It took the detonation of two atomic bombs and the threat of many more to finally convince the Japanese to surrender. Tens of thousands of GIs owe their lives to mankind's most destructive weapon. 2nd Lt. Paul Fussell, slated for the invasion of Japan, then an already-wounded 21-year-old rifle platoon leader, wrote long after the war:

"When the bombs dropped and news began to circulate that *Operation Olympic* would not, after all, take place, that we would not be obliged to run up the beaches near Tokyo assault-firing while being mortared and shelled, for all the fake manliness of our facades, we cried with relief and joy. We were going to live. We were going to grow up to adulthood after all."

on either side. U.S. troops were stunned to see how docile the Japanese behaved, while the Japanese were shocked to find Americans kind and generous toward their defeated enemy.

On Sept. 2, a few hours before the formal surrender, the Army's famed 1st Cavalry Division made its assault landing: 1st Brigade on the left and the 2nd Brigade on the right, teams abreast. Six days later, Pvt. Paul Davis of D Troop, 12th Cavalry, reputedly became the first U.S. enlisted man to "formally" enter Tokyo. Ultimately, 15 Army divisions, as well as the 2nd and 5th Marine divisions of the V Amphibious Corps, served on occupation duty in Japan.

"The 41st Infantry Division — 'Jungleers' — went ashore at Kure on southern Honsho, the first American troops landed there," remembered William Tschirhart. "We marched single file on both sides of the street at least five yards apart. We were all very tense because we did not see any people. We could feel that they were there, but they did not even look out the windows." The 41st had been slated for the invasion.

The Navy set up shop at Yokosuka and several other bases in southern

Marines of the 4th Regiment, chief element of the Third Fleet Landing Force, come ashore at Yokosuka Naval Base in Japan on Aug. 30, 1945.
National Archives

Above: An American military policeman comforts Japanese children, a typical interaction during the U.S. occupation of Japan from 1945 to 1952. U.S. Army

Right: Soldiers of the Army's 1st Cavalry Division march into Yokohama following Japan's surrender. Days later, the division was the first American unit to "officially" enter Tokyo and occupy the capital city in September 1945. U.S. Army

11th Airborne Division soldiers astride horses during occupation duty in Japan in the 1940s. Courtesy of 11th Airborne Division

Japan. The Fifth Air Force moved into Nagoya. The Twentieth Air Force, the big B-29 bomber fleet, kept its home bases in the Pacific islands, but was part of the occupation force.

Gen. Robert L. Eichelberger, head of the Eighth Army, became commander of all ground forces, including the XXIV Corps in Korea and two corps in Japan — I Corps at Kyoto and IX Corps at Sendai. U.S. Army troop strength in Japan reached a peak of 385,649 by December 1945.

Occupation forces worked fast and hard to feed hungry millions, erect new homes and factories, rebuild railroads and bridges and other infrastructures. By late 1948, most of the rubble was gone, and a new Japan was rising from the ashes.

Humanitarian activities — such as sponsoring orphanages — conducted by the average GI received virtually no public acknowledgement. Elliott Thorpe, chief of Counterintelligence in Japan, wrote: "Arriving in Japan fresh from the fighting field, these men [first wave of GIs who came in late summer 1945] showed a dignity and restraint that is hard to describe. They showed in their demeanor and action this was a time for a course of conduct that would help bring lasting peace to a worn-out people."

Phase II of the occupation was characterized mostly by political, economic and agricultural gains. With the "state of hostilities" officially declared over Dec. 31, 1946, only GIs on guard duty and in training remained armed. But sometimes the phases overlapped.

One of the few armed actions by the U.S. Army occurred in late 1947 when a large body of Koreans tried to take over the local government in Osaka. Gen. Eichelberger dispatched a regiment immediately to quell the disorder.

GIs also found caches of weapons, tanks in caves, artillery pieces hidden, and huge stocks of buried ammo when a local commander had not

Far East Occupation

Army and Marine divisions that served on occupation duty:

Japan

Americal	41st Infantry
1st Cavalary	43rd Infantry
2nd Marine	45th Infantry
5th Marine	77th Infantry
7th Infantry	81st Infantry
11th Airborne	97th Infantry
24th Infantry	98th Infantry
25th Infantry	**Korea**
27th Infantry	6th Infantry
32nd Infantry	7th Infantry
33rd Infantry	40th Infantry

Note: Fifth Air Force and numerous Navy ships also served in Japan. Though not technically considered occupation duty because the nations involved were Allies, divisions also served, after the surrender, in the Philippines (31st, 37th, 38th, 86th, 93rd and 96th) and North China (1st and 6th Marine.) The 3rd Marine Division was remained on Guam until Dec. 31, 1945.

Japan: For service between Sept. 3, 1945, and April 27, 1952. Service between Sept. 3, 1945, and March 2, 1946, is counted only if the Asiatic-Pacific Campaign Medal was awarded for service prior to Sept. 3, 1945. Time is not counted in eligibility if that time meets the requirements of the Korean Service Medal (1950–54).

Korea: For service between Sept. 3, 1945, and June 29, 1949. Service between Sept. 3, 1945, and March 2, 1946, is counted only if the Asiatic-Pacific Campaign Medal was awarded for service prior to Sept. 3, 1945.

Asiatic-Pacific Area: For duty between Sept. 2, 1945, and April 27, 1952, on shore or on ships in Japanese territories and in part of Korea and adjacent Korean islands. Service from June 27, 1950, determined to be eligible for the Korean Service Medal is not creditable toward the Navy Occupation Medal. The Navy Occupation Medal is not awarded for any service for which another medal is authorized, except as specified.

Navy Occupation Service Medal

Army Occupation Medal

turned them over to the Allied forces. One of the most amazing finds occurred in 1947 when the 5th Cavalry Regiment went on maneuvers on Chiba Prefecture, a thumb-like extension of land over the northern tip of Tokyo Bay. They found an entire balloon-bomb launching site, from which bombs had been sent up to fly over the Pacific and hit the U.S. Pacific Northwest. Troops had a field day blowing the whole place to bits.

Phase III, from 1949 to 1952, was mostly administrative. When the Korean War erupted in June 1950, only four divisions were stationed in Japan: 1st Cav, 24th, 25th and 7th Infantry. Those divisions were sent to Korea, and Japan became a staging area and medical base for American wounded. On April 27, 1952, U.S. occupation of Japan ended.

Eventually, the U.S. gave Japan about $1 billion dollars in aid, food, and supplies. This did not include $100 million worth of Army supplies donated to help the Japanese during the terrible winters of 1945 and 1946. And who can calculate the countless acts of individual kindness.

Perhaps the greatest tribute to GIs was paid by Edwin O. Reischauer, famed Asian scholar and former ambassador to Japan: "It is hard to imagine a conquering army that could have undertaken the physical and spiritual rehabilitation of the erstwhile enemy with greater good will and deeper sincerity."

An honor guard fires a salute as the body of a Marine is buried at sea.
U.S. Navy

'Invasion Without Gunfire': Occupation of Korea

When combat-seasoned GIs landed in Korea only a week after the official surrender of Japan, they soon found themselves "in the midst of a sullen and even hostile population," according to author Charles M. Dobbs, and "came to sense another source of hostility as well: the Russian occupation troops in the north."

Soldiers of the XXIV Corps (6th, 7th and 40th Infantry divisions), formerly based on Okinawa, were delegated the duty of carrying out the confused occupation of Korea. Eventually totalling 72,360 troops, the corps' leadership treated the landing at Inchon on Sept. 8–10, 1945, as an "invasion without gunfire."

After the wild outpourings of emotion in Seoul and the initial euphoria of liberation wore off, the Koreans saw the Americans as unwanted occupiers. Nevertheless, the men went about their jobs with little direction and in understrength units.

Within a few months of V-J Day, the battle-hardened corps had dwindled to a force of 45,000, many of them green draftees; and the 40th Division had returned to California. Remaining personnel were spread thinly.

The 6th Infantry Division occupied the southern half of the U.S. zone and was based in Pusan. The northern sector was covered by the 7th Infantry Division with headquarters in Seoul. Seoul itself was garrisoned by the 7th's 31st Infantry Regiment; the 17th Regiment handled the countryside; and the 32nd Regiment patrolled the 38th parallel.

Comprising only 5,000 men, the 32nd was responsible for 150 miles of hostile frontier. Dr. Clinton E. Berryhill of Williamsburg, Iowa, then an 18-year-old with the regiment during 1947, recalls: "I was a scout, sniper and squad leader in the Intelligence & Reconnaissance Platoon of the 32nd's HQ Company based in Seoul. The regiment was grossly understrength, and living conditions were primitive. Russians broadcast they would wipe us out. We were ready to fight, but thankfully war never came then."

Says Richard Stinson, who served with C Battery, 48th Field Artillery Battalion, 7th Division, in 1948–49, "Infantrymen manned checkpoints and road 'shotgun' on trains that were sometimes ambushed. After Korea was officially granted independence on Aug. 15, 1948, North Korean infiltrators — known as 'green arm bandits' — became even a greater problem."

U.S. troops began withdrawing from Korea in September 1948. In December of that year, the Truman Administration decided to leave only one combat unit there. The newly formed 5th Regimental Combat Team, 7,500 men-strong, was selected. It finally set sail for Hawaii on June 30, 1949.

"It seems as though we are the forgotten men who served our country at a time and place we were needed," laments veteran Al Hall of South Dakota. Adds Stinson, "Back in Washington, the brass's eyes were focused on Berlin and occupied Germany, we were forgotten."

Pvt. Oduel Fruge and Pvt. Robert Shropshire, members of the 31st Infantry, 7th Infantry Division, man a .30-caliber machine gun in guarding the dividing line above Chunchon, Korea, during the occupation in 1946.
U.S. Army

A U.S. Military Guard stands at attention in front of Tuk Soo Palace in Seoul, Korea, where American and Soviet officials came to an impasse in 1949 with Korean officials over free elections vs. Communist control.
U.S. Army

Plight of the POWs

"To be a prisoner of the Japanese was like being caught in a 20th century version of the Black Plague, a Yellow Death," wrote Gavan Daws, author of *Prisoners of the Japanese*. A more graphic and concise summation of the Allied POW experience in Asia and the Pacific would be hard to come by. When Wake Island and Guam fell in December 1941, the first of 25,600 American prisoners of war were captured in the Pacific Theater. By war's end, 34 percent were dead.

When the *USS Houston* was sunk on Feb. 28, 1942, during the Battle of the Sunda Strait, some 368 survivors made it to shore but were quickly captured by Japanese forces and taken to a former Dutch army camp in Batavia, now Djakarta. They ended up in Burma.

American servicemen trapped on the Bataan Peninsula and nearby Corregidor Island in the Philippines were force-marched, then loaded onto rail cars for internment at Camp O'Donnell near Tarlac or on to the massive POW camp at Cabanatuan, 75 miles north of Manila. Some 22,000, or 85 percent, of U.S. POWs in the Pacific were taken in the islands.

Three years later, during the massive bombing raids over Japan in 1945, American airmen were shot down and taken prisoner. These and thousands of other "guests of the emperor" were condemned to a living hell.

Conditions at the various camps depended on the country and period of the war. But they were all universally deplorable.

At Camp O'Donnell, originally built to train Filipino soldiers, prisoners arrived by railroad cars packed like sardines in a can. Pvt. Robert Body, a machine gunner with the 31st Infantry on Bataan, recalled being loaded onto a train and transported to Capos station, then on to O'Donnell: "We had to stand in the oven-like interior, for there was no room to move. As the train moved, we felt we were suffocating. Many died. They remained upright in death, for we were packed in like sardines and they couldn't fall."

Survivors of the *USS Houston*, along with members of the 2nd Bn. (the "Lost Battalion"), 131st Field Artillery Regt., 36th Div. (Texas National Guard), became slave laborers on the "railroad of death" — the Burma-Thailand Railway — from 1942–45. Of the 668 Americans consigned to the railway, 133 died. Another 12,267 Allied prisoners perished there. Reckoned one historian, "Each mile of the 'Railroad of Death' was paid for with lives of 64 Allied POWs, and 240 coolie slaves."

Conditions in the isolated camps along the railway route were horrendous. "They slept on filth-encrusted floors overrun with vermin," noted Daws. "Open drainage ditches served as toilets and soon overflowed. Rice, their staple, was often rotten and contained rat droppings and little white

Many prisoners of war at Camp O'Donnell in the Philippines held a bleak outlook following the torturous Bataan Death March. Survivors told how the enemy would rifle their pockets and in rough English shout, "Go you to hell." National Archives

"

To be a prisoner of the Japanese was like being caught in a 20th century version of the Black Plague, a Yellow Death.

"

— GAVAN DAWS
Author, *Prisoners of the Japanese*

Typically, POWs during the infamous "Death March" had their hands tied behind them and were tortured or beaten along the way by Japanese troops referred to as the "Buzzard Battalions." One survivor reported, "The Japanese would lean out of passing trucks and hit us with their rifle butts. They seemed to particularly pick on guys wearing steel helmets." National Archives

worms similar to common maggots." Of the food, Raymond D. Reed, a medic (with the 131st Artillery), said, "It wasn't a matter of picking out anything. You just looked that ol' worm in the eye and chewed him up. The weevils you'd just drink down. You soon passed the picky stage. It was food."

To appease the persistent Red Cross, which attempted to check camp conditions, the Japanese later set up a "model camp" at Mukden in Manchuria.

"Prisoners who had served at other camps in Asia considered the Mukden camp to be one of the best," noted Brig. Gen. W. E. Brougher, interned there during the final months of the war. Yet it was no picnic; 236 American POWs died there at the rate of 12 percent.

"I was a POW at Mukden and other camps in Manchuria and can personally testify that conditions were harsh. The first winter we had more than 400 men die in camp. An Allied bomb fell on our camp, killing 18 men and wounding 32. Treatment only improved when the Japanese knew the war was lost in 1945," wrote Norman Pysher.

POWs relocated to camps in Japan were often paraded in the streets to be ridiculed and spat upon by women and children. And when U.S. bombers targeted Japanese cities, American POWs would be executed. After 558 planes struck Tokyo on May 24, 1945, 62 POWs in the local military prison were tortured and killed. American airmen were selected for especially brutal treatment, resulting in agonizing death.

"The torturers *par excellence* were the dreaded *Kempei Tai*, the Japanese counterpart of the Nazi Gestapo," wrote Edward Russell in the book *Knights of Bushido: The Shocking History of Japanese War Atrocities*. These Japanese military policemen tortured thousands of Allied prisoners, employing a variety of techniques such as removing fingernails with pliers. They also used the water cure, kendo sticks, iron bars, knotted ropes, wooden clubs, baseball bats and thumbscrews.

"No POW ever had enough rice to eat, but the *Kempei Tai* always had rice to spare for torture — they would force it down a prisoner's throat by the fistful, pour water into him by the gallon until he swelled up inside to bursting, then jump on his belly. POWs were forever short of cigarettes, but the *Kempei Tai* always had enough for burning ears and noses and eyes," wrote Australian author Daws.

Left: Though given little to eat and ravaged by disease, prisoners working on the "Railway of Death" were expected to do heavy labor. Those who couldn't pull their load were executed. This photo was taken by fellow prisoner George Aspinall, with a camera he kept hidden throughout his internment.
Courtesy of Tim Boden

Top: POWs from the infamous Burma-Thailand Railway camps were walking skeletons at the time of their release in August 1945. Some 133 Americans perished building the "railroad of death."
Courtesy of Otto Schwarz, *USS Houston* Survivors Association

In the spring of 1945, POWs at a camp in Japan pose for a photo shot with a pinhole camera made clandestinely by fellow prisoner Terence Kirk. The man in the center of the photo is too weak to stand alone, so he is supported by someone standing behind him. Courtesy of Terence Kirk

Even some Japanese regulars had a sadistic streak and made sport of watching POWs suffer. That was also true of the Korean guards employed in Southeast Asia.

Poor nutrition from the lack of food, combined with the tropical elements — extreme heat and humidity, disease-carrying mosquitoes and mites — created a breeding ground for diseases, which ran rampant through the camps. Without medicine, open sores soon festered. Injuries went untreated yet prisoners struggled to continue working, knowing those who could not perform heavy labor were deemed useless and thus killed.

Despite such deplorable conditions, few Allied prisoners even attempted to escape. "Of all white prisoners, one in three died in captivity at the hands of the Japanese, starved to death, worked to death, beaten to death, dead of loathsome epidemic diseases that the Japanese would not treat," noted Daws.

"Even so, the prisoners stayed and took it. For them the stakes were: try to escape, with the chances of suffering and dying about a hundred percent, or stay, with what turned out to be a two-to-one chance of surviving," wrote Daws. "The final gross score was: died trying to escape, next to none; died as prisoners, tens of thousands."

Japanese doctors used POWs as guinea pigs — the term was *maruta*, meaning "logs of wood" — for a variety of pseudo-experiments. Severing an artery and draining all the blood, vivisections and amputations without anesthetics were among the sickening experiments. The most notorious experiments were performed by the infamous Unit 731 at Harbin, Manchuria: the "Japanese Auschwitz." Also, at Kyushu University in Japan, eight U.S. airmen were dissected alive in May 1945 in grotesque experiments.

Prisoners were often herded onto transports that unknowingly became targets for Allied planes and submarines. According to Japanese figures,

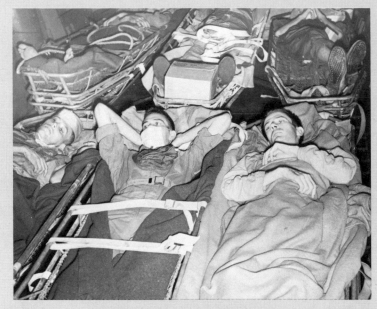

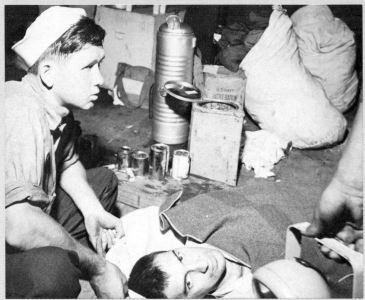

"

They put us in the hold of an old flat-bottomed ship that had been used to haul cattle. It was a 62-day trip, and it was holy hell! We were made to kneel, and your knees were in some-body else's back, and somebody else's knees were in your back.

There were no sanitary facilities whatsoever. You cannot imagine or comprehend what it's like for approxi-mately 250 men to crowd into an area this small. You get seasick; the dysentery is rampant; there's no food or water, no fresh air.

There was complete chaos down in the hold. From time to time you could hear the pings from the sonar of American submarines bouncing off the hull of the ship. Those subs were shadowing our convoy, and daily you could hear torpedoes hitting those ships.

Of course, we were below water level, and the sound would carry, and it would seem like the torpedo had hit right next to us. I guess we were fortunate that this old scow was so sorry that it wasn't a decent war prize.

"

— PVT. J. L. "JACK" GUILES
Headquarters Squadron
Far East Air Forces

Top left: U.S. prisoners of war detained at the Omori Prison Camp in Japan and too weak to walk on their own were carried by litter to U.S. hospital ships following their release in August 1945. U.S. Navy

Middle left: A Navy corpsman tends to an American prisoner released from the Omori Prison Camp in Japan in August 1945. National Archives

Bottom left: Allied POWs at the Omori Prison Camp at the war's end in August 1945. National Archives

Above: Hundreds of American, English and Dutch prisoners at Omori Prison Camp in Japan cheer for their U.S. Navy liberators. The makeshift sign on the roof instructs Army Air Forces' pilots where to drop relief supplies. National Archives

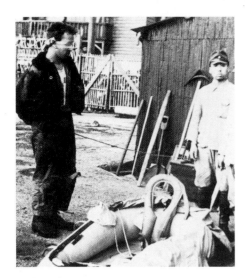

After his plane was shot down over Japan, a blindfolded American flier is "put on display" in Kobe with his inflatable raft and life vest.
Courtesy Mainichi Shimbun, Tokyo

"

American planes started coming over the Tokyo area around the first of November. After this, the bombing raids began to increase in intensity and frequency. I was between Tokyo and Yokohama and got a chance to see many of these raids. "Evidently our bombers, which were big babies used Mount Fuji as their gathering point before making their run on Tokyo. We weren't allowed to watch, but when the Japs hit the ground we sneaked little looks.

"

—STAFF SGT. JAMES CAVANAUGH
American POW at Subcamp No.2
Kawasaki, Japan

about 25 ships carrying POWs were bombed or torpedoed. Of the 50,000 POWs they shipped, 10,800 died at sea.

One of the worst disasters at sea involved the transport *Arisan Maru*, with 1,802 prisoners aboard. It left the Philippines on Oct. 21, 1944, and was torpedoed three days later. Only eight prisoners survived. Crammed below decks, POWs were trapped with no way out. Those who managed to escape were often shot in the water.

Outright atrocities were commonplace, too. On Wake Island, for instance, Japanese guards massacred 96 U.S. prisoners on the beach during the first week of October 1943, then fled.

On Palawan, an island in the south Philippines, soldiers of the 186th Regimental Combat Team, 41st Inf. Div., made a grisly discovery in February 1945, at a camp near Puerto Princera. Remains of 150 American POWs were found in two incinerated air-raid shelters. POWs who managed to escape the massacre, were sheltered by guerrillas, and told of the atrocity, which occurred in December 1944.

As Allied forces continued to drive the Japanese back toward the home islands, Tokyo sent out orders concerning the 100,000 Allied prisoners: "It is the aim to annihilate them all and not leave any traces."

Orders given at Taihoku prison on Formosa stated: "Whether they are destroyed individually or in groups, or however it is done, with mass bombing, poisonous smoke, poisons, drowning, decapitation, or what, dispose of the prisoners as the situation dictates. In any case it is the aim not to allow the escape of a single one, to annihilate them all, and not to leave any traces," according to the Japanese headquarters journal.

Even the emperor's demand to surrender after the second atomic blast over Nagasaki could not save hundreds of Allied POWs, who were executed by their humiliated captors in final acts of brutality in August 1945.

"After the emperor spoke, the last five [downed American airmen] were taken to a military cemetery [in Osaka]. Three were shot, two beheaded. The same day, hours into the peace, Japanese officers at Fukuoka on Kyushu took their samurai swords, and chopped 16 airmen to death. And it was 12 days after the emperor's broadcast before the Japanese at Ranau on Borneo killed the last 30 of their surviving prisoners," Daws noted.

Of the 132,134 documented Allied prisoners — Dutch, Australian, English and American — 35,756 died while in captivity. "In German prison camps, the POW death rate was only 4 percent," wrote Daws. "In Japanese prison camps, it was 27 percent. The American rate was higher, 34 percent."

On Sept. 23, 1945, the Japanese turned over urns containing the ashes of 2,600 Allied POWs, closing the curtain on this aspect of the Pacific war. Or so they thought.

After the war, American POWs received all back pay, but they had to fight for disability ratings from the Veterans Administration. What the POWs wanted most and have yet to receive are reparations payments and apologies from the Japanese.

Behind Bamboo: American POWs in the Pacific

Estimated number captured, died and returned to U.S. control

Captured by Country		
	Philippines	22,000
	Wake Island	1,555
	Java (Indonesia)	890
	Guam	400
	Japan & elsewhere	300
	Celebes (Indonesia)	255
	China	200
		25,600
Killed or Died in Captivity by Country	Philippines	5,135
	On prison ships	3,840
	Japan	1,200
	Manchuria (China)	175
	Burma	130
	Wake Island	100
	Korea	70
		10,650
POWs Liberated by Country	Japan	11,400
	Philippines	1,500
	Manchuria (China)	1,200
	Burma-Thailand	480
	Celebes (Indonesia)	200
	Korea	150
	China	20
		14,950

Source: *Surrender and Survival: The Experience of American POWs in the Pacific, 1941-1945* by E. Bartlett Kerr (N.Y., William Morrow & Co., 1985, pp. 339-40)

> "
> *Nagoya was devastated with fire bombs in March of 1945. It seemed that the bomb run was right over our camp. All night they came over. Music to our ears. They must have been no more than 500 feet off the ground. The city was burned to the ground. We didn't go to work for a long time because the steel mill had been crippled. They also didn't want us to see the destruction. And oh God, the stench of all those dead bodies was horrible.*
> "
>
> — SGT. RALPH LEVENBERG
> POW at Narumi Subcamp No. 2
> Nagoya, Japan

"I would like Japan to render an apology for the atrocities they rendered upon their enemies," said Ralph Levenberg, head of special projects for the American Defenders of Bataan and Corregidor. He was a POW from April 1942 to August 1945.

"We were treated very inhumanely. We were the victims of the most atrocious treatment known to mankind. The basis of our petition [submitted to the United Nations Human Rights Commission in 1995] is that we prisoners were forced into slave labor and exposed to atrocious treatment."

To date, the Japanese have refused to issue any apology. They claim that by signing the Treaty of Peace on Sept. 8, 1951 — which ended all war claims against Japan on March 31, 1952, and allowed Allied countries to seize Japanese assets to settle war claims — they are not obligated, financially or morally, to compensate Allied POWs.

Tokyo on Trial: War Crimes Exposed

Within days after Japan's surrender, Hideki Tojo summoned his doctor and asked exactly where his heart was. (Some Americans would probably say that Tojo — former Japanese prime minister — didn't have a heart.)

The doctor marked his patient's chest at exactly the right spot with black paint. Knowing he would soon be arrested, Tojo planned to shoot himself rather than be arrested for his crimes and didn't want to botch his own suicide. He would not be paraded before a military tribunal and humiliated simply because Japan had the unfortunate fate of losing the war.

In mid-September 1945, as American military policemen surrounded his house with press photographers in tow, someone shouted out, "Tell this yellow bastard we've waited long enough. Bring him out." But a shot rang out from inside the house and Tojo slumped to the floor, blood pulsing from his chest. Beside him was a U.S. handgun.

MPs rushed in and photographers shot the dramatic scene, with some onlookers callously dipping pieces of paper in the pooled blood, for souvenirs. But Tojo, as it turned out, was a poor shot and after being rushed to the hospital, was pumped with transfusions and peniccillin. Two months later, on Dec. 8, he was deemed well enough to be moved to the Sagamo Prison in Tokyo, where other war criminals were being housed.

Tojo was considered an A Class war criminal, a designation for Japanese leaders who had conspired to wage aggressive war. Specifically, he had ordered that food be denied any prisoners who could not work. He knew this would lead to mass brutalities such as those that occurred on the Bataan Death March. The International Military Tribunal of the Far East (IMTFE) was set up in Tokyo to handle A Class criminals.

By April 1946, 28 Japanese leaders were indicted for crimes against humanity and peace, murder and other more conventional wrongdoings. Though public outrage in the West demanded that the emperor also be put on trial (a June 1945 Gallop poll showed 70 percent of Americans favored executing the monarch), leaders in the U.S. felt that doing so would incite the Japanese people, requiring additional occupation troops to quell any rebellion.

According to Gavin Daws, Australian author of *Prisoners of the Japanese: POWs of World War II in the Pacific*, "Twenty-five of these A Class criminals were convicted and sentenced, 7 of them to death, 16 to life. (Two had died in prison.) 5,700-plus B and C Class criminals were brought to trial, about 3,000 were convicted and sentenced; 920 were executed."

Two prominent criminals sentenced to die were Yamashita Tomoyuki — the "Tiger of Malaya" — and Homma Masaharu, commander of Japanese troops in the Philippines during the Bataan Death March and the brutalities that followed at Cabanatuan and Camp O'Donnell. Yamashita was sentenced to death by hanging, while Homma was executed by a firing squad (considered a more honorable way to die).

Ironically, while imprisoned and awaiting the conclusion of his own trial, Tojo required dental work. A U.S. Navy dentist provided new upper

dentures, but not until he engraved "Remember Pearl Harbor" in Morse Code on them.

On Dec. 23, 1948 — more than seven years after the Japanese attack on Pearl Harbor — Hideki Tojo was hanged, along with three other criminals. Today, at the Yasukuni Shrine in Tokyo, the spirits of these war criminals are worshiped as deities.

Secondary criminals, B and C Class, were put on trial for ordering, or committing crimes, or allowing them to occur without intervening. Some 2,200 tribunals in Singapore, Indonesia, China, the Marshall Islands, the Philippines, Guam and elsewhere, between 1945 and 1951 tried these prisoners in the countries where the atrocities occurred.

"As for specific crimes in the B and C categories, the Allies developed a list of more than 300,000 and they stopped only because they had to stop somewhere," Daws noted.

All the Allied tribunals were important for what they showed the public regarding the potential consequences of a protracted conflict with Japan. Though barely remembered, they certainly should be.

"The 14 months I spent as a member of Gen. MacArthur's staff investigating Japanese war crimes committed in the Philippines during the course of the war showed me in horrible, unforgettable detail what could well have happened to members of an invasion force on Japanese soil and to American prisoners," wrote former Marine Louis L. Goldstein.

★ ★ ★

American prosecutors and defense counsellors in Yokohama talk with Japanese prisoners who were accused of war crimes. Of the more than 5,700 B and C Class criminals brought to trial, 3,000 were sentenced and 920 executed. U.S. Army

The International Military Tribunal of the Far East (IMTFE), chartered Jan. 19, 1946, was set up in Tokyo to handle A Class criminals. Judgments were not handed down until Nov. 4, 1948: 25 criminals were convicted with seven being sentenced to death. Dept. of Defense

Pacific Produced Five Presidents

Five American Presidents served as junior naval officers during WWII in the Pacific Theater.

John F. Kennedy was the skipper of *PT-109*, a torpedo boat that harassed enemy transports and warships in "The Slot" off Guadalcanal in 1943. That Aug. 2, the *PT-109* was rammed by a Japanese destroyer. With the injured in tow, Kennedy and the surviving crewmen swam to a nearby island. To evade enemy patrols, the *PT-109* crew hid on other islands until they were rescued.

Kennedy returned to PT boats two months later, but malaria and recurring back problems forced him to leave the Navy in December 1944.

Lyndon B. Johnson was a U.S. representative from Texas when the attack on Pearl Harbor occurred. As a Naval Reserve officer, he asked President Roosevelt for permission to be activated, which was granted a week after war was declared. By May 1942, Johnson was on Fiji as a naval inspector. He flew on one bombing mission aboard the B-26 *Heckling Hare* on June 9 over New Guinea.

Roosevelt decided, on July 1, 1942, that Johnson and all members of Congress serving in the military would be more useful on Capitol Hill: Johnson was back there by July 16.

Richard M. Nixon served as an operations officer with the South Pacific Combat Air Transport Command on New Caledonia in 1943. Later, wanting to be closer to the fight-

John F. Kennedy (President, 1961–63) commanded PT-109 in the South Pacific. While operating in the Solomons Islands, his torpedo boat was rammed by a Japanese destroyer on Aug. 2, 1943. Kennedy and surviving crew members swam to a nearby island and were eventually rescued.

Courtesy John F. Kennedy Library, Boston.

Lyndon B. Johnson, future President from 1964–68, became the first congressman to join the military after Pearl Harbor. President Roosevelt sent him to the Solomons as the President's personal observer.

Courtesy Lyndon Baines Johnson Library, Austin, Texas.

ing, he was transferred to Bougainville in the Solomans, where he endured frequent air raids by enemy bombers. He was discharged in March 1946.

Gerald R. Ford joined the Navy in 1942 and was assigned to the light aircraft carrier *USS Monterey* as a navigation officer and physical training director.

The *Monterey* saw action in the Gilbert Islands, Marshalls, Carolines and Marianas. During a typhoon, on Dec. 18, 1944, Ford was blown overboard but landed on a catwalk. Several other crewmen were killed and virtually all of the *Monterey's* planes were damaged in the typhoon.

Ford was discharged from the Navy in February 1946.

George Bush was just 18 when he became the youngest Navy pilot in WWII, flying an Avenger torpedo-bomber. He joined June 12, 1942, against his father's wishes.

Bush was assigned to the light carrier *USS San Jacinto*, which was part of *Task Force 58*. His unit was VT-51 Torpedo Squadron attached to U.S. Fifth Fleet.

Bush was twice forced to ditch at sea, once immediately after take-off from the *San Jac* and another time after being hit by anti-aircraft fire over ChiChi Jima Island in the Bonin Islands. He would fly 58 combat missions by the time his time overseas ended in December 1944.

Gerald R. Ford, destined to become President in 1974, served aboard the light carrier *USS Monterey* when it caught fire from planes bursting into flames on its deck during a typhoon in December 1944.

Courtesy Gerald R. Ford Library, Ann Arbor, Michigan.

While operating a rest camp for fatigued aviators on Bougainville, Navy Lt. Cmdr. Richard M. Nixon was away from his tent when it was destroyed during an air raid. As a Quaker, Nixon could have avoided service, but he volunteered and requested combat duty. Nixon was chief executive from 1969–74.

Courtesy Ed Printiss Photography, Whittier, California.

George Bush, later to become President in 1988, was at 18 the youngest man flying in the Navy during WWII. He was rescued at sea after his torpedo bomber was shot down by the Japanese fire in 1944.

Courtesy National Archives

In Your Own Words

Personal accounts of action on Land, at Sea and in the Air

> Suddenly the hill rocked under us. There was a roar to the left, to the right, and then several back to our rear. The Japs had moved the field guns into position around us on Cabcaben Field.
>
> 'Why the dirty bastards!' the man next to me said. 'They're using us as a shield to fire on Corregidor.' It was true. We should have realized then what to expect as their prisoners.
>
> A flight of enemy bombers were flying over Corregidor. Our officers cautioned us not to watch them because if our anti-aircraft fire hit any of them we would cheer in spite of ourself. Our chief worry was, would Corregidor return fire on the guns that surrounded us?

— CPL. HUBERT GATER
200th Coast Artillery (AA)
Bataan

Liberation of Manila

I was a 15-year-old civilian POW in Old Bilibid Prison, Manila and was one of a few fortunate internees to have had an eyewitness, over-the-wall spectacular view of American tanks rumbling down Quezon Boulevard the evening of Feb. 3, 1945. When we initially viewed the tanks, we became speechless. Our hearts stopped. The tanks came to an abrupt halt.

The entrenched Japs, located in the Far Eastern University (also Philippine Kempetai secret police headquarters) across the street from Bilibid, suddenly opened fire on the tanks. Bright horizontal white streaks flashed to our left and toward the tanks. Those tanks made an immediate response with brilliant red-orange-white streaks from their mighty guns toward the university and accompanied with deafening and earth-shaking *whomps!* A big chunk of the entire corner of the two story structure was blown to bits! Thus, we realized those tanks were *American*. Hot dogs! Yippee! and Hallelujah! The Americans had come at last and our liberation occurred the following morning, Feb. 4, 1945.

For 50 years, I have wondered the identity of those brave GIs who actually drove those beautiful tanks as the spearhead thrust into Manila, south on Quezon Boulevard, as it intersects with Azcarraga and Espana streets at the corner of Old Bilibid Prison.

A heartfelt *thank you* to all those courageous, wonderful GIs from Manila to Berlin whose devotion to their country made our *freedom* possible.

God Bless You All!! and God Bless America!

— BETSY HEROLD HEIMKE
Civilian Internee

Incoming!

We had heard of, but never saw, such a display of force before. LCI (Landing Craft, Infantry) equipped with rockets were in close, sending salvo after salvo ashore. Then the destroyers were pounding away, working close to the beach. The cruisers were next hammering away. Farther back were the battleships firing over our heads. Each projectile had a sound of its own. Some thundered, others screamed, still others whispered as they passed over.

Our ringside seat had a price though . . . we were next. A half mile from the beach the water was red with blood. We were cautioned to keep our heads down. That order was unnecessary. It was raining artillery and mortar shells, and heavy machine gun bullets. The closer to the beach we got, the harder it was to see where we were going, because the shells filled the air with spraying water laced with shrapnel.

— HOMER E. DRAUGHN
A Battery, 1st Battalion
11th Marine Regiment
1st Marine Division

Occupation of Japan

References to those units of the military that were awarded the Army of Occupation Medal by Gen. Douglas MacArthur on May 1, 1947, unfortunately did not include those military forces that had fought the long, hard war against Japan up from Australia, New Guinea, and the Philippine Islands and Okinawa. I know, since I was on Okinawa at Motobu Airstrip just before the atom bombs were dropped on Nagasaki and Hiroshima.

Our aircraft at that time were lined up wing-tip to wing-tip and nose-to-tail by the hundreds all loaded with fuel dripping from the wing tank vents and bomb bays fully loaded — A-20s, A-26s, B-25s, etc. We were scheduled as a part of the massive military invasion force to bring Japan to her knees. Our assignment to take Atsugi Airport north of Tokyo and secure it with .30 caliber carbines while we turned the aircraft around for fast reprisals against any further resistance.

I would not now have been writing this letter if this had occurred, because of the anticipated casualties. However, we did go in as an occupation force and we landed at Wakayama Beach at 4 a.m. Japan time in early November of 1945. We were stationed near Takarazuka in the dormitory of a munitions factory. We were not awarded the Army of Occupation Medal since most of us returned to the states for the Christmas holiday.

— CPL. SEYMOUR WOFSEY
Aircraft Serviceman
30th Air Service Squadron
Fifth Air Force

Rescued Twice — By a Football Player

After the bombardment stopped we made the landing on Morotai in the Molucca or Spice Islands [Indonesia] on Sept. 15, 1944, but I was only 5-foot-three inches short and so when I stepped off the landing craft the water was over my head. I reached up for help and this big sergeant — a football player from Fordham — told me to grab onto his back and he'd carry me in. Once ashore I didn't see him again.

A few months later I'm making the landing at Lingayen Gulf and when I come off the damn boat again I'm in deep water and about to drown! I reach up for help and I end up grabbing this big sergeant again and he says, 'What the hell are you doing . . . making a habit of this or what!?'

— DANNY WAMBOLT
534th Amphibian Engineers
Engineer Boat & Shore Regiment

Danny Wambolt displays a pair of machine guns on Morotai Island in the Moluccas (now part of Indonesia) during September 1944. U.S. Army

"

Playfully, we went downtown. I must have looked like a mangy dog. I saw a Korean woman barber and on the spur of the moment I decided to get a shave and haircut. We hadn't seen a woman for a long time. I also hadn't been in a barbershop and it seemed, oh so wonderful, to lie back in that chair. When I saw her razor I was a little hesitant. It was a hacksaw blade which had been fashioned into a razor. But the guys urged me on, so I let her get at me. She shaved between my eyebrows, my cheeks, and my chin. Afterward, my face was one sore mess. It was awful, but I was happy.

"

— PFC. LEE DAVIS
Divisional POW Camp
Jinsen, Korea

SEA

> 66
>
> *I was aboard the* USS Marathon *(APA-200) on July 22, 1945, when an explosion killed 37 men. Anchored in Buckner Bay, it took a torpedo from a kaiten — a Japanese one-man, suicide submarine. The men we lost were just 18 and 19 years old. I myself was only 18 and came so very close to dying that day, but it just was not my time.*
>
> 99
>
> — JIMMY BASYE
> USS *Marathon*
> Okinawa

The First Kamikaze Attack

The first *kamikaze* attack occurred during the first offensive action against the Japanese in the Marshall and Gilbert Islands.

In January 1942, two weeks after Pearl Harbor, the USS *Enterprise*, Adm. Halsey commanding, with the destroyer *Ralph Talbot* and other destroyers and cruisers, bombed and shelled those islands.

The Japanese sent over nine bombers wing-to-wing. The *Ralph Talbot* anti-aircraft fire hit the right wing bomber, which dropped out of formation, banking and smoking.

The combat air patrol came down through our anti-aircraft fire and shot down the rest of the bombers. The one the *Ralph* had hit was overlooked; it kept going in a slow circle and all of a sudden, it was approaching the carrier's stern.

The carrier started to turn, but the bomber crashed into the stern, cutting a parked plane in half and fell into the wake. A sailor on the carrier jumped into the rear cockpit and fired the machine guns into the wake.

From the Marshall and Gilberts we went to Wake Island and Marcus Island — 700 miles off Japan's coast. When we tied up at Pearl Harbor, we got a standing ovation from sailors and yard workers on the dock.

— DAVID W. GILMARTIN
Chief Machinist Mate
Ralph Talbot

Bagging Infiltrators at Peleliu

I was a rifleman aboard a rocket ship — USS LCI(G) 347 — in Flotilla 3, Group 8, Amphibious Forces of the Pacific Fleet, and recalled 'gaming' activity off the coast of Peleliu in the Palau Islands where the Japanese practiced infiltration methods during the night.

We would shoot at infiltrators running along the coral reefs in the early morning hours, using machine guns and cannons in the light of star shells lobbed by destroyers. We had great sport doing this. One morning we captured a Jap and had the Marines come pick him up. The Marine sarge said, 'If you get any more of these boogers, just shoot them and toss them over. Don't bother us with them.'

— CLYDE H. COLMAN
Marine Rifleman
LCI (G) 347
Peleliu, September 1945

The captain gave orders to move the ship up one length. No sooner had we done this than a shell hit exactly where we were sitting. They (the Japanese) were zeroed in on us.

We were bombarding in preparation for our troops' landing and their (Japanese) shells were splashing all around us. One of our lieutenants was pointing out toward the islands at artillery flashes when a shell exploded right off the front of our bow. It blew his arm off and wounded four other men.

— EDGAR EICHLER
Machinist Mate 3rd Class
USS *Bennion*

Atomic Bomb as Savior

One the day that Hiroshima was bombed, our crew flew a mission to another city in Japan. As we were leaving landfall, I was still in my position as central fire control gunner. I happened to look up and saw three B-29s heading into Japan at much higher altitude.

I called this in to the airplane commander, as was normal procedure. Our airplane commander ordered the navigator to make a note of the time and position the sighting.

When we were in the interrogation room after the mission, I reported this sighting to the intelligence officer. Our navigator backed me up. The intelligence officer didn't comment, but made a note.

I believe what I saw was the three B-29s heading into Hiroshima to drop the nuclear weapon. As we were leaving interrogation, we heard about the "atomic bomb." Our pilot remarked that he had heard that the bomb looked like a giant electric light bulb.

We thought the war was over, but were to fly one more mission. The day the treaty was signed, our crew — all of us — participated in the "show of power" mission over Tokyo Harbor. It was quite a day. About 500 B-29s flew over Tokyo and the harbor at 500 feet altitude!

I am one of the perhaps half million WWII veterans who believes his life may have been saved by using nuclear bombs. Many things could have happened between Sept. 2, 1945, and the second planned invasion of Japan in February 1946.

The Japanese, while no longer defending their country with fighter aircraft, to any extent, were still putting up tremendous defenses with antiaircraft fire. Then there were always midair collisions and explosions to contend with, not to mention mechanical malfunctions that could always take out an aircraft and its crew.

— MASTER SGT. MERLE E. BOUGES
B-29 crewman, 73rd Wing, Saipan

AIR

> 66
>
> *The operation over the Himalayan Mountains was known as the 'Hump' airlift. We flew that airlift over the highest mountains in the world, in good weather or bad, over large areas of territory inhabited by the enemy and by savage tribes, even headhunters, and with a confusing variety of planes.*
>
> 99

— LT. GEN. WILLIAM H. TUNNER
Commander General
Ferrying Division
Air Transport Command

CAMPAIGNS AND CASUALTIES

A Concise Reference Section

In Remembrance of Battle

Campaign Credits Awarded by Service

Asiatic-Pacific Campaign

Army/Army Air Forces

Philippine Islands	Dec. 7, 1941 – May 10, 1942
Burma, 1942	Dec. 7, 1941 – May 26, 1942
Central Pacific	Dec. 7, 1941 – Dec. 6, 1943
East Indies	Jan. 1 – July 22, 1942
India-Burma	April 2, 1942 – Jan. 28, 1945
Air Offensive, Japan	April 17, 1942 – Sept. 2, 1945
Aleutian Islands	June 3, 1942 – Aug. 24, 1943
China Defensive	July 4, 1942 – May 4, 1945
Papua	July 23, 1942 – Jan. 23, 1943
Guadalcanal	Aug. 7, 1942 – Feb. 21, 1943
New Guinea	Jan. 24, 1943 – Dec. 31, 1944
Northern Solomons	Feb. 22, 1943 – Nov. 21, 1944
Eastern Mandates	Jan. 31 – June 14, 1944
Bismarck Archipelago	Dec. 15, 1943 – Nov. 27, 1944
Western Pacific	June 15, 1944 – Sept. 2, 1945
Leyte	Oct. 17, 1944 – July 1, 1945
Luzon	Dec. 15, 1944 – July 4, 1945
Central Burma	Jan. 29 – July 15, 1945
Southern Philippines	Feb. 27 – July 4, 1945
Ryukyus	March 26 – July 2, 1945
China Offensive	May 5 – Sept. 2, 1945

Navy/Coast Guard

Pearl Harbor-Midway
Wake Island
Philippine Islands operation
Netherlands East Indies engagements
Pacific raids (1942)
Coral Sea
Midway
Guadalcanal-Tulagi landings
Capture and defense of Guadalcanal
Makin raid
Eastern Solomons
Buin-Faisi-Tonolai raid
Cape Esperance
Santa Cruz Islands
Gaudalcanal (Third Savo)
Tassafaronga
Eastern New Guinea operation
Rennel Island
Consolidation of Solomon Islands
Aleutians operation
New Georgia Group operation
Bismarck Archipelago operation
Pacific raids (1943)
Treasury-Bougainville operation
Gilbert Islands operation
Marshall Islands operation

Asiatic-Pacific raids (1944)
Western New Guinea operations
Marianas operation
Western Caroline Islands operation
Leyte operation
Luzon operation
Iwo Jima operation
Okinawa Gunto operation
Third Fleet operations against Japan

Kurile Islands operation
Borneo operations
Tinian capture and occupation
Consolidation of the Southern Philippines
Hollandia operation
Manila Bay-Bicol operations
Escort, anti-submarine, armed guard and
    special operations
Submarine War Patrols (Pacific)

Marine Corps

Pearl Harbor-Midway	Dec. 7, 1941
Guam	Dec. 8–10, 1941
Wake Island	Dec. 8–23, 1941
Bataan and Corregidor (Philippines)	Dec. 8, 1941 – May 6, 1942
Battle of Badoeng Strait (East Indies)	Feb. 19, 1942
Battle of the Coral Sea	May 4 – 8, 1942
Battle of Midway	June 3 – 6, 1942
Guadalcanal-Tulagi Landings	Aug. 7 – 9, 1942
First Savo Battle (Naval-Air)	Aug. 9, 1942
Capture and Defense of Guadalcanal	Aug. 10, 1942 – Feb. 8, 1943
Makin Island Raid (Gilberts)	Aug. 17 – 18, 1942
Battle of the Eastern Solomons	Aug. 23 – 25, 1942
Battle of Cape Esperance (Naval)	Oct. 11 – 12, 1942
Battle of Santa Cruz Island (Air)	Oct. 26, 1942
Battle of Guadalcanal (Naval-Air)	Nov. 11 – 15, 1942
Battle of Tassafaronga (Naval)	Nov. 30 – Dec. 1, 1942
Battle of Komandorski Island (Aleutians)	March 26, 1943

New Georgia Group

New Georgia-Rendova-Vandunu Occupation	June 20 – Aug. 31, 1943
Battle of Kula Gulf (Naval)	July 5 – 6, 1943
Battle of Kolombangara (Naval)	July 12 – 13, 1943
Vella Lavella Occupation	Aug. 15 – Oct. 16, 1943
Cape Gloucester (New Britain) Operation	Dec. 26, 1943 – March 1, 1944
Green Islands Landing	Feb. 15 – 19, 1944

Treasury-Bougainville Operation

Treasury Island Landing	Oct. 27 – Nov. 6, 1943
Choiseul Island Diversion	Oct. 28 – Nov. 4, 1943
Occupation and Defense of Cape Torokina	Nov. 1 – Dec. 15, 1943
Tarawa Operation (Gilbert Islands)	Nov. 20 – Dec. 8, 1943
Occupation of Kwajalein and Majuro Atolls (Marshall Islands)	Jan. 31 – Feb. 8, 1944
Occupation of Eniwetok Atoll (Marshall Islands)	Feb. 17 – March 2, 1944
Capture and Occupation of Saipan	June 15 – Aug. 10, 1944
Capture and Occupation of Guam	July 21 – Aug. 15, 1944
Capture and Occupation of Tinian	July 24 – Aug. 10, 1944
Capture and Occupation of Peleliu	Sept. 15 – Oct. 14, 1944
Leyte (Philippines) Landings	Oct. 20, 1944
Battle of Leyte Gulf (Naval Air)	Oct. 24 – 26, 1944
Iwo Jima Operation	Feb. 19 – March 16, 1945
Assault and Occupation of Okinawa Gunto	April 1 – June 21, 1945

Asiatic-Pacific Campaign Medal

Established on Nov. 6, 1942, it was awarded to all officers and enlisted men of the U.S. armed forces who, between Dec. 7, 1941, and March 2, 1946, served on active duty in the prescribed area or upon certain ships. Note: Though eligible, many ex-servicemen never actually received the medal.

Pacific Theater Battle Deaths by Campaign

Campaigns are listed in order of highest ground combat deaths.

★ U.S. Army

Campaign	Dates	Ground KIA	Air KIA	Total KIA	% of All KIA
Leyte/Luzon/S.P.I.[1]	17 Oct. 1944–4 July 1945	14,694	1,539	16,233	29.4%
Philippines	7 Dec. 1941–10 May 1942	10,460	3,387	13,847	25.1%
Ryukyus (Okinawa, Ie Shima, Keramarettos)	26 March–2 July 1945	4,700	18	4,718	8.5%
New Guinea	24 Jan. 1943–31 Dec. 1944	2,151	2,533	4,684	8.4%
Air Offensive (Japan)	17 April 1942–2 Sept. 1945		3,602	3,602	6.5%
Western Pacific[2] (Saipan, Guam, Marianas, Tinian, Palaus)	15 June 1944–2 Sept. 1945	2,141	925	3,066	5.5%
Burma/India	7 Dec. 1941–28 Jan. 1945	875	1,922	2,797	5.0%
Northern Solomons (New Georgia, Bougainville)	22 Feb. 1943–21 Nov. 1944	1,368	406	1,774	3.2%
Aleutians (Alaska)	3 June 1942–24 Aug. 1943	579	239	818	1.4%
Guadalcanal (Solomons)	7 Aug. 1942–21 Feb. 1943	562	150	712	1.2%
Central Burma	29 Jan.–15 July 1945	195	357	552	1.0%
Central Pacific	7 Dec. 1941–6 Dec. 1943	157	360	517	All the
East Indies (Dutch Indonesia)	1 Jan.–22 July 1942	34	427	461	remainder
Eastern Mandates[3] (Marshall Islands)	31 Jan.–14 June 1944	216	218	434[4]	less than
Bismarck Archipelago (New Britain, Admiralities)	15 Dec. 1943–27 Nov. 1944	82	264	346	1.0%
Papua	23 July 1942–23 Jan. 1943	239	104	343	
China Defensive	4 July 1942–4 May 1945	2	192	194	
China Offensive	5 May–2 Sept. 1945	3	44	47	
Total		**38,458**	**16,687**	**55,145[5]**	

[1] The war in the Philippines, especially in northern Luzon, continued right up until the armistice on Aug. 15, 1945. During this period, 155 soldiers were KIA and 495 WIA on Luzon.
[2] Air 17 April 1944–2 Sept. 1945
[3] Air 7 Dec. 1943–16 April 1944
[4] Conflicts with total of 787 KIA notes in official history.
[5] Designated campaign tally excludes 2,141 KIA not categorized by campaign, which brings the grand total to **57,286** KIA.

Note: Of Army battle deaths in the Pacific, 69.7% were on the ground and 30.2% in the air.

Source: Computed from Dept. of the Army, Army Battle Casualties and Non-Battle Deaths in WWII: Final Report. Washington, D.C., 1953.

★ U.S. Navy

Action	Dates*	Battle Deaths	Percent of Total
Pacific/Asia (Unspecified)	Dec. 1941–Aug. 1945	4,567	14.7%
Philippines–Invasion, Leyte Gulf, etc.	Oct. 1944–July 1945	4,336	13.9%
Okinawa	1 April–22 June 1945	4,022	12.9%
Undetermined Actions	Dec. 1941–Aug. 1945	1,769	5.7%
Pearl Harbor	7 Dec. 1941	1,763	5.6%
Dutch East Indies (Makassar Strait, Java Sea, etc.)	23 Jan.–1 March 1942	1,762	5.6%
Solomons (Remaining)	29 Jan.–25 Nov. 1943	1,302	4.1%
Guadalcanal/Tulagi Landings	7 Aug. 1942–21 Feb. 1943	1,198	3.8%
After July 1, 1945 (USS Indianapolis, etc.)	July–Aug. 1945	1,119	3.6%
Guadalcanal (Naval)	12–15 Nov. 1942	993	3.1%
Iwo Jima	19 Feb.–26 March 1945	982	3.1%

Kyushu/Japan (Bombardment)	Spring/Summer 1945	970	3.1%
Philippines – Fall of	7 Dec. 1941–May 1942	969	3.1%
Savo Island	8–9 Aug. 1942	947	3.0%
Tarawa (including Liscome Bay)	20–28 Nov. 1943	727	2.3%
Marianas Islands (Saipan, Guam, Tinian)	15 June–15 Aug. 1944	557	1.8%
Coral Sea	4–8 May 1942	544	1.7%
Tassafaronga	30 Nov. 1942	397	1.2%
Midway	3–6 June 1942	310	1.0%
Formosa/Indochina	Oct. 1944–July 1945	280	All the remainder
Santa Cruz Islands	26 Oct. 1942	247	less than 1%
Palau Islands (Peleliu)	15 Sept.–25 Nov. 1944	195	
Marshall Islands (Kwajalein, Roi Namur, Eniwetok)	Jan.–March 1944	191	
Aleutians/Alaska (Attu, Kiska, Kormandorski)	26 March 1943–Aug. 1945	178	
Biak/New Guinea (Landings)	27 May–22 June 1944	170	
Cape Esperance	12 Oct. 1942	169	
Cape Gloucester	26 Dec. 1943–1 March 1944	154	
Eastern Solomons	22–25 Aug. 1942	89	
Truk (Carolines)	16–17 Feb. 1944	81	
Pacific Raids	1942	44	
Total		**31,032**	

*Dates for some of the actions are approximate.

Note: Coast Guard: According to the Coast Guard Historical Office, a breakdown by theater is not available. Of the 1,035 Coast Guardsmen who died overseas during WWII, 574 were KIA and another 432 were WIA. The Coast Guard, of course, operated as part of the Navy during the war.

Source: *The History of the Medical Department of the Navy in World War II. Appendix Table 14 — Casualties Due to Enemy Action*, pp. 170–174. (Washington, D.C.: GPO, 1953). VFW staff arranged order of statistics.

★ U.S. Marine Corps

Action	Dates	Combat Deaths	Percent of Total
Iwo Jima	19 Feb.–26 March 1945	5,931	26.3%
Okinawa	1 April–22 June 1945	3,443	15.3%
Saipan	11 June–10 July 1944	3,152	14.0%
Guam	21 July–15 Aug. 1944	1,568	6.9%
Guadalcanal	7 Aug. 1942–8 Feb. 1943	1,504	6.6%
Peleliu	6 Sept.–14 Oct. 1944	1,336	5.9%
Tarawa	20 Nov.–8 Dec. 1943	1,085	4.8%
Solomons–New Britain (Air)	9 Feb. 1943–15 March 1945	783	3.4%
Bougainville	28 Oct. 1943–15 June 1944	732	3.2%
Bataan/Corregidor	7 Dec. 1941–6 May 1942	570	2.5%
Cape Gloucester	26 Dec. 1943–1 March 1944	438	1.9%
Kwajalein/Majuro	29 Jan.–8 Feb. 1944	387	1.7%
Tinian	24 July–1 Aug. 1944	368	1.6%
Eniwetok	17 Feb.–2 March 1944	258	1.1%
Sea Duty (Naval Battles)	7 Dec. 1941–2 Sept. 1945	242	1.0%
New Georgia	20 June–16 Oct. 1943	221	All the remainder
Marshalls, Carolines, Palau, Philippines, Volcano and Bonin Islands (Air)	Feb. 1944–June 1945	200	less than 1%
Wake Atoll	7–23 Dec. 1941	69	
Gilberts, Marshalls, Marianas (Air)	Nov. 1943–Aug. 1944	65	
Midway Islands	7 Dec. 1941–6 June 1942	48	
Talasea (New Britain)	6 March 1944	37	
Makin (Gilberts)	17–18 Aug. 1942	30	
Guam (Marianas)	7–10 Dec. 1941	10	
Arawe, Russell Is., Treasury Island	1943–1944	2	
Total		**22,479 ***	

*Most sources cite 19,733, leaving a discrepancy of 2,746 battle deaths.

Source: VFW staff arranged order of statistics. The figures originated with the Statistics Unit, Personnel Accounting Section, Records Branch, Personnel Department, U.S. Marine Corps, December 1952. Tables reprinted in *A Portrait of the Stars and Stripes (Vol. II): Chronology of U.S. Armed Forces, 1919–1945* by Bud Hannings (Glenside, Pa.: Seniram Publishing, 1991), pp. 875–79.

Pacific Theater Ground Casualties by Division

Listed in descending order

During World War II, the U.S. Army deployed 20 divisions to the Pacific Theater of Operations for combat. An additional division, the 98th, was stationed on Hawaii.

Those infantry, cavalry and airborne divisions suffered 60% of all Army ground deaths in the theater. As usual, the infantry, by far, absorbed the greatest percentage of casualties in WWII: 80% of Army killed in action.

While it is popularly assumed that the Pacific was essentially a Navy and Marine war, Army ground forces, in fact, sustained 35% of all battle deaths in the Pacific. Per capita, however, the Marine Corps had a far greater proportion of casualties in terms of the ratio of men fielded in combat to the number killed.

★ U.S. Army

Division	Combat Deaths	Wounded in Action
7th Infantry	2,334	7,258
96th Infantry	2,036	7,181
32nd Infantry	1,985	5,627
27th Infantry	1,853	4,980
77th Infantry	1,850	5,935
24th Infantry	1,689	5,621
25th Infantry	1,497	4,190
43rd Infantry	1,406	4,887
37th Infantry	1,344	4,861
American (23rd)	1,157	3,052
1st Cavalry	970	3,311
41st Infantry	960	3,504
38th Infantry	784	2,814
40th Infantry	748	2,407
11th Airborne	614	1,926
33rd Infantry	524	2,024
81st Infantry	515	1,942
6th Infantry	514	1,957
31st Infantry	414	1,392
93rd Infantry	17	121
Total	**23,211**	**74,990**

★ U.S. Marine Corps

Division	Combat Deaths	Wounded in Action
1st Marine	3,470	14,438
4th Marine	3,345	12,045
2nd Marine	2,795	9,975
5th Marine	2,414	7,159
3rd Marine	2,371	8,045
6th Marine	1,630	7,700
Total	**16,025**	**59,362**

Notes:
1. Keep in mind that these figures reflect only division casualties. Army ground units — such as separate Infantry regiments — incurred an additional **15,247** combat deaths. Also, another **6,454** Marine battle deaths are not included.
2. The Office of Air Force History does not have a break down available for individual AirForces' — 5th, 7th, 10th, 11th, 13th, 14th, 20th and Far East — casualties in the Pacific during WWII.

Source: Order of Battle, U.S. Army World War II by Shelby L. Stanton (Navato, Calif.: Presidio Press, 1984). "Combat Casualties By Division." Personnel Accounting Section, April 3, 1950, Marine Corps Historical Center.

Ship	Type	Cause	Battle/Place	Date	Killed
Arizona	B	Aircraft Bombs	Pearl Harbor	12/7/41	1,103
Indianapolis	HC	Sub. Torpedo	Philippine Sea	7/29/45	883
Franklin	AC	Aircraft Bombs	Off Coast of Japan	3/18/45	724
Juneau	LC	Sub. Torpedo	Guadalcanal	11/13/42	683
Houston	HC	Gunfire/Torpedo	Sunda Strait	3/1/42	655
Liscome Bay	EAC	Sub. Torpedo	Gilbert Islands (Tarawa)	11/24/43	646
Oklahoma	B	Aircraft Torpedo	Pearl Harbor	12/7/41	415
Bunker Hill	AC	Kamikaze	Okinawa	5/11/45	396
Quincy	HC	Torpedo	Savo Island	8/9/42	389
Mount Hood	AS	Explosion	Manus, Admiralty Is.	11/10/44	372
Vincennes	HC	Torpedo	Savo Island	8/9/42	342
Bismarck Sea	EAC	Kamikaze	Iwo Jima	2/21/45	326
Hoel	D	Gunfire	Leyte Gulf	10/25/44	268
Serpens*	CS	Explosion	Guadalcanal	1/29/45	253
Spence	D	Typhoon	Philippines	12/18/44	249
Astoria	HC	Gunfire	Savo Island	8/9/42	238
Birmingham	LC	Explosion	Philippines	10/24/44	237
Jarvis	D	Aircraft	Guadalcanal	8/9/42	233
Sims	D	Aircraft	Coral Sea	5/7/42	225
Lexington	AC	Aircraft Torpedo	Coral Sea	5/8/42	216
Princeton	AC	Aircraft Bombs	Leyte Gulf	10/24/44	208
Hull	D	Typhoon	Philippines	12/18/44	202
Cooper	D	Torpedo	Ormoc Bay, Leyte	12/3/44	191
Meredith	D	Bomb/Torpedo	Guadalcanal	10/15/42	187
Johnston	D	Gunfire	Leyte Gulf	10/25/44	186
New Orleans	HC	Torpedo	Tassafaronga	11/30/42	183
Neosho	O	Bomb	Coral Sea	5/7/42	181
Wasp	AC	Torpedo	Guadalcanal	9/15/42	173
Atlanta	LC	Torpedo	Guadalcanal	11/13/42	170
Helena	LC	Torpedo	Kula Gulf	7/6/43	168
De Haven	D	Bomb	Guadalcanal	2/2/43	168
Barton	D	Torpedo	Guadalcanal	11/13/42	165
Asheville	PG	Gunfire	Java	3/3/42	161
Morrison	D	Kamikaze	Okinawa	5/4/45	159
Drexler	D	Kamikaze	Okinawa	5/28/45	158
Monaghan	D	Typhoon	Philippines	12/18/44	154
Halligan	D	Mine	Okinawa	3/26/45	153
Luce	D	Kamikaze	Okinawa	5/4/45	149
Monssen	D	Gunfire	Guadalcanal	11/13/42	145
Ticonderoga	AC	Kamikaze	Formosa	1/21/45	144
Nashville	HC	Kamikaze	Philippines	12/13/44	133
Twiggs	D	Kamikaze	Okinawa	6/16/45	126
Pensacola	HC	Torpedo	Tassafaronga	11/30/42	125
Saratoga	AC	Air Attack	Iwo Jima	2/21/45	123
Hornet	AC	Torpedo	Santa Cruz Islands	10/25-26/42	118
Preston	D	Gunfire	Guadalcanal	11/14-15/42	117
Pillsbury	D	Gunfire	Java	3/1/42	116
McKean	HST	Torpedo	Bougainville	11/17/43	116
Underhill	DE	Human Torpedo	Luzon	7/24/45	113
Brownson	D	Air Attack	Cape Gloucester	12/26/43	108
Boise	LC	Gunfire	Cape Esperance	10/11-12/42	107
West Virginia	B	Torpedo/Bomb	Pearl Harbor	12/7/41	105
Samuel B. Roberts	DE	Gunfire	Leyte Gulf	10/25/44	102
Wasp (CV18)	AC	Bomb	Okinawa	3/19/45	101
Gambier Bay	EAC	Gunfire	Leyte Gulf	10/25/44	100

Abbreviations: AC—Aircraft Carrier; AS—Ammunition Ship; B—Battleship; CS—Cargo Ship; D—Destroyer; DE—Destroyer Escort; EAC—Escort Aircraft Carrier; HC—Heavy Cruiser; HST—High Speed Transport; LC—Light Cruiser; O-Oiler; PG-Patrol Gunboat.

Source: Dictionary of American Naval Fighting Ships. Washington, D.C.: Navy History Division, 1963–1991.

U.S. Submarine Service: The 52 U.S. submarines lost in WWII represented 18% of all the subs that saw combat duty. Some 3,505 submariners were killed. This loss rate was among the highest — if not the highest per capita — of any branch of the U.S. armed forces during WWII.

Medal of Honor Recipients by Battleground

Battleground	Current Country	Medals Awarded	Percentage
Philippines Luzon (30) Leyte (11) Corregidor (2) Mindanao (2) Negros (1) Samar (1)	Philippines	47	21.36
Solomon Islands Guadalcanal (11) Solomons (10) * Savo Island (5) * New Georgia (3)	Solomon Islands	29	13.18
Iwo Jima	Japan (Volcano Is.)	27	12.27
Okinawa	Japan (Ryukyu Is.)	22	10.00
New Guinea N.E. New Guinea (10) Bougainville (5) New Britain (3) Admiralty Is. (1)	Papua New Guinea	19	8.36
Pearl Harbor	U.S. (Hawaii)	16	7.27
Pacific (air war)	—	8	3.63
Peleliu	Belau	8	3.63
Marshalls	Marshall Islands	6	2.72
Saipan	N. Marianas (Commonwealth)	6	2.72
Coral Sea	S.E. of New Guinea	4	1.81
Guam	U.S. Commonwealth	4	1.81
Tarawa	Kiribati	4	1.81
Dutch East Indies Celebe Islands (1) Dutch New Guinea (1) (Irian Jaya) Halmahera Island (1)	Indonesia	3	1.36
Midway Island	U.S.	2	.91
off Japan	—	2	.91
Philippine Sea	east of Philippines	2	.91
Tinian	N. Marianas (Commonwealth)	2	.91
Attu, Aleutian Islands	U.S. (Alaska)	1	.46
Bismarck Sea	N.E. of New Guinea	1	.46
Burma	Myanmar	1	.46
China	China	1	.46
Gilbert Islands	Kiribati	1	.46
Ie Shima	Japan (Ryukyu Is.)	1	.46
Java Sea	off Indonesia	1	.46
off Korea	—	1	.46
Wake Island	U.S.	1	.46
Total in Pacific Theater		220	100.00

* Earned at sea during naval battles.

Medal of Honor Recipients: A Select Few

Sgt. Robert A. Owens, 1st Battalion, 3rd Marines, 3rd Marine Division, charged into the mouth of a steadily firing cannon at Cape Torokina, Bougainville, Solomon Islands on Nov. 1, 1943. In silencing the deadly weapon, he sacrificed his own life for the sake of his fellow Marines.

Cmdr. Eugene B. Fluckey, commanding officer of the submarine *USS Barb,* was leading his famous sub on its 11th war patrol along the east coast of China from Dec. 19, 1944, and Feb. 15, 1945, when he encountered a concentration of 30 enemy ships. Despite the treacherous waters and circumstances, he brought the *Barb* through to safety in addition to sinking Japanese vessels.

Maj. Richard I. Bong, Far East Air Forces, was "America's ace of aces" with 40 confirmed kills to his credit. Between Oct. 10 and Nov. 15, 1944 alone, he shot down eight Japanese aircraft with his P-38 over Balikpapan, Borneo and Leyte, Philippines. Tragically, he was killed testing a P-80 over California on Aug. 6, 1945.

Navy Lt. Edward H. O'Hare, Squadron 3, *USS Lexington,* became the Navy's first ace of WWII on Feb. 20, 1942, 400 miles from Rabaul, New Britain. In his F-4F Wildcat, he shot down five enemy bombers in just four minutes in what has been called "the most daring, single-action in the history of combat aviation." He disappeared without a trace on Nov. 26, 1943, while on a night flight over the Gilbert Islands.

The National Memorial Cemetery of the Pacific near Pearl Harbor, Hawaii — known as The Punchbowl — is the final resting place for thousands of WWII servicemen who died fighting in the Pacific campaign. Engraved tablets at the Courts of the Missing list those still unaccounted for. (The missing and killed in action from Korea and Vietnam are also honored at the Punchbowl.)

Thousands more are buried in cemeteries in foreign lands, such as the American Cemetery and Memorial at Fort McKinley in Manila, the Philippines.

J. Richard Salerno (inset), a veteran of the 24th Infantry Division who landed at Leyte in October 1944 and returned for the 50th anniversary, found the grave marker of a fellow soldier from New York.

Recommended Reading: Books by Battle

Single-Volume History of World War II
Gilbert, Martin. *The Second World War: A Complete History*. N.Y.: Henry Holt & Co., 1989. 846p.

General Histories of Theater
Costello, John. *The Pacific War*. N.Y.: Rawson, Wade Publishers, Inc., 1981. 829p.
Spector, Ronald H. *Eagle Against the Sun: The American War With Japan*. N.Y.: Free Press, 1985. 589p.

Air War (Pacific)
Boyne, Walter J. *Clash of Wings: World War II in the Air*. N.Y.: Simon & Schuster, 1994. 415p.
Lindley, John W. *Carrier Victory: The Air War in the Pacific*. Talisman-Parrish Bks., 1978.
Miller, Nathan. *The Naval Air War, 1939–1945*. Annapolis: Naval Institute Press, 1991. 213p.

Admiralties
U.S. War Department. *The Admiralties: Operations of the 1st Cavalry Division (29 Feb.–18 May 1944)*. Washington, D.C.: GPO, 1945. 151p.

Aleutians/Attu
Garfield, Brian. *The Thousand-Mile War: World War II in Alaska and the Aleutians*. N.Y.: Doubleday, 1969.
Hutchinson, Kevin D. *World War II in the North Pacific: Chronology and Fact Book*. Westport, Conn.: Greenwood Press, 1994. 288p.

Atomic Bomb Raids
Goldstein, Donald M., et al. *Rain of Ruin: A Photographic History of Hiroshima and Nagasaki*. Washington, D.C.: Brassey's, 1995. 175p.
Thomas, Gordon and Max Morgan Witts. *Ruin From the Air: The Enola Gay's Atomic Mission to Hiroshima*. N.Y.: Scarborough House, 1990. 386p.

Atrocities
Russell, Lord. *The Knights of Bushido: The Shocking History of Japanese War Atrocities*. N.Y.: Dutton, 1958.

Bismarck Sea
McAulay, Lex. *Battle of the Bismarck Sea*. N.Y.: St. Martin's Press, 1991. 226p.

Borneo
Morison, Samuel E. "Borneo, February–August 1945" in *The Liberation of the Philippines*. Boston: Little, Braum & Co., 1959.

Bougainville
Gailey, Harry A. *Bougainville: The Forgotten Campaign*. Lexington: Univ. of Kentucky Press, 1991

Burma
Fischer, Edward. *The Chancy War: Winning in China, Burma and India in World War II*. N.Y.: Crown Publishing Group, 1991. 250p.
Moser, Don. *China, Burma, India*. Alexandria, Va.: Time-Life, 1978. 208p.

Cape Esperance
Cook, Charles. *The Battle of Cape Esperance*. Annapolis: Naval Institute Press, 1992. 184p.

China
Cornelius, Wanda and Short, Thayne. *Ding Hao: America's Air War in China, 1937–1945*. Pelican, 1980. 502p.
Miles, Milton E. *A Different Kind of War: The Unknown Story of the U.S. Navy's Guerrilla Forces in World War II China*. N.Y.: Doubleday & Co., 1967. 629p.

Coast Guard
Willoughby, Malcolm F. *The U.S. Coast Guard in World War II*. Annapolis: Naval Institute Press, 1989. 347p.

Coral Sea
Millot, Bernard A. *The Battle of the Coral Sea*. Annapolis: Naval Institute Press. 1974. 163p.

Doolittle Raid
Schult, Duane. *The Doolittle Raid*. N.Y.: St. Martin's Press, 1988. 325p.

Fireballoons
Webber, Bert. *Silent Siege: Japanese Attacks on North America in WWII*. Medford, Ore.: Webb Research Group, 1988.

Firebombings
Caidin, Martin. *A Torch to the Enemy: The Fire Raid on Tokyo*. N.Y.: Ballantine, 1960.
Kerr, E. Bartlett. *Flames Over Tokyo: The U.S. Army Air Forces' Incendiary Campaign Against Japan, 1944–1945*. N.Y.: Fine, 1991. 288p.

Gilberts (Tarawa and Makin)
Hoyt, Edwin P. *Storm Over the Gilberts: War in the Central Pacific 1943*. N.Y.: Mason/Charter, 1978. 162p.

Guadalcanal
Frank, Richard B. *Guadalcanal: The Definitive Account of the Landmark Battle*. N.Y.: Random House, 1990. 800p.

Guadalcanal (Naval)
Hammel, Eric. *Guadalcanal: The Carrier Battles*. N.Y.: Crown Publishing, Inc., 1987. 505p.

Guam
Gailey, Harry. *The Liberation of Guam: 21 July–10 August, 1944*. Novato, Calif.: Presidio Press, 1988. 231p.

"Hump"
Koenig, William. *Over the Hump: Airlift to China*. N.Y.: Ballantine Books, 1972. 158p.

Indianapolis, USS
Kurzman, Dan. *Fatal Voyage: The Sinking of the USS Indianapolis*. N.Y.: Pocket Books, 1990. 336p.

Iwo Jima
Ross, Bill D. *Iwo Jima: Legacy Of Valor*. N.Y.: The Vanguard Press, 1985. 376p.

Java Sea
Van Ooster, F.C. *The Battle of the Java Sea*. Annapolis: Naval Institute Press, 1976. 128p.

Komandorski Islands
Loreli, John A. *The Battle of the Komandorski Islands*. Annapolis: Naval Institute Press, 1984.

Leyte Gulf
Cutler, Thomas J. *The Battle of Leyte Gulf, 23–26 October 1944*. N.Y.: HarperCollins, 1994. 343p.

Makassar Strait
Smith, S.E. "Macassar Merry-Go-Round" by Rear Adm. William P. Mack in *The U.S. Navy in WWII*. N.Y.: Morrow, 1966. pp.73–77.

Makin
U.S. War Department. *Makin*. Washington, D.C.: GPO, 1946. 136p. (See also Gilbert Islands.)

Marianas (Saipan, Guam, Tinian)
Hoyt. Edwin P. *To The Marianas: War in the Central Pacific, 1944*. N.Y.: Van Nostrand Reinhold Co., 1980. 277p.

Marshalls (Roi-Namur, Kwajalein, Eniwetok)
Heinl, Robert D. and John A. Crown. *The Marshalls: Increasing the Tempo*. Washington, D.C.: GPO, 1954. 188p.

Midway

Lord, Walter. *Incredible Victory.* N.Y.: Harper & Row, 1967. 331p.

Naval War

Hoyt, Edwin P. *Now Hear This: The Story of American Sailors in World War II.* N.Y.: Paragon House, 1993.

Smith, S.E. *The U.S. Navy in World War II.* N.Y.: William Morrow, 1966. 1,049p.

van der Vat, Dan. *The Pacific Campaign: WWII — The U.S. Japanese Naval War, 1941-1945.* N.Y.: Simon & Schuster, 1991. 430pp.

New Britain

Miller, John. *Cartwheel: The Reduction of Rabaul.* Washington, D.C.: Dept. of Army, 1959. 418p.

USMC. *The Campaign on New Britain.* Washington, D.C.: GPO, 1952. 220p.

New Georgia

Horton, D. C. *New Georgia: Pattern for Victory.* N.Y.: Ballantine Books, Inc., 1971. 160p.

Hammel, Eric. *Munda Trail.* N.Y.: Avon Books, 1989. 298p.

New Guinea (Papua/Buna)

Mayo, Lida. *Bloody Buna.* N.Y.: Doubleday, 1974. 212p.

Vader, John. *New Guinea: The Tide Is Stemmed.* N.Y.: Ballantine Books Inc., 1971. 160p.

New Guinea (Dutch)

Prefer, Nathan. *MacArthur's New Guinea Campaign, March-August 1944.* Harrisburg, Pa.: Stackpole Books, 1995. 288p.

Riegelman, Harold. *Caves of Biak.* N.Y.: Dial Press, 1955.

Occupation of Japan

Schaller, Michael. *The American Occupation of Japan: The Origins of the Cold War in Asia.* Oxford: Oxford Univ. Press, 1985.

Sheldon, Walt. *The Honorable Conquerors: The Occupation of Japan 1945-1952.* N.Y.: Macmillan Co., 1965. 336p.

Okinawa

Belote, James H. & William M. Belote. *Typhoon of Steel: The Battle for Okinawa.* N.Y.: Harper & Row, 1970. 368p.

Operation Downfall

Allen, Thomas B. and Norman Polmar. *Code-Name Downfall: The Secret Plan to Invade Japan — and Why Truman Dropped the Bomb.* N.Y.: Simon & Schuster, 1995. 351p.

Pearl Harbor

Weintraub, Stanley. *Long Day's Journey into War: December 7, 1941.* N.Y.: Truman Talley Books, 1991. 706p.

Peleliu/Palaus

Falk, Stanley. *Bloodiest Victory: Palaus.* N.Y.: Random House, 1974. 160p.

Ross, Bill D. *Peleliu: Tragic Triumph: The Untold Story of the Pacific War's Forgotten Battle.* N.Y.: Random House, 1991. 381p.

Philippine Sea

Y'Blood, William T. *Red Sun Setting: The Battle of the Philippine Sea.* Annapolis.: Naval Institute Press, 1981. 257p.

Philippines

General (Leyte, Luzon, S. Philippines)

Breuer, William B. *Retaking the Philippines.* N.Y.: St. Martin's Press, 1986.

Falk, Stanley L. *Decision at Leyte.* N.Y.: W.W. Norton, 1966.

Morison, Samuel Eliot. *The Liberation of the Philippines.* Boston: Little, Brown, 1959. 320p.

Steinberg, Rafael. *Return to the Philippines.* Alexandria, Va.: Time-Life Books, 1980. 208p.

Bataan

Whitman, John W. *Bataan Our Last Ditch.* N.Y.: Hippocrene Books, Inc., 1990. 754p.

Knox, Donald. *Death March: The Survivors of Bataan.* N.Y.: Harcourt Brace Jovanovish, 1981. 482p.

Corregidor

Belote, James & William. *Corregidor: The Saga of a Fortress.* Harper & Row, 1967.

Devlin, Gerard M. *Back to Corregidor: America Retakes the Rock.* N.Y.: St. Martin's Press, 1992. 261p.

Manila

Cortesi, Lawrence. *The Battle for Manila.* N.Y.: Kensington Publishing, 1984. 288p.

Prisoners of War

Daws, Gavan. *Prisoners of the Japanese.* N.Y.: William Morrow & Co., 1994. 462p.

Kerr, E. Bartlett. *Surrender and Survival: The Experience of American POWs in the Pacific, 1941–1945.* N.Y.: William Morrow & Co., 1985.

LaForte, Robert S., Himmel, Richard L. and Marcello, Ronald E. *With Only the Will to Live: Accounts of Americans in Japanese Prison Camps, 1941–1945.* Denton, Texas: Univ. of N. Texas, 1994. 320p.

Saipan

Jones, Don. *Oba, The Last Samurai, Saipan 1944–45.* Novato, Calif.: Presidio Press, 1986. 241p.

Santa Cruz Islands

The Battles of Cape Esperance and Santa Cruz Islands. Washington, D.C.: Naval Historical Center, 1994. 100p.

Savo Island

Clark, Chris and Loxton, Bruce. *The Shame of Savo: Anatomy of a Naval Disaster.* Annapolis: Naval Institute Press, 1994. 346p.

Warner, Denis & Peggy. *Disaster in the Pacific: New Light on the Battle of Savo Island.* Annapolis: Naval Institute Press, 1994. 320p.

Solomons

Hoyt, Edwin P. *The Glory of the Solomons.* N.Y.: Stein and Day, 1983. 348p.

Solomons (Naval Battles)

Kilpatrick, C.W. *The Naval Night Battles in the Solomons.* Fla.: Exposition Press of Florida, 1987. 315p.

Kurzman, Dan. *Left to Die: The Tragedy of the USS Juneau.* N.Y.: Pocket Books, 1994. 325p.

Submarine Service

Alden, John D. *U.S. Submarine Attacks During WWII.* Annapolis: Naval Institute Press, 1989.

Blair, Clay. *Silent Victory: The U.S. Submarine War Against Japan.* Philadelphia: Lippincott, 1974.

Tarawa

Graham, Michael B. *Mantle of Heroism: Tarawa and the Struggle for the Gilberts, November 1943.* Novato, Calif.: Presidio Press, 1993. 360p. (See also Gilberts.)

Typhoon (Dec. '44)

Adamson, Hans Christian & George Francis Kosco. *Halsey's Typhoons.* N.Y.: Crown Publishers, Inc., 1967. 206p.

Calhoun, Raymond. *Typhoon: The Other Enemy — The Third Fleet and the Pacific Storm of December 1944.* Annapolis: Naval Institute Press, 1981. 247p.

Wake Island

Cressman, Robert J. *'A Magnificent Fight': The Battle for Wake Island.* Annapolis: Naval Institute Press, 1994. 352p.

Schultz, Duane P. *Wake Island: The Heroic Gallant Fight.* N.Y.: St. Martin's Press, 1978. 247p.

War Crimes Trials

Brackman, Arnold C. *The Other Nuremberg: The Untold Story of the Tokyo War Crimes Trials.* N.Y.: Morrow, 1987.

Minear, Richard H. *Victors' Justice: The Tokyo War Crimes Trial.* Princeton: Princeton Univ. Press, 1971.

Piccigallo, Philip R. *The Japanese on Trial: Allied War Crimes Operations in the East, 1945–1951.* Austin: University of Texas Press, 1979. 292p.

U.S. Army Division Shoulder Patches Pacific Theater

★ U.S. Army — Ground

1st Cavalry	6th Infantry	7th Infantry	11th Airborne	23rd Infantry (Americal)
24th Infantry	25th Infantry	27th Infantry	31st Infantry	32nd Infantry
33rd Infantry	37th Infantry	38th Infantry	40th Infantry	
41st Infantry	43rd Infantry	77th Infantry	81st Infantry	
93rd Infantry	96th Infantry	98th Infantry		

U.S. Army Air Forces — Pacific Theater
U.S. Marine Corps

| 5th | 7th | 10th | Far East Air Force |

| 11th | 13th | 14th | 20th |

| 1st Marine | 2nd Marine | 3rd Marine | 4th Marine |

| 5th Marine | 6th Marine |

Profiles

EDITORS

RICHARD K. KOLB
Editor-in-Chief, *VFW Magazine*

As magazine editor, he conceived the four-year series — "50 Years Ago This Month" — upon which this book was built. He determined the content and edited and created the copy at all stages of development.

Kolb joined the magazine in 1989, and became publisher in 1990. He writes often for the magazine. His 36-part series on the *Saga of America's Overseas Veterans* appeared 1989–94.

Previously, Kolb was a staff writer and editor for corporate and association publications in the petroleum industry. As a free-lance writer, he contributed more than 50 articles, mostly on military history and veterans issues, to 20 national publications.

A Vietnam veteran (4th Infantry and 101st Airborne divisions), he holds a degree in political science (University of Alaska), with emphases in international relations, history and journalism.

Long active in veterans affairs, he chaired the Vietnam Veterans Leadership Program in Houston, Tex., coordinating a public outreach and employment campaign during the 1980s.

He resides in Kearney, Mo., and belongs to VFW Post 5717.

GARY L. BLOOMFIELD
Senior Editor, *Faces of Victory*

He contributed feature articles to the WWII series and was photography editor for the entire project. He also wrote many of the book's sidebars and sections.

He worked on the *VFW Magazine* staff from 1989 to 1995, and was a civilian Army public affairs specialist in Kansas City previously. He holds degrees in English (Avila College) and liberal arts (Baker University).

During his 10 years in the Army, he served two tours in Korea, and in Germany. He earned recognition as Army Journalist of the Year (1977), U.N. Command Best Journalist (1978) and USAREC Best Journalist (1989). Photos he shot have appeared in numerous national and international publications.

He resides in Belton, Mo. and belongs to VFW Post 9879 in San Francisco.

TIMOTHY K. DYHOUSE
Staff Writer, *VFW Magazine*

The newest member of the magazine staff, he wrote several of the sidebars for the Pacific volume. He also played a part in the proofing process.

A 1994 graduate of the University of Kansas' William Allen White School of Journalism, he lent a fresh perspective to the project.

ROBERT WIDENER
Art Director, *VFW Magazine*

He created the cover of the book, plus lent extensive input into the design and the photo spreads. He was responsible for design and layout of the WWII series. Widener moved from a Kansas City advertising agency to the magazine in 1989.

After earning a degree in English from Emporia State University, he spent several years in advertising, primarily in graphic design. He has more than 10 years' experience as a graphic arts specialist.

He resides in Kansas City, Mo.

MICHAEL McKENZIE
Consulting Editor, Addax Publishing Group

He served as the publisher's copy editor.

A regional correspondent for *Sports Illustrated* and local sports radio commentator, McKenzie has worked since 1965 as an editor, columnist and reporter for newspapers and magazines, including *The Kansas City Star & Times* and *The Atlanta Journal,* as well as a broadcaster.

As part of a reporting team with the *Kansas City Star & Times,* he shared a Pulitzer Prize in 1981. To his credit are one book and two anthologies.

His B.A. degree from Westmar College (Iowa) is in English. He was an information and broadcast specialist with the U.S. Army during 1967–70 at Redstone Arsenal, Ala.

He resides in Shawnee Mission, Kan.

MICHAEL B. GRAHAM

Graham is author of *Mantle of Heroism: Tarawa and the Struggle for the Gilberts* (1993). He wrote 12 articles for *VFW Magazine's 50 Years Ago This Month* Pacific series. He also wrote the section, "Mobilizing for the War Against Japan."

He is a U.S. government foreign affairs officer. During the war with Iraq, he served on the State Department's Kuwait/Gulf War Task Force as a public affairs specialist. He is also founding vice president of Sigma Mu Sigma, the international military studies college and professional honor society.

Graham holds degrees in journalism and international relations (Marshall University), is a graduate of the Foreign Service Institute post-graduate school of foreign area studies, and is a post-graduate student in strategic studies at American Military University.

DOMINIC J. CARACCILO

Author of the *Ready Brigade of the 82nd Airborne in Desert Storm* (1993), he contributed several articles to the "50 Years Ago This Month" series on the Pacific.

Caraccilo teaches systems engineering at the U.S. Military Academy, his alma mater, at West Point.

He commanded HQ Co., 2nd Bde., 82nd Airborne Division — the Ready Brigade of the National Command Authority — during the Persian Gulf War, 1990–91. A member of the VFW, he resides at West Point, N.Y.

OTHER CONTRIBUTORS

John Cloe is an Air Force historian based in Alaska and author of *The Aleutian Warriors* (1990).

John F. Foltz, Sr. is an Oklahoma newspaperman and veteran of the Army of Occupation.

Kent DeLong is the author of *War Heroes: True Stories of Congressional Medal of Honor Recipients* (1993).

Bill Gruver was a professor at the Walter Cronkite School of Journalism and Telecommunications, Arizona State University.

Roy A. Parmelee is a free-lance writer based in Tampa, Fla.

Bill Wagner is a free-lance writer based in St. Paul, Minn.

THE SATURDAY EVENING
POST
OCTOBER 13, 1945   10¢